Alaska
National Interest Lands
The D-2 Lands

Volume 8, Number 4 / 1981 / Alaska Geographic®

The Alaska Geographic Society

To teach many more to better know and use our natural resources

ALASKA GEOGRAPHIC®, ISSN 0361-1353, is published quarterly by The Alaska Geographic Society, Anchorage, Alaska 99509. Second-class postage paid in Edmonds, Washington 98020. Printed in U.S.A.

THE ALASKA GEOGRAPHIC SOCIETY is a nonprofit organization exploring new frontiers of knowledge across the lands of the polar rim, learning how other men and other countries live in their Norths, putting the geography book back in the classroom, exploring new methods of teaching and learning — sharing in the excitement of discovery in man's wonderful new world north of 51°16'.

MEMBERS OF THE SOCIETY RECEIVE *Alaska Geographic®*, a quality magazine which devotes each quarterly issue to monographic in-depth coverage of a northern geographic region or resource-oriented subject.

MEMBERSHIP DUES in The Alaska Geographic Society are $30 per year; $34 to non-U.S. addresses. (Eighty percent of each year's dues is for a one-year subscription to *Alaska Geographic®*.) Order from The Alaska Geographic Society, Box 4-EEE, Anchorage, Alaska 99509; (907) 274-0521.

MATERIAL SOUGHT: The editors of *Alaska Geographic®* seek a wide variety of informative material on the lands north of 51°16' on geographic subjects — anything to do with resources and their uses (with heavy emphasis on quality color photography) — from Alaska, Northern Canada, Siberia, Japan — all geographic areas that have a relationship to Alaska in a physical or economic sense. In late 1981 editors were seeking material on the following geographic regions and subjects: Alaska fish and fisheries, the Seward Peninsula, Canada's Northwest Territories, and mining and geology. We do not want material done in excessive scientific terminology. A query to the editors is suggested. Payments are made for all material upon publication.

CHANGE OF ADDRESS: The post office does not automatically forward *Alaska Geographic®* when you move. To insure continuous service, notify us six weeks before moving. Send us your new address and zip code (and moving date), your old address and zip code, and if possible send a mailing label from a copy of *Alaska Geographic®*. Send this information to *Alaska Geographic®* Mailing Offices, 130 Second Avenue South, Edmonds, Washington 98020.

MAILING LISTS: We have begun making our members' names and addresses available to carefully screened publications and companies whose products and activities might be of interest to you. If you would prefer not to receive such mailings, please so advise us, and include your mailing label (or your name and address if label is not available).

Library of Congress cataloging in publication data:
Hunter, Celia.
    Alaska national interest lands, D-2 lands.
    (Alaska geographic, ISSN 0361-1353 ; v. 8, no. 4)
    "Celia Hunter and Ginny Wood . . . contributed the text for this issue" — T. p. verso.
    Includes bibliographies.
    1. National parks and reserves—Alaska—Guide-books.
2. Alaska—Description and travel—1959- —Guide-books. 3. Alaska—Public lands. I. Wood, Ginny.
II. Title. III. Series.
F901.A266 vol. 8, no. 4 [F902.3] 917.98'045 81-10979
ISBN 0-88240-159-9   AACR2

The Cover: Monarch of the Alaska Range, Mount McKinley, also known as Denali, rises 20,320 feet, more than 3,000 feet above its highest neighbor, Mount Foraker. This view shows Wonder Lake which lies near the end of the 90-mile road through Denali National Park and Preserve. (Rick McIntyre)

Title page: This angler tests the fish of Lake Schrader in the Franklin Mountains of the Arctic National Wildlife Refuge. (Gary Dobos)

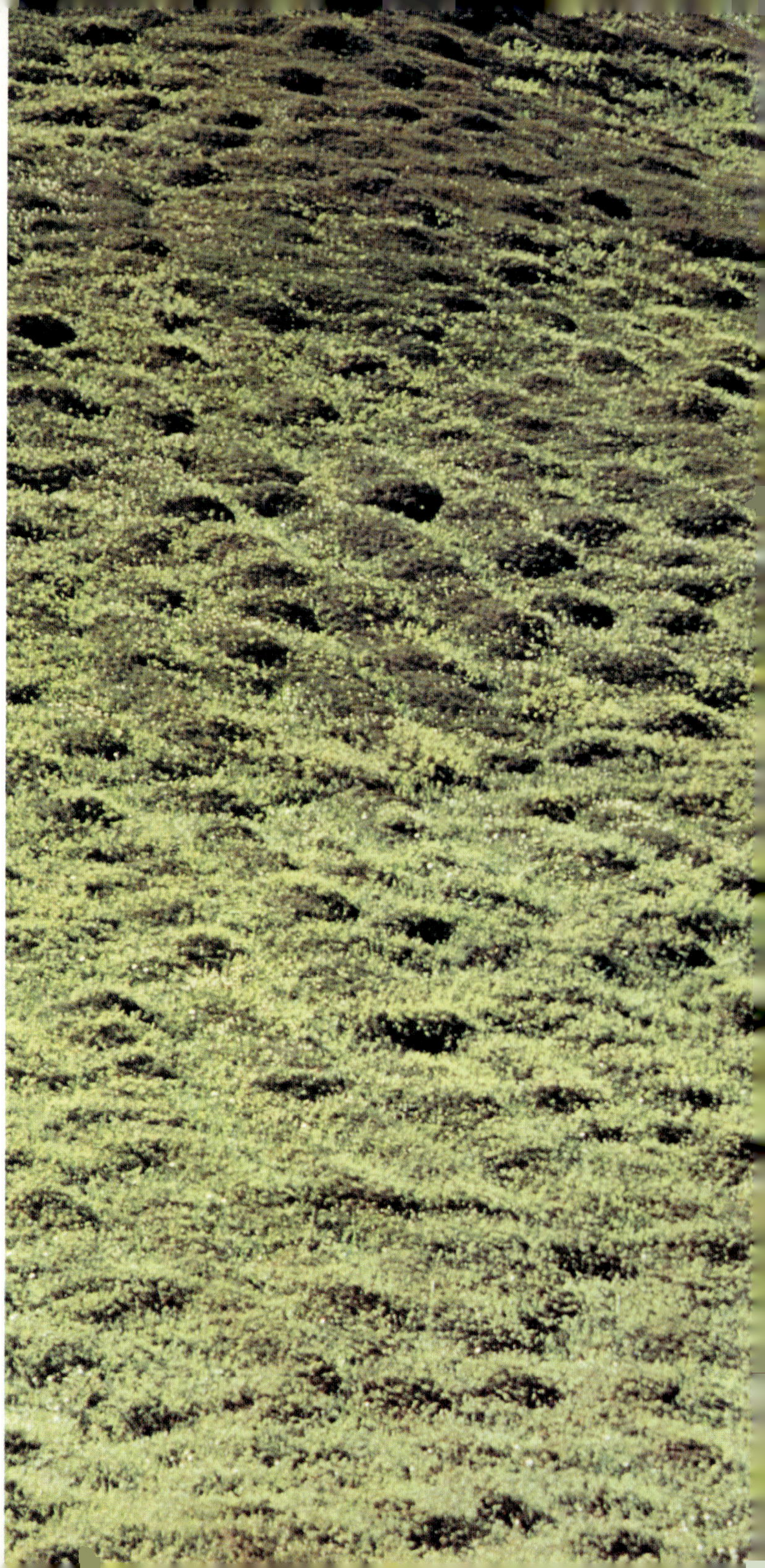

About This Issue:

Celia Hunter and Ginny Wood, long-time Alaskans, contributed the text for this issue. They are both widely recognized conservationists and founders of Camp Denali, a wilderness camp in the Denali area. Celia writes on environmental matters for *ALASKA®* magazine and for the *Daily News-Miner* in Fairbanks.

We thank the many photographers who shared their images of Alaska National Interest Lands, and we appreciate the assistance of staff from the National Park Service, U.S. Fish & Wildlife Service, U.S. Forest Service and Bureau of Land Management.

Editors: Robert A. Henning, Barbara Olds, Penny Rennick
Editorial Assistant: Kathy Doogan
Designer: Dianne Hofbeck
Cartographer: Jon.Hersh

Far left: Hummocks — soft, spongy, unstable bumps in the tundra — dot much of the arctic area's landscape and add immeasurably to the difficulties of cross-country hiking. (John and Margaret Ibbotson)

Left: Ferns are a common sight in lush southeastern rain forests. (Pat Powell)

Contents

Right: A winter sun returns, following sunset in mid-November, to Takahula Lake in the Alatna valley in Gates of the Arctic National Park on January 22. (Tom Falley)

Opposite: One of Glacier Bay National Park and Preserve's many glaciers winds down to the sea, through the valley it has carved out of the mountains. (John and Margaret Ibbotson)

Introduction

Editor's note: *The Alaska lands bill deals with many of the complex issues involving disposition of non-military federal land in Alaska, but boundaries and total acreages in some areas are still not final. State and Native land selections will also influence the ultimate shape and size of units established under the d-2 bill.*

This issue is designed to be an overview, not a comprehensive account, of federal units established in Alaska under d-2 legislation. For a detailed account of any particular area, contact the agency which administers that particular unit.

Two national historical parks, Sitka and Klondike Gold Rush, are not included in this issue because d-2 legislation did not affect their total acreage.

Government agencies administering lands with the word "fiords" in the unit's title do not spell the word in the same way. The National Park Service spells the word with a "j" as in Kenai Fjords National Park; the U.S. Forest Service uses an "i" as in Misty Fiords National Monument. In this issue we will use the "i" spelling except with the official park service designation of Kenai Fjords National Park.

USGS topographic series maps referred to in this issue are scaled 1:250,000 (1 inch equals 4 miles) and are not adequate for use in hiking. The U.S. Geological Survey publishes maps for much of Alaska on a scale of 1:64,500 (1 inch equals 1 mile). A free copy of Index to Topographic Maps of Alaska *is available from any large map supplier who carries USGS topographic materials on Alaska or by writing: Branch of Distribution, U.S. Geological Survey, Box 25286 Federal Center, Denver, CO 80225.*

On December 2, 1980, President Jimmy Carter signed into law the Alaska National Interest Lands Conservation Act, also known as the d-2 lands bill or the compromise HR 39. By this stroke of his pen, an area larger than California was designated for conservation.

This act places more than 97 million acres of Alaska into new or expanded parks and refuges, doubling the size of both the National Park System and the National Wildlife Refuge System. The act protects 25 free-flowing Alaska rivers in the natural state, almost doubling the size of the Wild and Scenic River System. And by classifying 56 million acres of these lands as wilderness, the law tripled the size of the National Wilderness Preservation System.

This huge land transfer originated in passage of the Alaska Native Claims Settlement Act (ANCSA) in December 1971 by which Alaska Natives received both land and money in settlement of their aboriginal land claims. Under Section 17 (d)(2) of that act, the Secretary of the Interior was authorized to withdraw from "all forms of appropriation under the public land laws, including the mining and mineral leasing laws . . . ," and from state and Native regional corporation land selections "up to, but not to exceed, eighty million acres of unreserved public lands . . . which the Secretary deems are suitable for addition to or creation as units of the National Park, Forest, Wildlife Refuge, and Wild and Scenic Rivers System." Congress was given until December 1978 to enact legislation implementing this section.

In 1972, Rogers Morton, secretary of interior, first withdrew most of Alaska's unreserved federal land for study, and later, in 1973, submitted an administration proposal recommending more than 83 million acres of new units for the four conservation systems.

In December 1977 Representative Morris Udall introduced HR 39 which would have set aside 140 million acres as national parks,

Previous page: A cruise ship sails up Muir Inlet, in Glacier Bay National Park and Preserve. This view is from White Thunder Ridge and shows Wolf Point in the foreground. (Ginny Wood)

Right: Thousands of harbor seals haul out on a sand bar in the Moffett Point-Strawberry Point area of Izembek Lagoon, Izembek National Wildlife Refuge. (John Sarvis)

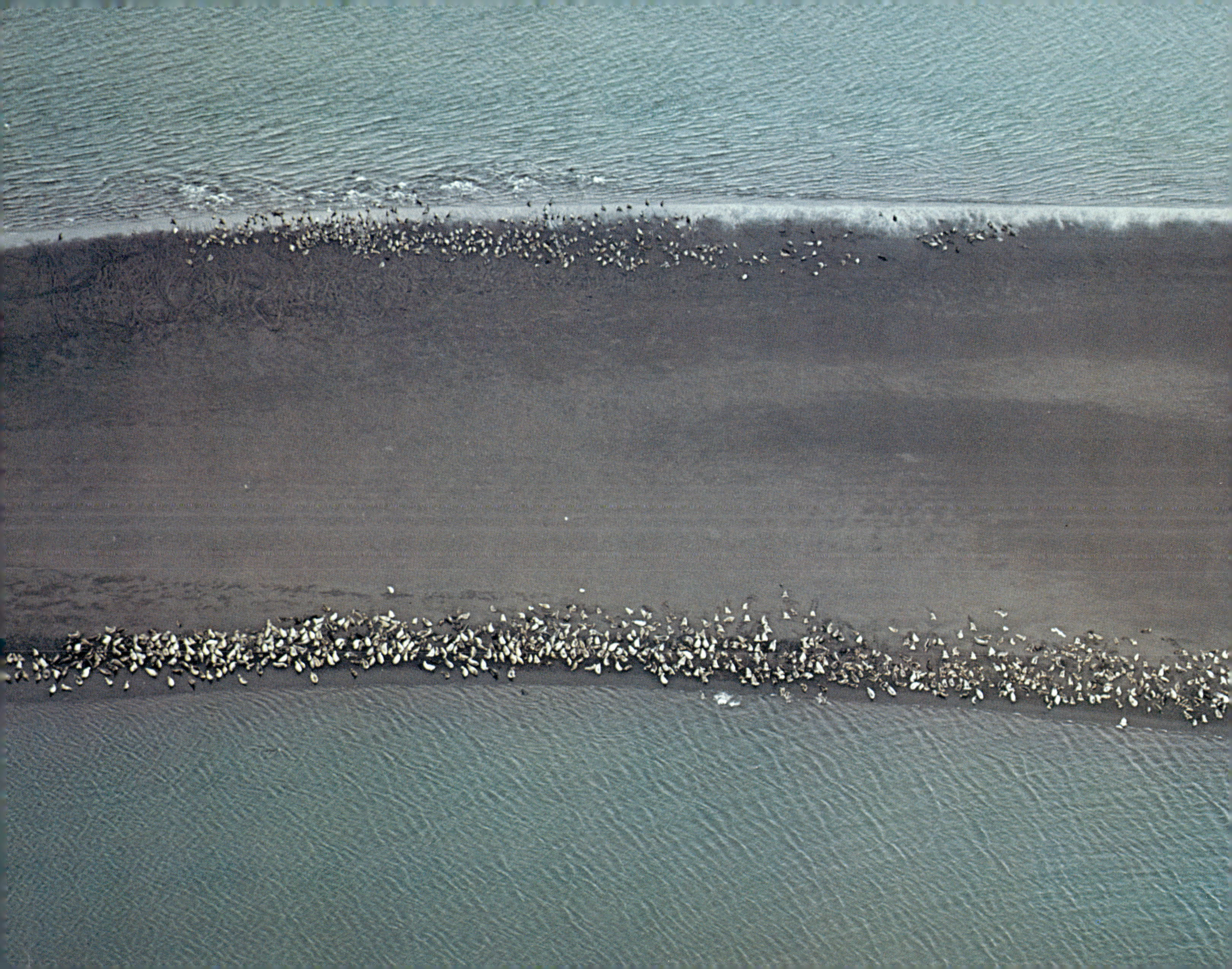

A visitor to Katmai
National Park and Preserve
gets a close look at the roiling
waters of the Ukak River as it
churns past ash cover hundreds
of feet thick. Novarupta
Volcano exploded in June 1912
covering 40 square miles of a
verdant valley with up to
700 feet of pumice and ash.
(John and Margaret Ibbotson)

wildlife refuges, wild and scenic rivers, and wilderness. This bill was passed by the U.S. House of Representatives in 1978, but failed to pass the U.S. Senate.

In late 1978, as the time limit set by ANCSA was about to expire, Interior Secretary Cecil Andrus withdrew lands included in the pending legislation under emergency authority prescribed by the Federal Land Policy and Management Act of 1976. President Carter designated 56 million acres of the lands so withdrawn as national monuments.

In February 1980 the House of Representatives passed a modified HR 39. In August 1980 the Senate passed a compromise version of the Alaska lands bill which created 106 million acres of new conservation units and affected a total of 131 million acres of land in Alaska. In November 1980 the House accepted the Senate version which President Carter signed in December.

The Alaska d-2 lands bill breaks new ground in a number of ways. A deliberate effort was made to include entire ecosystems in protected status. Along the Alaska Peninsula an effective continuity of wildlife habitat lands has been created, utilizing a variety of land classifications. In the Brooks Range, similarly, the protected habitat now extends from the Canadian boundary to very near the Bering Sea. Most of the Porcupine caribou herd's migration route lying within Alaska is protected, and attempts are being made to establish similar protection on the Canadian side.

A desire to maintain cultural integrity for Native communities and rural life styles within the newly created national parks generated provisions to continue subsistence activities including hunting, fishing and trapping by using motorized vehicles such as snow machines and motorboats where traditionally practiced.

In addition, the means of access to wilderness areas will include traditional methods such as airplanes and motorboats. Provisions for retaining, maintaining, and building new shelter cabins where required for public safety are also included.

Mineralized zones and areas with known oil and gas potential were excluded from designated areas to permit development, when economically feasible.

Cooperative management agreements between the state and federal agencies are being negotiated in areas where such agreements will provide better fulfillment of management guidelines.

With passage of the Alaska d-2 lands bill, the final step in the allocation of territory within Alaska is complete, save for minor adjustments. This allocation began in 1958, with passage of the Alaska Statehood Act by which the state was given the right to select 103 million acres of land as its statehood entitlement. Outstanding Native claims were settled by the Alaska Native Claims Settlement Act of 1971, which turned over about 44 million acres of land to 13 Native regional corporations and more than 200 village corporations. The national interest in Alaska lands resulted in the protection within conservation units of 131 million acres through passage of the compromise HR 39.

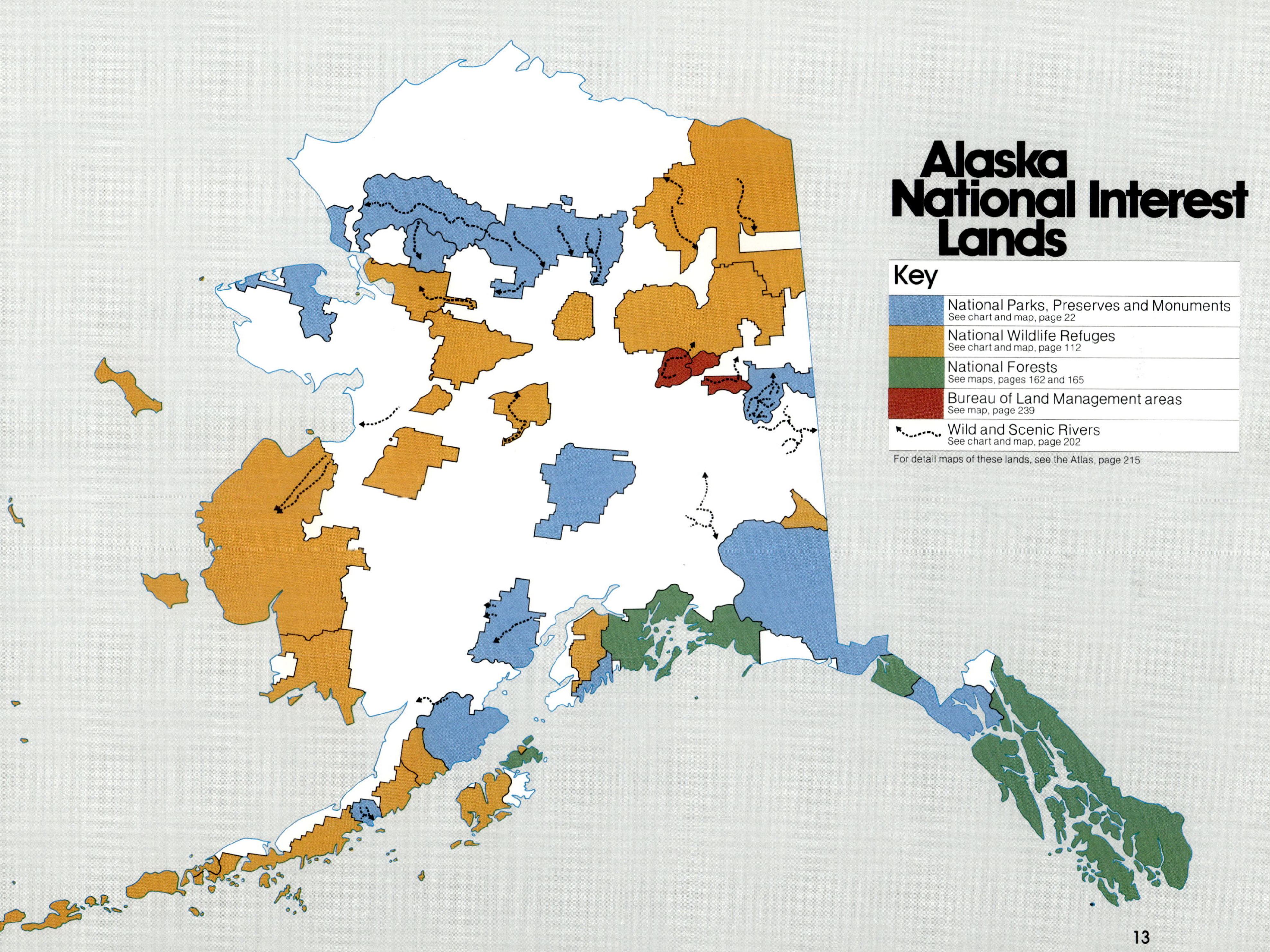

Alaska
National Interest
Lands
Key
National Parks, Preserves and Monuments
See chart and map, page 22
National Wildlife Refuges
See chart and map, page 112
National Forests
See maps, pages 162 and 165
Bureau of Land Management areas
See map, page 239
Wild and Scenic Rivers
See chart and map, page 202
For detail maps of these lands, see the Atlas, page 215

Above: The arctic poppy is a frequent colorful sight, most often found in sandy, gravelly soil. (Gil Mull)

Left: Three caribou herds — Mentasta, Chisana and Nelchina — graze within Wrangell-Saint Elias National Park and Preserve. The Chisana herd generally confines its movements to the northeast section of the park near Beaver Creek; the Mentasta and Nelchina herds share habitat between 2,000 and 5,000 feet in the northern and western Wrangells. (W.K. Almond)

Right: John Ibbotson crosses the tundra-covered slopes of Kugrak Valley which winds to the south of the Noatak River in Noatak National Preserve.
(John and Margaret Ibbotson)

Left: Mom and cub wait for salmon to return upriver on the Alaska Peninsula. Much of the peninsula has been designated national interest land and has been included in provisions of the d-2 bill. (Larry Aumiller)

Right: Mount Mageik (7,250 feet) towers above Katmai's Valley of Ten Thousand Smokes. (Pat Powell)

Below: Much of the land set aside under the d-2 bill protects vital habitat for Alaska's substantial wildlife populations. One of the state's larger mammals is the moose, largest member of the deer family. (Tom Walker)

Management Goals and Objectives of Federal Land Management Agencies

National Park Service:

The National Park Service has as its guiding principle the protection and preservation of the lands and related resources entrusted to its care to pass them on in unimpaired condition to future generations. However, their mission has two aspects: to preserve the values of these lands AND to provide for the use and enjoyment by people of the national parks. The key to resolving these often conflicting directives is the word "unimpaired" — all management and uses must be evaluated for their impact on the wide range of values represented in the national parks.

Alaska's new national park areas have added another dimension to National Park Service management. The areas established as parks under the Alaska lands act contain lands which have been traditionally used and occupied by indigenous peoples. To help preserve the culture of these people, which often depends upon the use of natural resources for subsistence and survival, the new park areas are directed by the act to permit subsistence activities to continue. Thus on the new parks, rural Alaskans are allowed to continue to hunt and fish, cut firewood and house logs, gather berries and other products, to trap for their own use and for items used in handcrafts. Traditional methods of transportation for subsistence activities are allowed, including the use of mechanized equipment, such as snow machines and motorboats.

Certain new areas, and portions of other new parks, have been classified under the act as national preserves. These national preserves are managed by the National Park Service in the same way as national parks with the exception that sport hunting and fishing and some trapping activities will be permitted. They are closed to the staking of mining claims, or other forms of entry, such as homesites.

Top: Ranger Stacy Studebaker greets visitors to Katmai National Park and Preserve. (Chlaus Lotscher)

Above: Black bear tracks in Great Kobuk Sand Dunes of Kobuk Valley National Park leave a firm warning to be alert for those following behind. (Manya Wik)

A traveler watches a gold-panning demonstration at a stream in the Kantishna District in the northern addition to Denali National Park and Preserve. (Ginny Wood)

U.S. Forest Service:

The national forests of the United States are managed for multiple use. Among uses recognized by forest service planners are watershed protection, protection of wildlife habitat, recreation, wilderness, timber harvesting, fisheries maintenance, mining and oil and gas production, grazing of domestic livestock and research.

The Alaska lands act established a number of wilderness areas, and two national monuments, to be managed by the U.S. Forest Service. These are located in southeastern Alaska within Tongass National Forest.

U.S. Fish & Wildlife Service:

The National Wildlife Refuge System is managed by the U.S. Fish & Wildlife Service. The major purpose of the refuge system is to protect the habitats of wildlife, fish, birds and marine mammals found within its boundaries. Other uses of lands within the National Wildlife Refuge system may be permitted as long as they do not impact adversely on this primary purpose.

Thus, wildlife refuges are open to hunting, fishing and trapping under appropriate state and federal regulations. At the discretion of the Secretary of the Interior, refuges may be opened to oil and gas exploration and leasing.

Below: Canoeists take it easy along the Swan Lake Canoe Trail in the Kenai National Wildlife Refuge. This 60-mile route connects 30 lakes with forks of the Moose River. Fishing is permitted on the refuge under state and federal regulations, and rainbow trout, Dolly Varden and silver salmon inhabit the trail's waterways.
(Jo Keller, U.S. Fish & Wildlife Service)

Left: Bob Uhl, long-time resident of the Krusenstern area, draws seal oil from fresh blubber stored in a seal poke at Sealing Point on Cape Krusenstern. For centuries Sealing Point has been a gathering place for hunters and among their chief prey has been *oogruk,* or bearded seal. Hunting seal and other traditional subsistence activities will be encouraged in the Cape Krusenstern National Monument. (Anore Jones)

Alaska Wilderness Areas

Passage of the Alaska National Interest Lands Conservation Act (ANILCA) on December 2, 1980, added millions of acres to the National Wilderness Preservation System. Administration of these wilderness areas is the responsibility of the agency under whose jurisdiction the land is situated. Agencies which administer wilderness areas in Alaska include the National Park Service, U.S. Fish & Wildlife Service, and the U.S. Forest Service. Although the Bureau of Land Management (BLM) has authority to manage wilderness in the public domain, no BLM wilderness areas exist in Alaska.

Wilderness allocations to different agencies in Alaska are:

Agency	Approximate Acreage
U.S. Forest Service	5,360,000
National Park Service	32,355,000
U.S. Fish & Wildlife Service	18,560,000

Wilderness, according to the Wilderness Act of 1964, is land sufficient in size to enable the operation of natural systems without undue influence from activities in surrounding areas, and should be places in which man himself is a visitor who does not remain. Wilderness management in the continental United States restricts the use of mechanized equipment for transportation and even such things as chain saws for use in clearing land within wilderness. Wilderness is assumed to be land maintained in a natural state — roadless, without maintained trails and without man-made structures.

Alaska wilderness regulations follow the stipulations of the Wilderness Act as amended by the Alaska lands act. Specifically designed to allow for Alaska conditions, the rules are considerably more lenient about transportation access, man-made structures and use of mechanized vehicles. The primary objective of a wilderness area continues to be the maintenance of the wilderness character of the land.

In Alaska wilderness areas, the following uses and activities are permitted:

1. Fishing, hunting and trapping will continue on lands within the national forests, national wildlife refuges and national park preserves. In national park wilderness fishing is allowed but not hunting.
2. Subsistence uses, including hunting, fishing, trapping, berry-gathering and use of timber for cabins and firewood will be permitted in wilderness areas by all agencies.
3. Public recreation cabins in wilderness areas in national forests, national wildlife refuges and national park preserves will continue to be maintained and may be replaced as needed. A limited number of new public cabins may be added if needed for health and safety reasons.
4. Existing special use permits and leases on all national forest wilderness lands for cabins, homesites or similar structures will continue. Use of temporary campsites, shelters and other temporary facilities and equipment related to hunting and fishing on national forest lands will continue as it has in the past.
5. Fish habitat enhancement programs, including construction of buildings, fish weirs, fishways, spawning channels and other accepted means of maintaining, enhancing and rehabilitating fish stocks will be allowed in national forest wilderness areas. In a designated wilderness, such structures should emphasize a rustic appearance and be in keeping with the wilderness nature of the area. Reasonable access including use of motorized equipment will be permitted.
6. Special use permits for guides and outfitters operating within wilderness areas in the national forests will be allowed to continue.
7. Private, state and Native lands surrounded by wilderness areas will be guaranteed access through the wilderness area.
8. Use of airplanes, motorboats and snow machines where *traditional* as a means of access into wilderness areas will be allowed to continue.

The blue water of Clearwater Slough, seen from the Kikahe River, Stikine-LeConte wilderness, is a bright contrast to the river's muddy appearance. (Staff)

National Park Service Parks, Preserves and Monuments

Lands administered by the National Park Service in Alaska consist of national parks, national preserves and national monuments since passage of the Alaska d-2 lands bill.

National parks are managed to preserve scenic, wildlife and recreational values for which they were set aside. Mining, logging and other forms of resource exploitation are not permitted within park boundaries, nor is hunting allowed under ordinary park regulations, and motorized access is restricted to automobile traffic on authorized roads.

Provisions for the new park service-administered areas in Alaska recognize the unusual situation in Alaska where the boundaries of some of the new units contain lands traditionally occupied and used by Alaska Natives and rural residents for subsistence activities. Thus all new parks, preserves and monuments and the additions to older parks will be managed to permit subsistence hunting, fishing and gathering activities, and the use of such motorized vehicles as snow machines, motorboats and airplanes, where such activities have been customary.

Also, in recognition of traditional uses of certain areas, the bill establishes national preserves which will be managed as national parks except that sport hunting will be permitted. Preserves accommodate subsistence activities, but they exist primarily to allow sport hunting to continue.

National Park Service Units in Alaska

Before 1971* Name	Acreage	As of December 2, 1980** Name (numbers refer to map)	Total Acreage	Monument	Park (Includes acreage classified as Wilderness)	Preserve	Wilderness (Lands within Parks and Preserves that are maintained as natural areas)
		1. Aniakchak National Monument and Preserve	514,000	138,000		376,000	
		2. Bering Land Bridge National Preserve	2,457,000			2,457,000	
		3. Cape Krusenstern National Monument	560,000	560,000			
Mount McKinley National Park	1,940,000	4. Denali National Park and Preserve	5,696,000†		4,366,000	1,330,000	1,900,000
		5. Gates of the Arctic National Park and Preserve	7,952,000		7,052,000	900,000	7,052,000
Glacier Bay National Monument	2,748,000	6. Glacier Bay National Park and Preserve	3,328,000†		3,271,000	57,000	2,770,000
Katmai National Monument	2,923,000	7. Katmai National Park and Preserve	4,268,000†		3,960,000	308,000	3,473,000
		8. Kenai Fjords National Park	567,000		567,000		
		9. Kobuk Valley National Park	1,710,000		1,710,000		190,000
		10. Lake Clark National Park and Preserve	3,653,000		2,439,000	1,214,000	2,470,000
		11. Noatak National Preserve	6,460,000			6,460,000	5,800,000
		12. Wrangell-Saint Elias National Park and Preserve	12,318,000		8,147,000	4,171,000	8,700,000
		13. Yukon-Charley Rivers National Preserve	1,713,000			1,713,000	
TOTAL ACREAGE:	7,611,000		51,196,000	698,000	31,512,000	18,986,000	32,355,000

*1971 — Section 17(d)(2) of the Alaska Native Claims Settlement Act (ANCSA) authorized the withdrawal of unreserved public lands by December 1978. However, Congress failed to meet the deadline, so late in 1978 these lands were withdrawn by the Secretary of the Interior under emergency authority prescribed by the Federal Land Policy and Management Act of 1976, and designated by the President as national monuments.

**In December 1980, The Alaska National Interest Lands Conservation Act established these lands as monuments, parks and preserves.

† Includes pre-1971 acreage

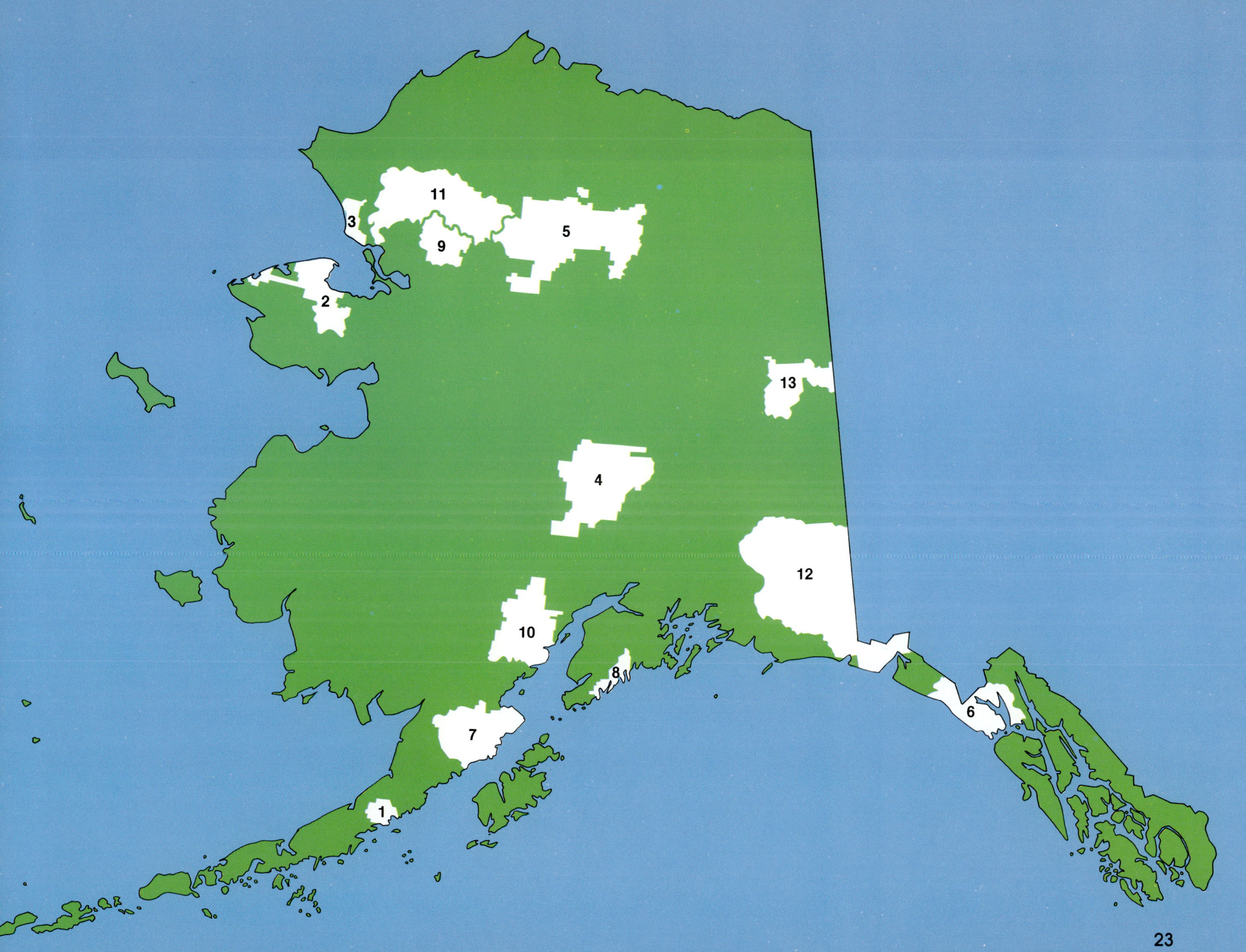

1
2
3
4
5
6
7
8
9
10
11
12
13

Aniakchak National Monument and Preserve

Location: Southwestern Alaska on Alaska Peninsula; ten miles east of Meshik (Port Heiden); 400 miles southwest of Anchorage.

Size: 514,000 acres (138,000 acres in monument; 376,000 acres in preserve).

Access: Scheduled airlines operate from Anchorage to King Salmon, and Anchorage to Meshik. Charter planes fly from King Salmon to Meshik (Port Heiden), a distance of 130 miles; floatplanes fly from King Salmon to Surprise Lake.

By foot from Meshik to monument boundary is ten miles of difficult walking; no trail.

See detail map, page 216.

Area Description: Aniakchak National Monument and Preserve contains a representative portion of the Alaska Peninsula ecosystem composed of four physiographic zones: coastal, river valley, upland and volcanic. The monument's major feature is Aniakchak caldera which chronicles a history of volcanic activity and the beginnings of revegetation and plant and animal succession.

The 30-mile-square caldera, one of the world's largest, is the giant crater of a collapsed volcano six miles in diameter, rimmed by 2,000-foot walls that once were the lower slopes of a large mountain. The valley floor, 1,100 feet in elevation at the lowest point, presents a bizarre landscape of vent cones, one rising 2,200 feet with its own snow-packed crater; extensive fields of ash and cinder; and lava flow material.

Aniakchak last erupted in 1931. Captain Halvorsen, superintendent of the Alaska Packers' cannery at Chignik, estimated that at least one pound of ash an hour fell on every square foot of ground at Chignik. Even as far north as the Kuskokwim area, 300 miles away, one-fourth inch of ash covered everything.

The Pacific Ocean forms the eastern boundary of the preserve with a coastline of rocky cliffs, extensive beaches, wide bays and sheltered coves. The western side of the monument slopes gently from the caldera to a broad, tundra plain, pockmarked with ponds, bordering Bristol Bay. This side of the Aleutian Range, adjoining the backbone of the Alaska

► Smaller cones and craters rupture the floor of Aniakchak caldera, a major feature of Aniakchak National Park and Preserve. At the time of Aniakchak's last eruption, in 1931, ash reached as far as the Kuskokwim area 300 miles to the north. (Keith Trexler, National Park Service, reprinted from *ALASKA GEOGRAPHIC*®)

► The Aniakchak River flows through the Gates, a breach in the east wall of Aniakchak caldera. (M. Woodbridge Williams, National Park Service)

► Moss and other hardy vegetation cling to the caldera's slopes. During the destructive eruption in 1931, ash falling on tundra hundreds of miles away ground the teeth of grazing reindeer down to the gums. (George Wuerthner)

Below: Surprise Lake in upper right and the rises of Vent Mountain (right) and smaller cinder cones stand out in this aerial photo of Aniakchak caldera taken from 14,000 feet. (M. Woodbridge Williams, National Park Service)

Right: Sweeps of ash partly cover lava ridges inside Aniakchak caldera. The crater was discovered and named in 1922 by R.H. Sargent and W.R. Smith of the U.S. Geological Survey. (Keith Trexler, National Park Service)

Peninsula, receives less precipitation than the Pacific side.

Aniakchak River, designated as a wild and scenic river, gushes out of Surprise Lake within the caldera to rush turbulently through a narrow gap in the crater's wall. Farther along, the river slows to a meander, finally reaching the Pacific Ocean. The Meshik River flows out of Meshik Lake westward into Bristol Bay.

Emerald-hued Surprise Lake, fed by warm springs, covers two and one fourth square miles in the northeastern part of the caldera. The lake and Aniakchak River contrast with the otherwise stark landscape of the crater. From the top of the crater's walls above the lake, an expanse of snow- and ice-covered peaks and uninhabited rolling hills and plains overlook both the Bering Sea and Pacific Ocean.

Fauna: Brown/grizzly bear, caribou, fox, moose and wolf are found on land; eagles, migratory waterfowl, and seabirds fly overhead. Sea lions, sea otters and seals inhabit coastal waters; salmon and trout abound in the streams.

Flora: The western Alaska Peninsula is treeless. Wet tundra with mosses, sedges, grasses and lichens cover most of the Bristol Bay coastal plain and the lower western slopes of the Aleutian Range. Brushy thickets grow along riverbeds.

Accommodations: None available in monument/preserve.

Recreational Opportunities:

Since very few persons other than Natives and a few scientists have ventured into this area, the prime attraction is an opportunity to explore on foot a wilderness area seldom visited. Possible activities include hiking, primitive camping, fishing, photography, natural history, river rafting on the Aniakchak National Wild and Scenic River (whose upper reaches are termed ''challenging'') and beach walking.

Human Use and Occupation:

Although most Natives who inhabit the Alaska Peninsula now call themselves Aleuts, they are descendants of the Koniag Eskimo culture, mixed with Russian lineage from the late-18th and 19th century Russian sea-otter-hunting era. Approximately 300 persons live in the area with population centers at Meshik (Port Heiden); and at Chignik, Chignik Lake, and Chignik Lagoon, 50 miles to the southwest.

Suggested Reading:
►*ALASKA GEOGRAPHIC®*, Vol. 4, No. 1, *ALASKA'S VOLCANOES*
►*ALASKA GEOGRAPHIC®*, Vol. 6, No. 3, *ALASKA'S NATIVE PEOPLE*
►*ALASKA GEOGRAPHIC®*, Vol. 5, No. 3, *BRISTOL BAY BASIN*

Further Information:
►Area Director, National Park Service
540 West 5th Avenue
Anchorage, AK 99501
►Superintendent, Katmai National Park and Preserve
National Park Service
Box 7
King Salmon, AK 99613

USGS Topographic Series:
Sutwick Island, Chignik, Bristol Bay, Ugashik

Bering Land Bridge National Preserve

Location: Central and northwestern Seward Peninsula, south of the Arctic Circle; 50 miles south of Kotzebue, 90 miles north of Nome, and 60 miles east of Siberia.

Size: 2,457,000 acres.

Access: Scheduled daily airline service operates to Kotzebue and Nome from Anchorage or Fairbanks. Bush planes from Nome or Kotzebue fly to Deering or Shishmaref. Floatplanes can land on Imuruk, Lava or Kuzitrin lakes.

North Killeak Lake forms in a maar crater in Bering Land Bridge National Preserve. These craters are formed by steam explosions associated with volcanic activity. (Pete Sanchez, National Park Service)

Area Description: Maritime climate influences the coastal area; continental climate predominates inland. The preserve is cold and windswept during dark winters when temperatures vary from 40°F. to -60°F. In summer temperatures can reach 85°F. May, June and July have 24-hour daylight. Annual precipitation is about eight inches, falling mostly as rain in summer.

The low profile of the landscape gives a sense of unobstructed vastness and exposure to the elements. The coastal area is flat, marshy and studded with ponds that furnish habitat for nesting waterfowl. The interior topography is rolling rather than jagged, and even the Bendeleben Mountains with elevations up to 3,700 feet have rounded contours.

Permafrost, permanently frozen soils and gravels found from one to five feet below the surface, has sculptured the ground with pingos (ice-cored domes), braided streams, solifluction lobes (frost movement on large volumes of loose material causing it to flow downhill and form lobes), and thaw lakes. Volcanic activity has produced extensive lava fields of the pahoehoe type (basaltic lava with a smooth or billowy surface) around Imuruk Lake, and maar lakes (low-rimmed, water-filled craters formed by steam explosions associated with volcanic activity).

Geothermal activity has produced Serpentine Hot Springs near the preserve's southern boundary.

This new unit of Alaska's National Park and Preserve System is different from others. It features ecological, geological, anthropological and historical processes rather than places. There are no spectacular features such as high mountains, glaciers, gorges or forests. Bering Land Bridge National Preserve will probably never attract large numbers of tourists or outdoor recreationists. But for scientists and those interested in the interaction of time and climate on the geology, geography, plants, animals and human use of the land, the preserve has much to offer.

Periodically, between 40,000 and 11,000 years ago, climatic changes caused the rise and ebb of great ice sheets of the Pleistocene era. During these periods, the water level in the Bering Sea would also fall and rise, causing the bottom to

See detail map, page 216.

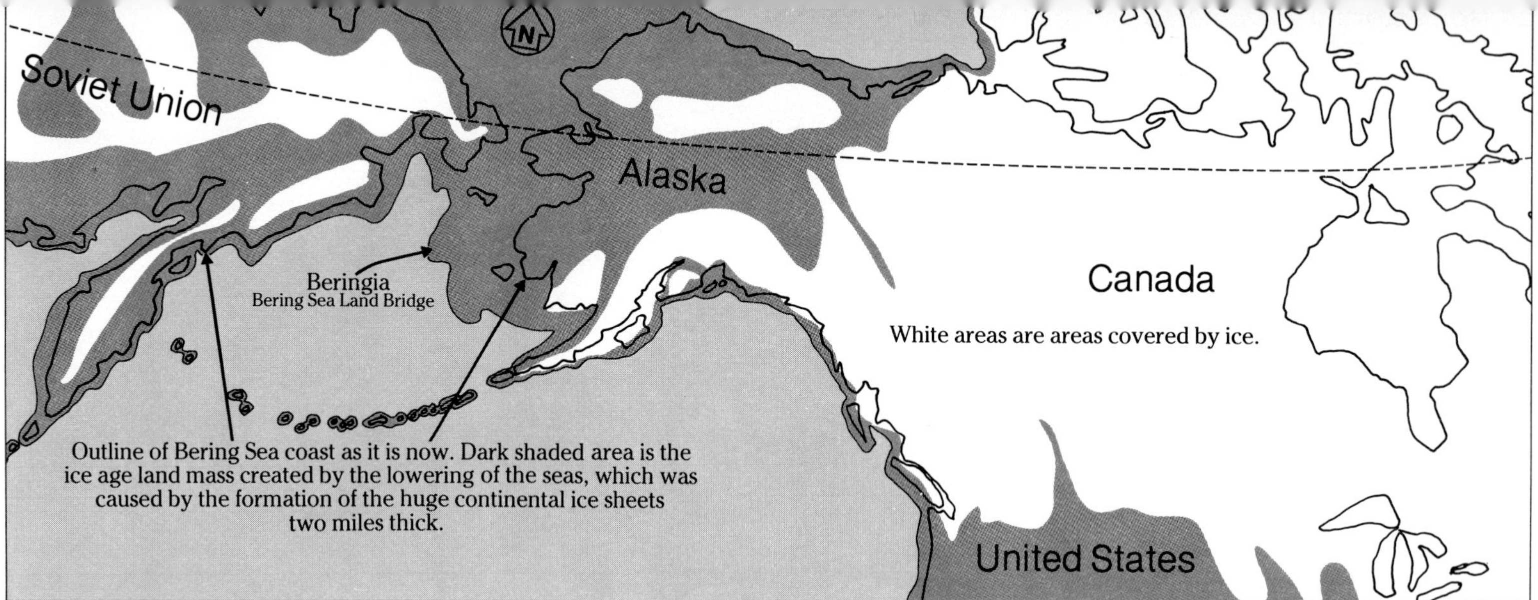

Reprinted from *The ALASKA JOURNAL*®

emerge for several thousand years, then submerge again.

During some of these periods, the land bridge from Alaska to Asia was up to 900 miles wide. While the two continents were connected, plants, animals and man migrated into Alaska, and probably down ice-free corridors to populate other parts of the western hemisphere.

The Bering Land Bridge National Preserve contains archaeological records, both discovered and undiscovered, of these migrations which furnish bits and pieces of the unfolding history of man. Today, the majority of Seward Peninsula's inhabitants are Eskimos, many following traditional patterns of a subsistence economy based on the resources which the sea and land provide. To preserve these resources is an important objective in the management of this preserve.

Fauna: Large concentrations of waterfowl and other migratory birds in the wetlands and estuaries along the coast are a major feature of the preserve. An inventory lists 137 species of birds here.

Offshore swim 15 species of marine mammals including bearded seal *(oogruk)*, walrus, hair seal, ribbon seal, and humpback, fin and bowhead whales.

Polar bears frequently visit offshore ice, while inland roam brown/grizzly bear, arctic fox, wolverine, mink, ermine, hare, ground squirrel, lemming, voles, and a once-rare but now common visitor, moose. Caribou, once numerous, have been replaced by a domesticated subspecies, reindeer, imported at the turn of the century from Siberia. Several herds are owned and tended by Eskimos who have permits to graze their herds within the preserve. The reindeer fill the caribou niche.

Flora: The preserve is devoid of trees, but a varied combination of plants make up different tundra communities ranging from sedges, mosses and grasses of moist lowlands to herbs and lichens of drier, better-drained ridges and hills.

Accommodations: There are none in the preserve.

Recreational Opportunities: The gentle terrain encourages roaming on foot with pack and binoculars. While much of the area is marshy, higher ground and dry tundra and lava flow areas provide easier walking. An opportunity exists for discreet observation and understanding of Native interaction with a harsh but biologically rich environment which has sustained them for centuries. Archaeological artifacts of past human migrations, fossil remains of prehistoric animals, history of explorations by Vitus Bering and Captain James Cook, epics of 19th century whalers and early 20th century gold seekers give the discerning visitor a sense of man's involvement with a land in which the forces or processes of nature still dominate.

Suggested Reading:
►*ALASKA GEOGRAPHIC®,* Vol. 6, No. 3,
ALASKA'S NATIVE PEOPLE

Further Information:
►Superintendent, Bering Land Bridge National Preserve
National Park Service
Nome, AK 99762

USGS Topographic Series:
Kotzebue, Shishmaref, Bendeleben, Teller

Clockwise from above:
► A visitor walks among the tors of Bering Land Bridge National Preserve. Tors are high, isolated pinnacles made up of much jointed, usually granitic rocks that have endured intense weathering. (T. Newman, National Park Service)
► Sedge tundra covers the coastal expanses of Bering Land Bridge National Preserve. This photo was taken near 798-foot Devil Mountain on the northern portion of the Seward Peninsula where it extends out to separate lower Kotzebue Sound from the Chukchi Sea. (Pete Sanchez, National Park Service)
► A wary female common eider keeps close watch for intruders while incubating her eggs in a well-hidden nest on the tundra. Common eiders are North America's largest ducks and just one of the several species of waterfowl found here. (Penny Rennick)

Cape Krusenstern National Monument

Some of the beach ridges — ancient beach fronts built up by shifting deposits of earth — for which Krusenstern is famous are visible in this aerial of the cape. Archaeologists have found evidence of several ancient cultures in diggings in the ridges. (Robert Belous, National Park Service, reprinted from *ALASKA GEOGRAPHIC®*)

Location: Northwestern Alaska along the Chukchi Sea coast, above the Arctic Circle; ten miles north of Kotzebue at its most southerly point, and approximately 450 miles northwest of Fairbanks.

Size: Approximately 560,000 acres.

Access: Daily scheduled airlines operate from Fairbanks and Anchorage to Kotzebue; bush planes land on beaches or lagoons within the monument. Small boats can be chartered at Kotzebue to cross Kotzebue Sound to Sisualik Spit in the monument.

See detail map, page 217.

With her can of insect repellent at hand to keep insects under control, Carrie Uhl prepares beluga muktuk and meat to store in seal oil in the cold storage behind the Uhls' camp at Sisualik in Cape Krusenstern National Monument. Beluga are small, light-colored, toothed whales found throughout many of Alaska's coastal waters. (Anore Jones)

Area Description: The influence of the maritime climate is cancelled much of the year by the freezing over of the Chukchi Sea. Gale force winds add a wind-chill factor to sub-zero temperatures during the winter. Summers are mild with temperatures ranging between 32°F. and 80°F. Twenty-four-hour daylight extends from May to mid-August.

An uninformed tourist at Cape Krusenstern might comment, "Where are the sights? Where is the monument? There is nothing here but ponds and endless monotonous ridges." But to archaeologists the scene is intriguing.

Ridges at the monument are a succession of beaches; each in turn was at one time a shoreline. As ocean currents and storms washed up new deposits of gravel, another beach was formed in front of the older one. From the air, the ridges look like furrows left in the wake of a gigantic plow. There are 114 beaches, six to eight feet high, extending up to eight miles long on the cape where the land bends northward from Kotzebue Sound to the Chukchi Sea.

Dr. Louis Giddings, a 1932 graduate of the University of Alaska who went on to achieve worldwide recognition as a chronicler of early man's occupation of the Arctic, first gazed on these ridges from the top of an old platform at the cape. In *Ancient Men of the Arctic* (1967), Giddings describes the cape:

No longer monotonous, the landscape becomes rich in detail. Immediately below, one sees half-buried logs of driftwood, probably tossed by storms to the height of the beach, and arrangements of weathered wood and whalebone, quite certainly the work of man. Belying its appearance from the sea, the first crest has been walked upon by many men, and signs of their tenting, digging, and storing soon become evident in patterns of rectangles and circles formed by the ground-hugging leaves of various plants. Similar areas on the surface of other crests, beyond, testify to their also having been the sites of human activity. Lines running along the crests were made by men and animals for whom the old, parallel beaches were natural highways. Between the crests, sheltered from the wind, the vegetation grows taller and in a variety of hues, and moist spots encourage sedges and thick-leaved plants. Far back from the ocean, some of the swales hold water, making canals. Still farther back, swales join to become ponds, and finally, in the distance, the continuous water of a wide lagoon stretches three miles to the slopes of Ingitkalik Mountain. . . . Ducks and dowitchers fly up from the ponds now and then, and a glitter in the distance is the sunlight reflected from the wings of wheeling terns.

Below: A woolly musk ox, ready for anything, looks out from tundra grass at Krusenstern. Alaska's original musk ox population was exterminated by hunters in the mid-1800s. However, animals were introduced from foreign stocks in the early part of this century and musk ox have now retaken some of their original range. (Peter Connors)

Right: Sweet pea is one of the common tundra flowers of the Krusenstern area. (Anore Jones)

A young American golden plover chick scoots out from under its parent's wing at Cape Krusenstern. Elegant golden plovers build their nests in tundra vegetation on drier slopes; they can be distinguished from black-bellied plovers by their smaller size and darker appearance. (James Young)

Giddings pondered the scene before him and speculated if these series of beaches might not also chronicle a series of many generations of hunters and travelers. "If they do, have we not, at Cape Krusenstern, an unequalled archaeological sequence — an orderly succession of people who resettled at the ocean edge whenever a new beach formed?" wondered Giddings. At the time of his death in 1964, Giddings had traced, by the distinctiveness of artifacts which he had excavated, a succession of cultures stretching from the present back to approximately 6,000 B.C. More clues to the past lie buried at Cape Krusenstern waiting to be discovered and analyzed. Eskimos still come here to hunt and gather. To protect this way of life as an ongoing link with the past, and to preserve the archaeological evidence of this continuity of man's relationship with the land is a major goal in the management of Cape Krusenstern National Monument.

Fauna: Large mammals — black and brown/grizzly bears, musk ox, caribou, reindeer, moose, and wolves — rely on the monument's vegetation or smaller animals for nourishment. Smaller mammals present here include wolverine, short-tailed weasel (ermine), mink, arctic and red foxes, arctic ground squirrel, tundra hare, lemming and voles.

Offshore swim walrus, polar bear, and several species of seals and whales.

A diversity of bird life nests on the wet, moist and alpine tundra of Cape Krusenstern National Monument. Some species are present only in summer when they migrate from warmer climates to breed, nest and raise young here. A few hardy varieties such as ravens, ptarmigans, and owls remain year-round. Summer visitors include but are not limited to waterfowl — arctic, common, and yellow-billed loons, whistling swans, Canada and white-fronted geese, pintails, and American wigeons; shorebirds — sandhill cranes, American golden plovers, black-bellied plovers, and semipalmated sandpipers; and passerines — barn and bank swallows, gray-cheeked thrushes, white and yellow wagtails, lapland longspurs, snow buntings, and several species of sparrows and finches.

Flora: The coastal strip from Cape Krusenstern north is classified as alpine tundra and supports such plants as

Willow and Arunya Jones
and Carolyn Connors
pick salmonberries in
the Krusenstern area.
(Peter Connors)

willows, dwarf birch, and alpine azalea; various herbs including saxifrages and moss campion; grasses, sedges, ferns, mosses and lichens.

Wet tundra characterizes coastal vegetation from near the cape east toward Sisualik. Here grow willows, dwarf birch, shrubby cinquefoil, bog cranberry, blueberry, cloudberry, herbs, grasses, sedges, lichens, mosses and liverworts.

Moist tundra dominates the monument's vegetation away from the coast and visitors must contend with ever-present cotton grass tussocks, the foe of hikers throughout much of Alaska. Mixed with the cotton grass are dwarf birch, Labrador tea, lingonberry, cloudberry, mountain avens, mosses, lichens and other hardy plants.

Accommodations: None in the monument but Kotzebue, ten miles distant, has hotels, restaurants and stores.

Recreational Opportunities: To the extent that visitors do not diminish the major purpose of the monument — to protect the past and present cultural heritage of the Eskimo people — they will be encouraged to experience and understand this unique environment and its resources. Visitors should be aware, however, that much river and beach front land is owned by local residents and as such should not be used as part of the national park areas.

Recreational activities include primitive camping, hiking, bird-watching, fishing, and the sense of history that comes with experiencing the land and elements just as those who camped here for centuries have done.

Suggested Reading:
►*Ancient Men Of The Arctic*, J. Louis Giddings, 1967
►*ALASKA GEOGRAPHIC*®, Vol. 6, No. 3, *ALASKA'S NATIVE PEOPLE*

Further Information:
►Superintendent, Cape Krusenstern National Monument
  National Park Service
  Kotzebue, AK 99752

USGS Topographic Series:
Noatak, Kotzebue, Point Hope, Delong Mountains

Denali National Park and Preserve

Location: Southcentral Alaska about 200 miles north of Anchorage. Denali National Park and Preserve encompasses both the original Mount McKinley National Park and additions to the north, south and west. Denali is bounded on the east by the Alaska Railroad and George Parks Highway and on the north by the 64th parallel. The area's southern boundary zigzags northeastward from just south of the Cathedral Spires to Denali State Park.

Moonlight illuminates Mount McKinley and Wonder Lake. The Alaska State Geographic Names Board has agreed to change the mountain's name to Denali, but the federal board has yet to approve this action. (Tom Ulrich)

Size: The original park was nearly 2 million acres; the additions bring the total acreage of park and preserve to 5,696,000 acres, with another 1,900,000 acres designated wilderness.

Access: Major access is via the original park and existing park road which extends into the northern addition terminating at the Kantishna airstrip, a 1,200-foot bush strip. Free shuttle bus service is offered from the visitor's center at the east entrance through the park to Wonder Lake, near the north addition.

The George Parks Highway parallels the eastern boundary of the park and preserve for 128 miles from Mile 132 in the Denali State Park area to Mile 260, but this offers mainly viewing opportunities since large rivers cut off foot access.

Foot traffic can reach the southern addition boundaries near the Tokositna River from the Peters Hills, terminus of a primitive 25-mile dirt road taking off to the west from the Parks Highway at Mile 115 near Trapper Creek.

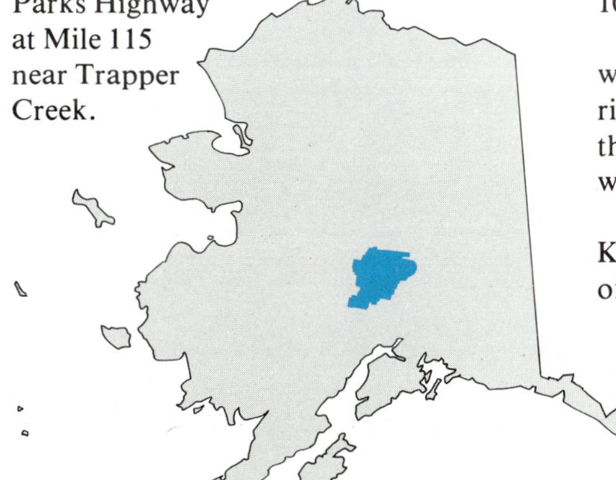

See detail map, page 217.

Charter flights to Lake Minchumina will offer access to the northwestern preserve area.

The Alaska Railroad stops at the park on trips between Anchorage and Fairbanks.

Area Description: Before passage of the Alaska National Interest Lands Conservation Act, and prior to establishment of Denali National Monument in 1978, the area known as Mount McKinley National Park was the second largest park in the national park system, covering 3,030 square miles.

The southern half of the original park contains the Alaska Range, dominated by Mount McKinley (also known as Denali), North America's highest mountain and the park's main attraction. The mountain has two peaks, known collectively as the Churchill Peaks. The north summit reaches a height of 19,470 feet; the south, 20,320 feet. The area is studded with mountains, many of them exceeding 10,000 feet, and is laced with glaciers.

To the north, the original park is dotted with hundreds of small lakes and many rivers and streams. This habitat supports the abundant and varied wildlife for which the park is famous.

The northern addition includes the Kantishna Hills, the westernmost portion of the "outer range" which encloses the

Mount Foraker, second highest peak in the park at 17,400 feet, rises to the west of
Mount McKinley. In 1899 Lt. J.S. Herron named the peak for Joseph Foraker
(1846-1917), a United States senator from Ohio. (John and Margaret Ibbotson)

Although not actually
the peak Robert Dunn
named in 1903 for his
aunt Anna F. Hunter,
this 14,575-foot peak
near Mount McKinley
has come to be known
as Mount Hunter.
(Brian Okonek)

Above: Ice cascades off the nearly vertical ridges
of The Mooses Tooth, 15 miles southeast of
Mount McKinley. (Courtesy of National Park Service)

Right: Overshadowed by their taller neighbors to
the northeast, the Cathedral Spires are sheer, stark,
knife-edged peaks rising from the core of the Alaska
Range about 60 miles southwest of Mount McKinley.
Highest peak in the group, Kichatna Spire (8,985 feet)
was not climbed until 1966.
(Staff, reprinted from *ALASKA GEOGRAPHIC®*)

Denali National Park's weather is normally better on the north side of the Alaska Range because slopes on the southern side catch storms moving in from the Gulf of Alaska. This tempest pushed its way north across the Alaska Range, however, and darkens the skies over Wonder Lake. (Brad Ebel)

road through the original park. Beyond the hills the ground slopes gently, interspersed with low hills, to the Kantishna River into which McKinley River, Moose Creek and other streams flow.

This land and the preserve lying south of Lake Minchumina were added to the original park to provide a more complete ecosystem for park wildlife such as wolf, brown/grizzly bear (generally known as grizzly in interior Alaska), caribou and moose. Only a portion of their habitat and range had been included within the original park boundary.

The southern addition, containing mostly snow, ice and rock, brings the massif of Mount McKinley as well as the vast glacier system flowing southward from McKinley and other Alaska Range peaks to the east, completely within park/preserve boundaries.

The southwest preserve extends considerably farther west than the original park boundary and encompasses the Cathedral Spires, granite, snow-capped, extremely steep-sided peaks interspersed with narrow, deep valleys.

The Kantishna Hills and the Dunkle Hills, just west of Cantwell, are both active mining areas in which the Alaska d-2 lands bill mandated study for three years to determine land use decisions.

Fauna: Wildlife found within the northern park addition and northwest preserve include caribou, moose, wolf, wolverine, fox, lynx, brown/grizzly bear and many smaller furbearers. A variety of waterfowl nest on streams and lakes within this area, and a hardy throng of spruce grouse, ptarmigans, gray jays, chickadees and other species make the area their year-round home. The spring and fall migration path for thousands of sandhill cranes passes over the northern portions of the park and preserve.

This bull displays the full rack characteristic of adult male caribou; females and young bulls also have antlers but they are much smaller than those of adult bulls.
(Mark Kelley)

41

Below: North America's only white wild sheep, Dall sheep rams (shown here) usually forage apart from females and young. The sexes come together to breed in late November through mid-December. (D.E. Luthy)

Below right: Dall sheep ewes and lambs graze on steep, rocky slopes of the Alaska Range in Denali National Park and Preserve. (George Wuerthner)

Flora: Much of the area is covered with ice and snow, but mixed spruce and birch are found in stream valleys and on upland slopes below tree line, which is about 2,700 feet altitude in the park addition.

Alpine tundra and moist tundra cover much of the remaining landscape. Between 3,000 and 4,000 feet sparse, low-growing vegetation characteristic of alpine tundra ekes out a meager existence in a harsh environment. Most mountain slopes above 4,500 feet are bare except for rock lichens.

Cotton grass and various other grasses, sedges, mosses, herbs and shrubs make up the moist tundra vegetation that covers much of the foothills.

Top: The only small hawk in Alaska with a reddish area on its back and tail, this American kestrel, or sparrow hawk, sits on a willow branch waiting for insects, mice or unwary smaller birds to pass by. (D.E. Luthy)

Above: Visitors, whether following the Denali Park road or traveling cross-country, are likely to spot willow ptarmigan, one of three ptarmigan species found in Denali National Park and Preseve. (Penny Rennick)

Left: These red currants, ready for picking in late summer, dangle from a branch in Denali National Park and Preserve. (John and Margaret Ibbotson)

Above: Delicate, star-shaped flowers of bog bean or buck bean add elegance to wet, low-lying areas. (John and Margaret Ibbotson)

Overleaf: Fall colors of dwarf willow and birch brighten the tundra north of the Alaska Range in Denali National Park. (Rick McIntyre)

A major attraction for visitors at Denali are the sled dog demonstrations held near park headquarters. During the winter the park's dog teams haul rangers and supplies.
(George Wuerthner)

Accommodations: Visitor facilities and accommodations can be found at the east entrance near McKinley Park Station on the Alaska Railroad. These include large campgrounds for vehicles and walk-in campgrounds for tent campers, as well as a youth hostel.

At Mile 87, two miles north of Wonder Lake in the original park, there is a wilderness vacation camp and an overnight tourist lodge, both situated within the park's northern addition. Tourist facilities are available along the Parks Highway, but none exist at either Peters Hills or Lake Minchumina.

Recreational Opportunities:

Excellent ice and rock climbing can be found in the southern addition to the park, and in the southwestern preserve centered around Cathedral Spires. A major takeoff point for climbs of 20,320-foot Mount McKinley is located at the 6,000-foot level on Kahiltna Glacier.

Hiking and backpacking with primitive camping can be enjoyed in the northern park addition, basing either at Kantishna or Lake Minchumina, or entering along the Lignite-Stampede pioneer access road.

Hunting in season will be permitted in the preserve, in accordance with state and federal regulations.

Suggested Reading:
►*The Wilderness of Denali,* Charles Sheldon, 1930
►*The Conquest of Mount McKinley,* Belmore Browne, 1913
►*The Ascent of Denali,* Hudson Stuck, 1914
►*A Naturalist in Alaska,* Adolph Murie, 1961
►*Mount McKinley: The Pioneer Climb,* Terris Moore, 1967
►*A Tourist Guide To Mount McKinley,* Bradford Washburn, 1980

Further Information:
►Superintendent, Denali National Park and Preserve
National Park Service
McKinley Park AK 99755

USGS Topographic Series:
McKinley, Talkeetna, Healy

Gates of the Arctic National Park and Preserve

Location: Northcentral Alaska, north of the Arctic Circle; 200 miles northwest of Fairbanks, 200 miles southeast of Barrow and 40 miles north and west of Bettles. Straddles the Brooks Range for about 200 miles from 157° to 150° longitude.

See detail map, page 218.

Size: 7,952,000 acres (7,052,000 in park; 900,000 acres in preserve), with 7,052,000 acres designated wilderness.

Access: Scheduled airlines operate from Fairbanks to Bettles, 40 miles south of the park, or to Anaktuvuk Pass, on the continental divide and north of the park.

Charter floatplanes fly out of Bettles to designated lakes and rivers. Chandler Lake on the north slope of the Brooks Range lies within Native land and is open to float and ski plane landings by permission of the Anaktuvuk village corporation. Wiseman, on the north Slope Haul Road, will be an access point now that most of the road is open to public use from June 1 to September 1.

Above: Prop wash from an ascending floatplane ruffles the waters of Circle Lake at the entrance to Arrigetch Valley. Floatplanes are a major means of access for travelers entering the Gates of the Arctic.

Right: On the south slope of the Brooks Range the channel of the Alatna River leaves oxbow lakes as it meanders past Takahula Lake, separated from the river by a low ridge, and flows south to join the Koyukuk. In the upper and lower portions of the photo smaller streams flow downhill to join the Alatna. A small, algae-filled lake occupies a crater at the top of a small hill at Takahula's north shore (to the left of the larger lake in this photo).
(Both by John and Margaret Ibbotson)

Area Description: Climate of the Gates of the Arctic area varies. South of the range summer temperatures are 32°F. to 85°F.; winter temperatures 32°F. to -60°F. North of the Brooks Range summer temperatures are much cooler; winter temperatures are somewhat milder but there is more wind. Precipitation records of eight to ten inches annually classify the area as semiarid, but this is hard to believe while experiencing frequent showers and boggy tundra during summer travels. Mid-May through mid-August the area receives 18 to 24 hours of daylight. North of the continental divide snow can fall every month of the year.

Landmark and highest point in the western Brooks Range is Mount Igikpak at 8,510 feet. (Kitt Marrs)

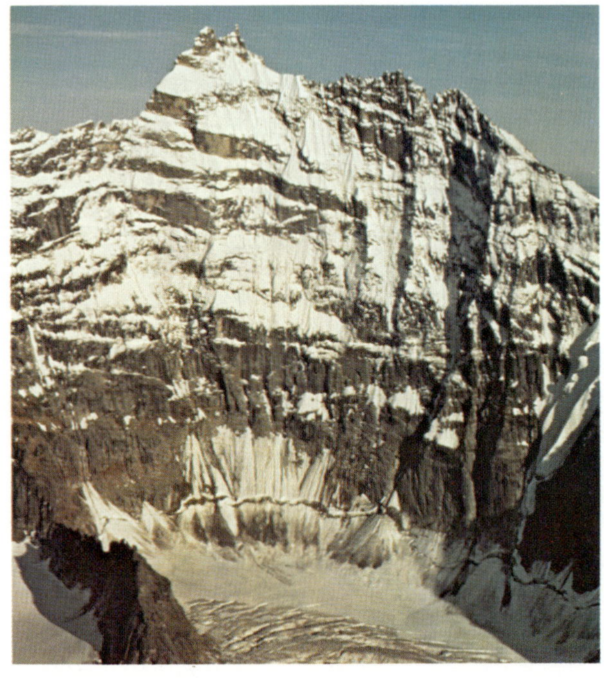

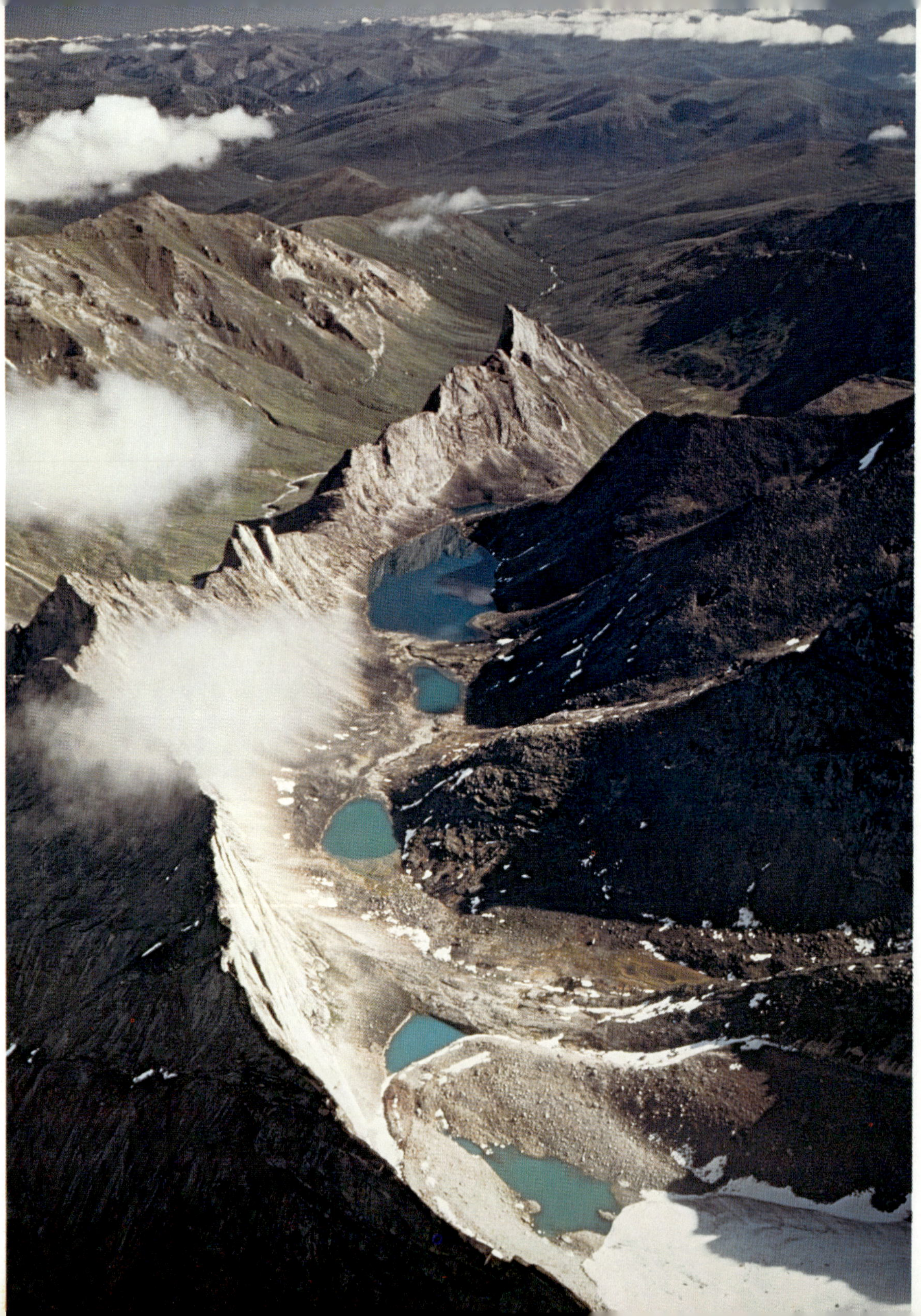

Left: Alpine lakes, many fed by glaciers, lie nestled in the bowl of a knife-edged ridge in the Arrigetch Peaks. (John and Margaret Ibbotson)

Below: In contrast to the granitic Arrigetch Peaks, altered basalts weather to rough pinnacles and rubble in the Angayucham Mountains in Gates of the Arctic. (Gil Mull)

When Robert Marshall first saw 6,666-foot Boreal Mountain, he dubbed the peak and its neighbor to the west, Frigid Crags, the Gates of the Arctic. (George Wuerthner)

The ground is permanently frozen starting from 2 to 30 feet below the surface, thus creating bogs and tussocks in low and poorly drained areas. Ridges and well-drained slopes are dry.

The major feature of Gates of the Arctic National Park and Preserve is the Brooks Range, actually a northern extension of the Rocky Mountains. Although not as high (rising to 8,500 feet) as the state's coastal mountains or Alaska Range, the seemingly endless mountain expanse from the Canadian border almost to the Chukchi Sea makes the Brooks Range one of the last and largest wilderness areas left in the United States.

Many rivers (flowing northward, southward and westward from glacier cirques) and numerous lakes form arteries for water travel by raft, canoe and kayak, and provide floatplane access for backpackers.

Just as the Teton Range forms a spectacular cluster of peaks in the Rocky Mountains, the granite spires of the Arrigetch Peaks in the Alatna River drainage jut against the skyline in the central Brooks Range. Mount Doonerak (7,610 feet) and Mount Igikpak (8,510 feet) and numerous other crags and glaciated peaks, many nameless, keep this range from being monotonous.

The Gates of the Arctic was the name that Robert Marshall, a forester who spent several summers and a winter exploring the then-unmapped areas north and west of Wiseman in the 1920s and 1930s, gave Boreal Mountain and Frigid Crags (both of which he named) that rise like sentinels on either side of the north fork of the Koyukuk River.

Below: Named by Robert Marshall for Ernie Johnson, the most famous trapper on the North Fork, Koyukuk River, Ernie Creek flows from a pass in the Brooks Range to the North Fork, Koyukuk, 28 miles southeast of Anaktuvuk Pass. (George Wuerthner)

Right: Awlinyak Creek flows northeast 18 miles to the Alatna River 21 miles southeast of Survey Pass. (Steve Jones)

No roads or trails exist in either the park or preserve. Traces of the "Hickel Highway," a bulldozed winter route bladed out prior to construction of the North Slope Haul Road to move supplies for haul road construction camps, can be seen along the John River and through the Anaktuvuk Valley. In summer the route resembles a canal along much of its length.

Six designated wild and scenic rivers flow within and out of Gates of the Arctic: the Noatak, Alatna, John, Kobuk, Tinayguk, and North Fork, Koyukuk. All but two comparatively small areas, one in the northeast extending along the Itkillik River to Itkillik Lake, and another small area surrounding Selby Lake in the southwest, have national park status. These two small areas are preserves where sport hunting is allowed. All of the land with national park status is classified as wilderness.

Abutting Gates of the Arctic National Park and Preserve is Noatak National Preserve and bordering that preserve to the south is Kobuk Valley National Park. These three National Park Service areas form a contiguous expanse of protected landscape of unique ecological, scenic and recreational importance from the North Slope Haul Road on the east almost to the Chukchi Sea coast on the west.

Fauna: Moose, caribou, Dall sheep, brown/grizzly and black bear, wolf, beaver, hoary marmot, wolverine, otter, marten, mink, weasel, lynx, red fox, porcupine and assorted small rodents reside or migrate through this area. More than 150 species of birds including hawks, owls, ptarmigan and migrating waterfowl are common here. A couple of uncommon resident birds are the arctic warbler and Smith's longspur.

Streams and lakes of Gates of the Arctic furnish habitat for salmon, lake trout, arctic grayling, arctic char, lingcod, whitefish, and northern pike. While many varieties of wildlife are represented in this far north habitat, productivity is low, each animal requires a lot of space, and the land cannot sustain heavy use or disturbance.

Flora: The south side of the Brooks Range gets more precipitation and warmer summer temperatures, and a taiga forest covers the river valley and slopes from 1,000 to 2,000 feet. Farther north the spruce forests give way to tundra that stretches all the way to the Arctic Ocean.

Caribou alternately graze and move up the steep slopes of Savioyok Pass northwest of Wiseman near the eastern boundary of Gates of the Arctic National Park. (George Wuerthner)

Left: Poplar leaves and bearberry create a colorful mosiac on the spongy tundra of Gates of the Arctic. (George Wuerthner)

Right: Colorful lichens and mosses cling to huge boulders along an unnamed alpine lake nestled among the Arrigetch Peaks in Gates of the Arctic National Park. (Shelley Schneider)

Left: From its head at a glacier in the Endicott Mountains, the Anaktuvuk River winds 135 miles northward to the Colville River. For centuries inland Inupiat Eskimos have hunted in this area. In recent years these Eskimos have established a village at Anaktuvuk Pass. (Stuart Pechek)

Right: Carrying heavy packs, backpackers move through the Anaktuvuk Valley. (Ginny Wood)

Accommodations: None available.

Recreational Opportunities:

Gates of the Arctic offers the backpacker a challenging and rewarding experience available in few places today: the opportunity to explore hundreds of square miles of pristine wilderness, almost unaltered by man, to chart one's own route marked only by the trails of animals, and to encounter nature on its own terms.

Human Use and Occupation:

Until the late 1940s, the Nunamiut, or inland Eskimos, hunted and camped in the Anaktuvuk River area, their subsistence life style little changed through the centuries. Now the Nunamiut are congregated at Anaktuvuk Pass where their sod huts decay among the plywood prefabs that modern civilization has brought.

Athabascan Indians along major river systems to the south of the mountains hunted and fished northward into the present park and preserve, but made no permanent settlements within present park boundaries. Both Eskimos and Indians still hunt, fish and gather berries in some parts of Gates of the Arctic. Native subsistence use will continue within the park and preserve under terms of the Alaska d-2 lands bill.

Suggested Reading:
► *Arctic Village*, Robert Marshall, 1933
► *Arctic Wilderness*, Robert Marshall, 1956
► *Arctic Wild*, Lois Crisler, 1958
► *ALASKA GEOGRAPHIC®*, Vol. 4, No. 2, *THE BROOKS RANGE*
► *Nunamiut: Among Alaska's Eskimos*, Helge Ingstad, 1954

Further Information:
► Superintendent, Gates of the Arctic National Park and Preserve
National Park Service
Fairbanks, AK 99701
► Field Office, National Park Service
Bettles, AK 99726

USGS Topographic Series:
Chandler Lake, Wiseman, Survey Pass, Killik River, Hughes, Ambler River, Philip Smith Mountains, Chandalar

Above: A kayaker enjoys the solitude of this sandy beach along the Alatna River. A major tributary of the Koyukuk, the Alatna flows southeast about 145 miles from the central Brooks Range to the village of Allakaket where it meets the Koyukuk. (Shelley Schneider)

Overleaf: Reflecting the stillness before winter storms, serenity pervades the South Arrigetch Creek Valley in this autumn photo. The creek flows out of the Arrigetch Peaks between Arrigetch Creek and Takahula River, to join with the Alatna River in Gates of the Arctic National Park and Preserve. (Shelley Schneider)

Glacier Bay National Park and Preserve

Location: Southeast Alaska, 50 miles west of Juneau near the northern end of the Alaska Panhandle. Bordered by Icy Strait and Cross Sound on the south, the Pacific Ocean on the west, and Canada on the north.

Size: 3,328,000 acres (3,271,000 in park; 57,000 in preserve), with 2,770,000 acres designated wilderness.

Access: Daily scheduled plane service operates from Juneau during the summer. Charter planes and boats also are available from Juneau. The landing field at Gustavus is ten miles from park head-

Muir Glacier calves into Muir Inlet, both named for naturalist John Muir. The glacier, part of Glacier Bay National Park and Preserve, has retreated 25 miles since 1892. (Ginny Wood)

quarters and Glacier Bay Lodge at Bartlett Cove. Daily boat trips operate during summer months from Bartlett Cove up to Riggs Glacier on Muir Inlet. Daily overnight tours during summer from Bartlett Cove to Johns Hopkins and Tarr inlets.

Area Description: With passage of the Alaska National Interest Lands Conservation Act of December 2, 1980, Glacier Bay National Monument, established in 1925 by President Calvin Coolidge, became a national park. Approximately 585,000 acres to the northwest were added to the park/preserve to protect fish and wildlife habitat and migration routes in Dry Bay and along the lower Alsek River, and to include the northwest slope of Mount Fairweather.

In Glacier Bay the dynamics of the Pleistocene epoch, which lasted more than one million years have been condensed into a "little ice age" that took place in 7,000 years. During this period

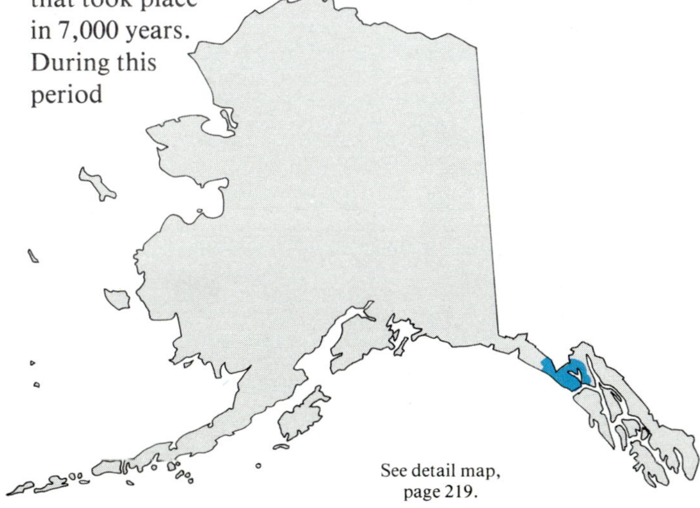

Left: Mount LaPerouse towers 10,728 feet above LaPerouse Glacier, named for French navigator Jean LaPerouse, who explored the area in 1786. (Chip Porter)

Above: Glacial flour, an accumulation of silt and debris, gathers at the edges of Vivid Lake, near Black Cap Mountain. (George Wuerthner)

glacier flowing a hundred miles down from the Saint Elias Range. Almost 100 years later, when John Muir built his cabin at Muir Point just north of Mount Wright, terminus of Muir Glacier as it was now called, was just to the north, 35 miles from where Vancouver had seen it. At present the terminus has retreated almost 25 miles more, leaving a broad bay and a long, narrow inlet.

Grand Pacific Glacier once was part of Muir Glacier. Now Grand Pacific lies at the head of Tarr Inlet, almost giving British Columbia a seaport 45 miles from where Glacier Bay forks to become Muir and Tarr inlets. Tributary glaciers have retreated correspondingly, leaving salt water to invade the space that ice once filled. Yet other glaciers to the west seem to have remained almost stable during this period of ablation. Some, including Grand Pacific, have started to advance, perhaps beginning the entire process over again. For scientists seeking to understand the dynamics of the great glaciers of the Ice Age from the waxing and waning of those of the "little ice age" still in progress, Glacier Bay is an invaluable outdoor laboratory.

Fauna: Land and marine wildlife abounds in Glacier Bay. A trip by water into the park's many fjords offers sightings of humpback whales, killer whales cutting the water with their tall dorsal fins, or hair seals poking their head up to stare at passing boats. During late spring hundreds of seals haul out on floating ice to give birth to their pups.

Along gravel beaches brown/grizzly, black, and occasionally rare glacier bears

(bluish color phase of the black bear) rummage for food. On high rocky ledges mountain goats are often sighted. In the rain forest roam moose, Sitka blacktail deer, lynx, marten and mink. More than 225 bird species have been reported from the park. Among the more common birds are black oystercatchers, cormorants, guillemots, puffins, gulls and terns.

four glacier readvances occurred, the last retreat from the maximum advance taking place in 230 years — the fastest recorded retreat anywhere on earth.

In 1794 when Capt. George Vancouver sailed through Icy Strait, he charted but did not enter Glacier Bay. The bay then was just a slight indentation in a wall of ice which marked the terminus of a broad

Above: Large-leaved avens. (William D. Boehm, reprinted from *ALASKA GEOGRAPHIC®*)

Right: Moss covered spruce and a blackwater pond are features of this bog near Bartlett Cove. (George Wuerthner)

Flora: For summer visitors the boat excursion from Bartlett Cove up Muir Inlet to calving Riggs Glacier is like watching a time lapse movie in reverse which condenses three centuries of glaciation and plant succession into a day. Leaving the dock, passengers watch vegetation along the shoreline change from moss-laden climax coastal hemlock forests to spruce forests as the boat chugs up Glacier Bay. Spruce trees, in turn, give way to thickets of willow and alder in Muir Inlet which is often full of floating pan ice and icebergs higher than the boat itself. Here and there the stumps of huge trees, buried by moraines centuries ago then exposed by erosion, stick out along a barren beach. At Goose Cove, the glacier's terminus in 1929, clumps of alders and a few young spruce have begun to invade the grass and lichens.

Clockwise from upper left: Marsh marigold, Luetkea, Purple mountain saxifrage, Mountain harebell.

Lupine

Glacial Gardens

Story and photos by William D. Boehm

Editor's note: This excerpt is from *GLACIER BAY: OLD ICE, NEW LAND,* Vol. 3, No. 1 of *ALASKA GEOGRAPHIC®* by William D. Boehm.

Glacier Bay's dramatic process of glacial recession creates conditions that bring a diversity of plant communities and life zones into the area. Where glacial fluctuations have occurred, plant diversity is seen, expressed in the process known as plant succession. Where glaciation has not disturbed the landscape, plant communities developed unhindered for several thousand years and became stratified into a series of life zones largely determined by altitude and moisture.

At sea level in the monument, moderate climatic conditions allow a temperate range of plant species that are also found in British Columbia and the State of Washington. The zone is typical Pacific coastal rain forest where giant hemlock and spruce trees grow.

Paintbrush

Dwarf fireweed

At about the 2,500-foot level, stunted and twisted forms of other, hardier trees and shrubs grope for existence in the subalpine zone. This zone ranges from the heartland of Alaska south to the higher mountain ranges of California.

At still higher elevations, climatic conditions approach those on the treeless arctic north slope. The plant community at this elevation is made up of both arctic and alpine plant species. Broad slopes of alpine meadows reach up to the barren rock and ice-covered high mountains of the monument.

Several decades after the recession of a glacier, newly bared land begins to change from sterile moraines to a mosaic of pioneering plants. At first the soil is low in critical nutrients, but hardy species such as dwarf fireweed, dryas, horsetail and mosses and lichens are able to colonize areas that are stable and have sufficient moisture.

Bordering the mature beaches well above high tide and adjacent to the forest edge are fireweed, red elderberry, alder and devil's club. Many edible herbs grow near the high tide mark. These include goosetongue, seashore plantain and Siberian spring beauty, along with scurvygrass and the tart sandwort.

In the arctic-alpine zone, between 2,500 and 5,000 feet, mature meadows have developed in areas that escaped recent waves of glaciation by being above the carved valleys. Here the warm summers are brief and the winters long. Plants native to this zone have adapted to unfavorable conditions — high winds, a short growing season, extremes in temperature and dehydration. Dehydration is a product of the intense solar radiation at higher elevations.

Plant adaptations usually involve structural changes that permit them to survive the extremes of the environment. For example, by acquiring a low profile and possessing specialized leaves that may be woolly, covered with a thick coat of wax or reduced in size, a plant minimizes dehydration from wind and solar radiation. A thick, tight mat of intertwined leaves and branches may increase the temperature around the plant, allowing it to grow in the often freezing temperatures of spring and summer.

The rich alpine meadows of northern Dundas Bay, Mount Wright, Red Mountain and the ridges of the outer coast support a wide variety of colorful flowers well adapted to climatic extremes. In areas where snow lingers through the summer and along alpine streams are found the bog violet, buttercups and the marsh marigold. On other slopes, the lupine, mountain harebell, paintbrush, leutkea and large-leaved avens grow.

At the upper limits of the zone, at 5,000 to 6,000 feet, the variety of alpine vegetation shrinks to a handful of the hardiest species, such as heath, saxifrage and crustose lichens.

Above: A waterway winds through the Beardslee Islands, near the mouth of Glacier Bay. The islands are made up of moraine and other material from the enormous glacier which at one time filled Glacier Bay. (William D. Boehm, reprinted from *ALASKA GEOGRAPHIC®*)

Right: The tour boat *Thunder Bay* is dwarfed by the cliffs of White Thunder Ridge along Muir Inlet. (Shelley Schneider)

Accommodations:
A resort lodge and campground are available at Bartlett Cove, and a small inn with family-style meals is open near Gustavus airport. No other designated campgrounds exist in the park or preserve, but campsites for primitive camping are plentiful. Take note of tides when beach camping.

Recreational Opportunities:

Glacier Bay offers endless opportunities for exploration by hand-propelled crafts as well as motorboats, but caution is advised for storms are sudden and floating ice can turn over or fracture off without warning. Fishing for halibut and salmon lure salt-water fishermen, while devotees of rod and reel can fish for trout in clear-running streams. Certain areas of the park furnish excellent cross-country hiking and backpacking possibilities while dense brush, glaciers and roaring glacial streams block access to others. There are many peaks more than 10,000 feet high to challenge the mountaineer experienced on snow and ice and patient enough to wait out the storms. A system of nature trails radiate out from the lodge and park head-quarters area near Bartlett Cove, the only maintained trails in the park and preserve.

Human Use and Occupation:

According to legend, Tlingit Indians fished, gathered plants and camped along the shores of the park's bays and inlets before the glaciers advanced, and returned to their traditional activities as the ice retreated.

Capt. James Cook sighted and named 15,300-foot Mount Fairweather in 1778. Mountaineers found the name ironic when they were pinned down for days by storms while attempting to climb the peak two centuries later. A Frenchman, La Perouse, made the first recorded landing in what is now the park at Lituya Bay in 1786.

Russians pursuing the sea otter with Aleut hunters, and prospectors looking for gold were the only white visitors into the vast wilderness until the late 19th century. In 1879 naturalist John Muir, with his Indian companions, paddled a canoe into Glacier Bay from Wrangell. What he saw that late October enticed him back for more explorations in 1880 and again in 1890 when he built a cabin at what is now called Muir Point. From this base Muir spent the summer scrambling about Muir Glacier, which was then just in front of his cabin, to measure the movement of the ice. Other scientists followed, and a few settlers, most of whom came to farm the outwash plain at Gustavus.

Suggested Reading:

▶ *Glacier Bay, The Land and the Silence,* Dave Bohn, 1967
▶ *Travels in Alaska,* John Muir, 1915
▶ *ALASKA GEOGRAPHIC®,* Vol. 3, No. 1, *GLACIER BAY*

Further Information:

▶ Superintendent, Glacier Bay National Park and Preserve National Park Service Post Office Box 1089 Juneau, AK 99802
▶ Superintendent, Glacier Bay National Park and Preserve Gustavus, AK 99826

USGS Topographic Series:

Mount Fairweather, Skagway, Yakutat

Al Sanders kayaks among the icebergs in the upper portion of Glacier Bay, near Gilbert Island. (George Wuerthner)

Katmai National Park and Preserve

Location: Southwest Alaska, approximately 250 miles southwest of Anchorage, at the beginning of the Alaska Peninsula.

Size: 4,268,000 acres (3,960,000 in park; 308,000 in preserve), with 3,473,000 acres designated wilderness.

Access: Daily scheduled air service operates from Anchorage to King Salmon on the park's western boundary, with floatplane connections to Brooks River Lodge, ranger station and public campground on Naknek Lake. The only road access to the park is an unimproved road leading ten miles from King Salmon to the western boundary.

Cape Douglas, named by Capt. James Cook in 1778 for his friend Dr. John Douglas, canon of Windsor, reaches into the Pacific Ocean along Katmai's eastern boundary.
(Gary Dobos)

Area Description: Katmai National Park and Preserve gets considerable rainfall and strong winds. Precipitation varies from 60 inches a year along the 140-mile coastline and in higher elevations, to 25 inches annually in the park's interior. Temperatures are mild by Alaska standards.

Established by presidential proclamation in 1918, Katmai National Monument was set aside to preserve the Valley of Ten Thousand Smokes, which was created by cataclysmic volcanic action in 1912 in one of the largest eruptions recorded in Alaska. Subsequent proclamations in 1931, 1942 and 1969 expanded the monument's boundaries to include 2.7 million acres of scenic and wildlife resources adjacent to the Valley of Ten Thousand Smokes whose "smokes" had subsided considerably by this time.

With passage of the Alaska lands bill, more than one million acres were added to the existing monument and the entire area was given national park status.

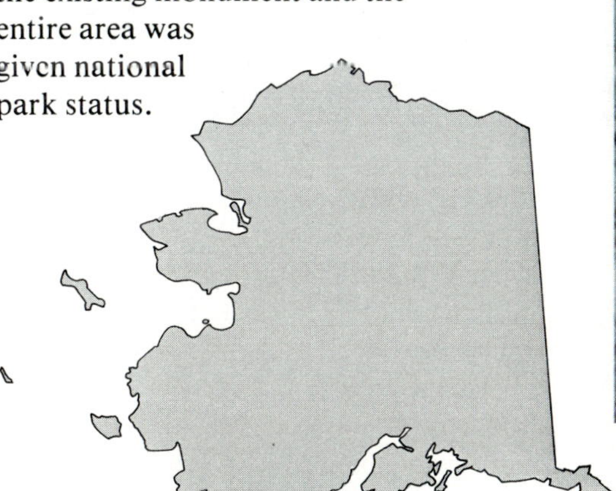

See detail map, page 219.

Nearly a million salmon return each year to the Naknek River system to spawn.
(John and Margaret Ibbotson)

This aerial taken near Kaflia Bay shows the rugged, indented coastline along Katmai's eastern boundary. (George Wuerthner)

Unlike monuments, only Congress, not a president, can alter boundaries of national parks. To the northwest, boundary lines were redrawn to include 308,000 acres designated as preserve. Almost all the original monument and additions are now in wilderness classification.

The upper portion of the Alagnak River, which flows out of Kukaklek Lake and Nonvianuk Lake through the preserve in the northwest to Bristol Bay outside park lands, is designated a wild and scenic river.

The new acreage adds to the old monument a representative portion of Bristol Bay lowlands and tundra land forms, the headwaters of watersheds which drain through the park that now ensure preservation of important sockeye (red) salmon spawning and nursery streams, and additional brown/grizzly bear habitat.

Covering more than 40 square miles, the Valley of Ten Thousand Smokes was named by a team of scientists, including Robert F. Griggs, who first made their way on foot into the area from Shelikof Strait in 1916. They found this once-verdant valley covered up to 600-700 feet in depth with ash, pumice and rocks that had been ejected by Novarupta volcano; and they noted thousands of fumaroles issuing from mini-craters in the valley floor. In his book, *The Valley of Ten Thousand Smokes* (1922), Griggs formu-

lated his theory of the causes of this gigantic explosion which sent ash around the world; and prophesied that this area, which in his view far surpassed Yellowstone in visitor appeal, would some day attract as many tourists as the famous Wyoming landmark. He was proved wrong however. The fumarole activity, unlike the geyser Old Faithful, soon began to diminish until by 1951, the first ranger patrol into the area since Grigg's expeditions could find but seven active "smokes."

Above: From the air the Valley of Ten Thousand Smokes appears as a huge gray mat cracked by erosion from rivers forging channels on their way from the Aleutian Range to the coastal lowlands of Bristol Bay. (George Wuerthner)

Left: R.F. Griggs named Mount Martin, or Martin Volcano (6,050 feet), for U.S. Geological Survey member George C. Martin, author of the first authoritative report of the Mount Katmai eruption. (R. Nichols, National Park Service)

A moose calf wanders along a lupine-studded shore. Much of the park's coastal and lakeland habitat supports moose that feed on willows, water plants and grasses.
(Larry Aumiller)

A big brownie, one of the huge coastal brown/grizzlies for which Katmai is famous, walks along a stream bank. Salmon moving upstream to spawn attract large numbers of bears to the area's salmon streams in summer.
(George Wuerthner)

Fauna: King of wildlife in Katmai is the brown/grizzly bear. Other wildlife likely to be seen are moose, river otter, marten, weasel, mink, lynx, muskrat, beaver and an occasional caribou that might wander into the western extension from Becharof National Wildlife Refuge. Seals, sea lions, sea otters and beluga and gray whales can be found off coastal waters along Shelikof Strait. Waterfowl, shorebirds, raptors and songbirds abound.

Flora: Vegetation varies from alpine tundra on the higher slopes, to moist tundra, dense willow-alder thickets and mixed spruce-birch forests on lower elevations.

Accommodations:
Wien Air Alaska operates a lodge and campground on the shores of Naknek Lake, a fishing camp at Grosvenor Lake and a lodge at Kulik Lake to the north. Nearby communities of King Salmon (population 300) and Naknek (population 472) offer a hotel or other lodging.

Recreational Opportunities:
When Northern Consolidated Airlines (now part of Wien Air Alaska) began tourist operations in the monument with tent camps on the Brooks River and Colville Lake in 1950, sport fishing was the attraction, not the Valley of Ten Thousand Smokes which was only accessible by extremely arduous backpacking. Now a four-wheel-drive van takes visitors along a primitive road to a point overlooking the volcanic devastation.

And canoeing, kayaking and other recreational activities have replaced the spectacular fishing as the park's major appeal. The serene Grosvenor River, the swift-flowing Savonoski River and a series of large lakes connected by a portage form a circular waterway of almost 100 miles for canoeists and kayakers. Most backpacking is done in the Valley of Ten Thousand Smokes where several types of terrain can be encountered. Backpacking in other areas, while possible, is arduous because of the dense brush and high grass.

Wildlife and bird-watching is superb. Spawning salmon draw bears to the mouths of streams where visitors can safely watch the antics of these huge shaggy animals as they feed.

Human Use and Occupation:

Archaeological sites have revealed occupation along Shelikof Strait, and the Savonoski and Brooks rivers, that date back 6,000 years. Before the eruption in 1912, Eskimo villages existed within the present boundaries of Katmai. These were abandoned because of ash fall. Before the same volcanic outburst, a well-used trade trail, pioneered by Natives, then used by Russians and finally by gold seekers, ran from the Pacific Ocean coast through what is now Valley of Ten Thousand Smokes to Bristol Bay.

Suggested Reading:
►*The Valley of Ten Thousand Smokes,* Robert F. Griggs, 1922
►*Rambles Through An Alaskan Wild; Katmai And The Valley of the Smokes,* Dave Bohn, 1979
►*ALASKA GEOGRAPHIC®,* Vol. 4, No. 1, *ALASKA'S VOLCANOES*

Further Information:
►Superintendent, Katmai National Park and Preserve
National Park Service
Post Office Box 7
King Salmon, AK 99613

USGS Topographic Series:
Katmai, Naknek, Iliamna

Above: Tales of fabulous fishing lured travelers to Katmai during the park's early development. Today backcountry exploration attracts a great number of visitors; but a chance at some of the region's fine trout, such as this angler is holding, still draws many to Katmai. (George Wuerthner)

Right: Two hikers cross a snowfield between Mount Mageik (7,250 feet) and Mount Cereberus (3,687 feet) in the Katmai Pass area. (Chlaus Lotscher)

Kenai Fjords National Park

Location: Southcentral Alaska on the southeast edge of the Kenai Peninsula.

Size: 567,000 acres.

Access: Scheduled airlines and buses operate to Seward which is connected by the Seward Highway to Anchorage, 127 miles to the north. Boat or floatplane charters to Kenai Fjords are available.

From the west across Kachemak Bay the ice fields of Kenai Fjords resemble a frosting poured over rugged Kenai Mountains. Kenai National Wildlife Refuge encompasses much of the territory between the bay and the park.
(Chlaus Lotscher)

Since the eastern boundary of the park extends nearly to Seward, difficult foot access is possible from the seaport. This effort, however, is more a snow-and-ice mountaineering venture than a simple hike. The Alaska Marine Highway ferry between Seward and Kodiak passes offshore of the park, but does not stop en route.

Area Description: The maritime climate brings heavy rains and snows, with the least rainfall in May. Summer temperatures range from 40°F. to 60°F. Snow and freezing temperatures can occur any month on the ice fields and winter storms begin in September.

Kenai Fjords National Park is an active vestige of the last ice age with all its forces and processes still evident. The 700-square-mile Harding Icefield is a remnant of the large ice cap that once covered the Kenai, Chugach, and Saint Elias mountains during the Pleistocene. The Kenai Fjords were formed when the ice cap spilled into the sea and left long, deeply-scoured inlets when the ice retreated and was replaced by sea water. The fiords themselves are indented with numerous bays and coves, and at the heads of some, glaciers reach tidewater, calving huge chunks of ice into the inlet.

In addition to the fiords, the Harding Icefield, named for U.S. President Warren Harding, forms the other major physiographic feature of the park. Fed by an average of 400 inches of precipitation per year, the ice cap stretches for miles and miles as a plain of uninterrupted ice and snow. On the skyline are nunataks, mountain tops with their lower slopes submerged by thousands of feet of ice.

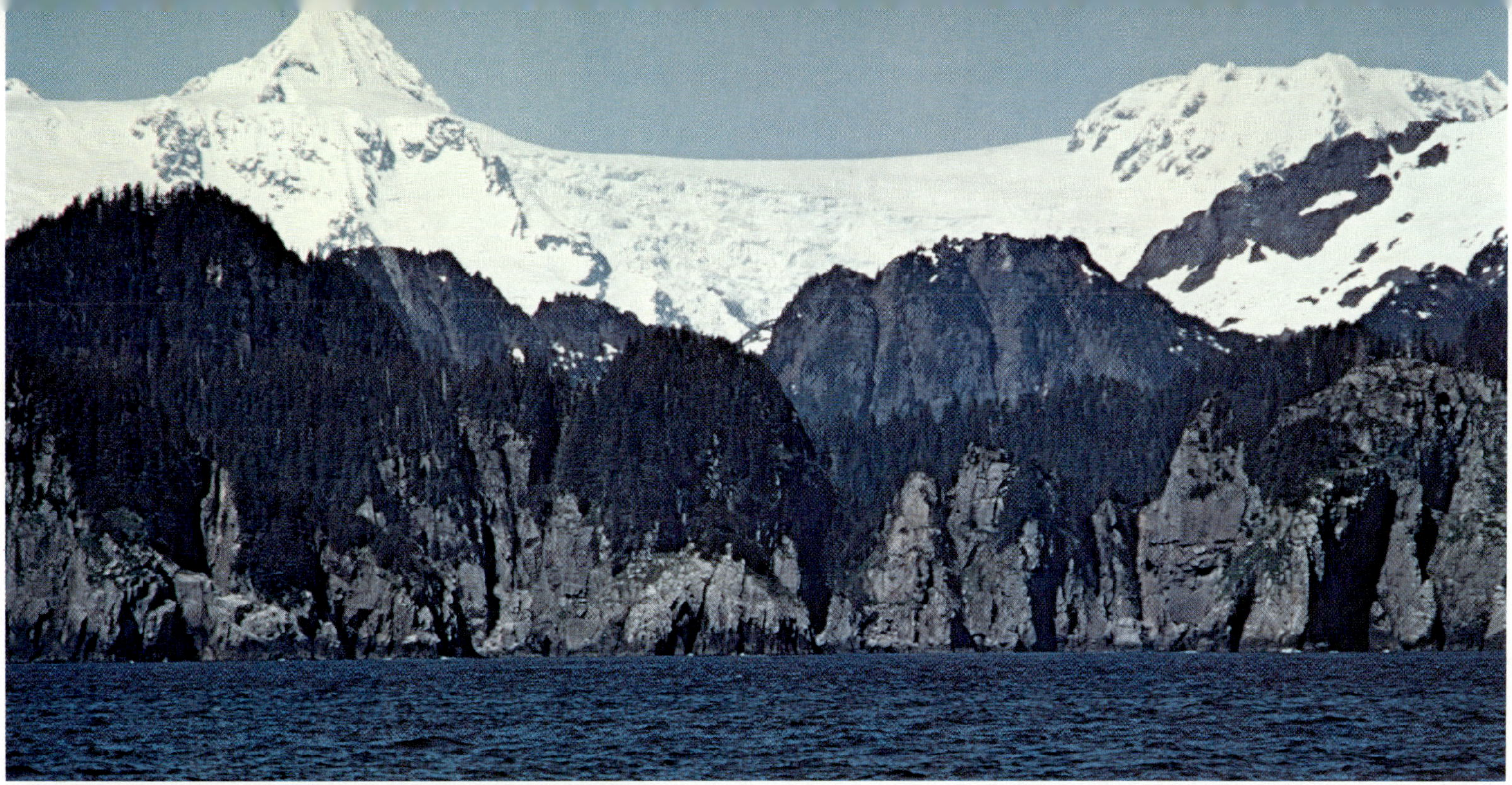

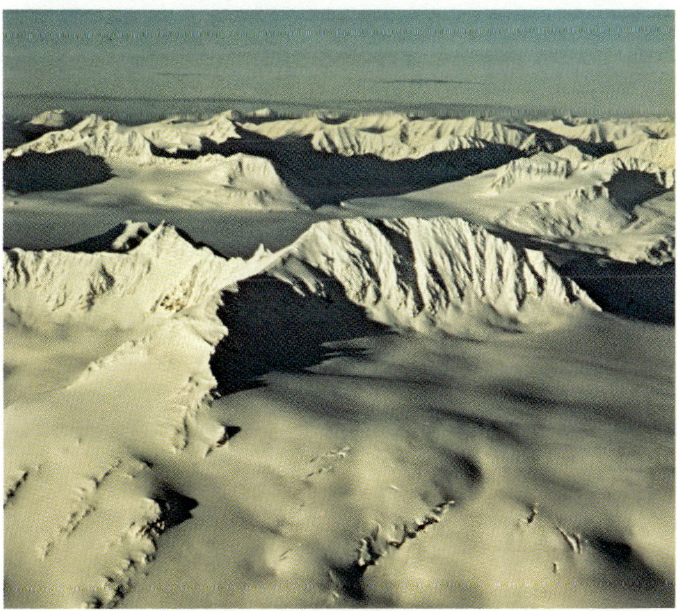

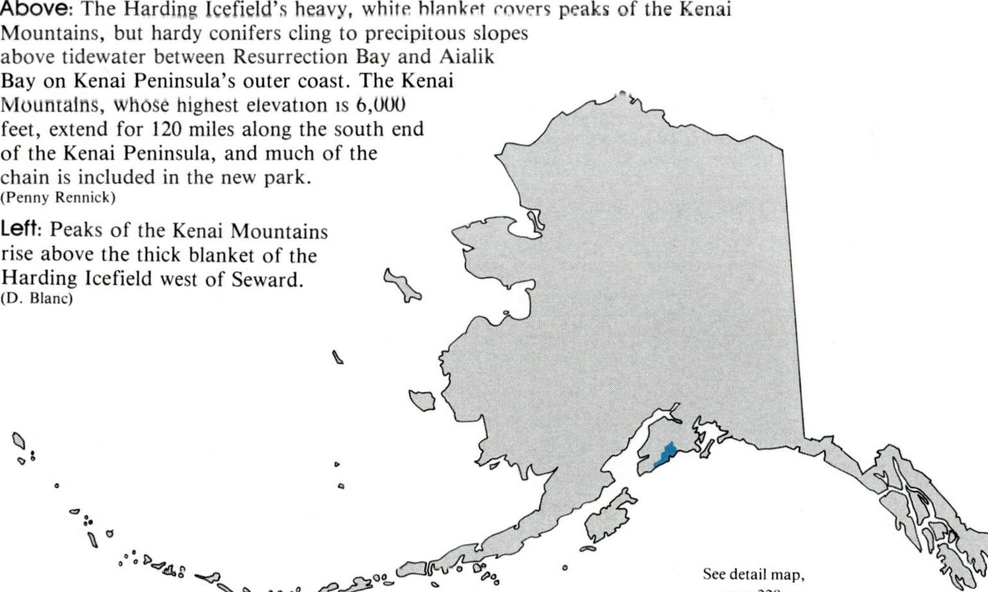

Above: The Harding Icefield's heavy, white blanket covers peaks of the Kenai Mountains, but hardy conifers cling to precipitous slopes above tidewater between Resurrection Bay and Aialik Bay on Kenai Peninsula's outer coast. The Kenai Mountains, whose highest elevation is 6,000 feet, extend for 120 miles along the south end of the Kenai Peninsula, and much of the chain is included in the new park.
(Penny Rennick)

Left: Peaks of the Kenai Mountains rise above the thick blanket of the Harding Icefield west of Seward.
(D. Blanc)

See detail map, page 220.

Left: About 80 species of birds commonly occur in Kenai Fjords; many other species use the park's habitat sporadically. Here black-legged kittiwakes swoop and swerve near a rocky point in Resurrection Bay. (Penny Rennick)

Right: Harbor seals rest and bear their young on ice floes at the base of some Kenai Fjords glaciers.
(M. Woodbridge Williams, National Park Service)

Fauna: The Kenai Peninsula shelters mountain goats, moose, Dall sheep and black and brown/grizzly bear. Lower elevations abound in small furbearers including mink, weasel, marten, lynx, fox, wolverine, coyote, hoary marmot, hare and squirrels.

Marine life near the park is rich and abundant. Both sea otters and Steller sea lions are now restored to former population levels on the south coast, which also shelters large numbers of harbor seal. Offshore swim 14 species of whales including some species listed as endangered. Both the right whale dolphin and the Pacific white-sided dolphin frequent the Gulf of Alaska near Kenai Fjords.

Coastal areas provide habitat for 62 species of birds, some seldom seen elsewhere. Among the seabirds present in the area are horned and tufted puffins, and shearwaters that breed in Australia and Tasmania and migrate in huge flocks extending for miles. Loons, cormorants, eagles, murrelets, murres, auklets and waterfowl make the fiords a birder's paradise.

Flora: Vegetation in the park tells the story of plant succession with the retreat of each glacier. At lower elevations, there is some forest land, made up of coastal hemlock and Sitka spruce, which is replaced by alpine tundra and barren ground higher up.

Accommodations: None at present in the park. Seward (population 1,842) offers motels, restaurants and two campgrounds.

Recreational Opportunities:
Some visitors enjoy water travel in Kenai Fjords, either by small boat or kayak, but turbulent Gulf of Alaska weather and strong tides and currents make it essential to have local knowledge and good skill in small boat handling. Anyone venturing into Kenai Fjords on his own should obtain detailed information on local landing sites, weather and navigational hazards.

Boat travel for bird-watching, observing marine life, and visiting tidewater glaciers in various bays and lagoons is popular. Camping and hiking opportunities are extremely limited.

Recreation on the Harding Icefield includes hiking, and cross-country skiing. Some knowledge of glacier travel is advisable.

Sightseeing flights over the ice field are available from Seward.

Suggested Reading:
►"Kenai Fjords: A National Park in Waiting," *Audubon*, July, 1978

Further Information:
►Area Director, National Park Service
540 West Fifth Avenue
Anchorage, AK 99501

USGS Topographic Series:
Seward, Blying Sound, Seldovia

Kobuk
Valley
National
Park

Location: Northwest Alaska, about 350 miles northwest of Fairbanks and 75 miles east of Kotzebue.

Size: Approximately 1,710,000 acres, with 190,000 acres designated wilderness.

Access: Scheduled airlines operate from Anchorage or Fairbanks to Kotzebue. From Kotzebue chartered planes or boats will provide transportation into the park. Another way to reach the park is via scheduled flights to Bettles, then by charter plane to the headwaters of the Kobuk River where a float trip downriver will give access to the park.

Upstream from the park about eight miles, the village of Ambler (population 192) has charter planes available, and residents may also furnish boat transportation into the park. Downstream, two small villages, Kiana (population 344) and Noorvik (population 490), may have charter plane and boat service available.

Area Description: The Kobuk Valley is influenced by an arctic continental weather system and experiences cool, moist summers, and very dry, cold winters. Mean annual temperature in July is about 57°F.; mean temperature in January about -10°F. Temperatures can sometimes reach into the 80s on a mid-summer day, and go as low as -30°F. in winter. Most precipitation occurs in summer. Visitors should be prepared for rain, but periods of warm, sunny weather do exist. Annual precipitation for the Kobuk Valley is about 18 inches, most of it as rain in the summer. The region enjoys 24-hour daylight from late May to early August.

Words like "gentle," "protected," "a friendly wilderness," come to the mind of the visitor who first looks out or down on Kobuk Valley National Park, depending on whether he first experiences the area floating down the Kobuk River or from an airplane flying above it. This is especially true if he or she has experienced other parts of the Brooks Range where adjectives such as "stark," or "exposed" are more likely to be used.

Cradled by the Baird Mountains to the north and the low-lying Waring Mountains to the south, the Kobuk River flows through a wide forested valley. Unlike many Alaska streams, neither the Kobuk nor the streams that flow into it are fed by glaciers so their waters run clear instead of silty. One of these tributaries, the Salmon, has been classified a wild and scenic river.

The Kobuk River, designated a wild and scenic river from where it flows out of Walker Lake to the western boundary of Gates of the Arctic National Preserve, meanders serenely to the sea after two sets of rapids near its headwaters which are usually portaged. Flowing 280 miles to empty into an inlet of Kotzebue Sound, the Kobuk has for centuries served as a transportation artery for coastal Eskimos coming into the interior to hunt land animals and for inland Eskimos traveling to the coast for subsistence from the sea.

During the Pleistocene epoch, the Kobuk Valley offered an ice-free corridor joined to the land bridge that periodically

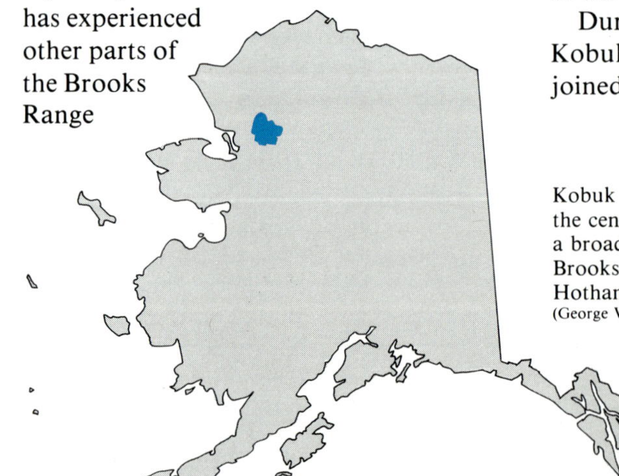

Kobuk Valley National Park encompasses the central portion of the Kobuk River Valley, a broad watershed which stretches from the Brooks Range more than 300 miles to enter Hotham Inlet southeast of Kotzebue.
(George Wuerthner)

See detail map, page 220.

formed to connect Alaska to Siberia as the ice ages waxed and waned. The valley contains stratified artifacts dating 10,000 years of human occupation. At Onion Portage, where the Kobuk almost loops back on itself near the eastern boundary of the park, Dr. J. Louis Giddings, the same archaeologist who made the discoveries at Cape Krusenstern, found what has been described as the most important archaeological site ever unearthed in the Arctic. For 18 feet below the surface in two acres, 30 layers of middens and old dwellings chronicle the cultural history of inland Eskimos and their predecessors.

The major anomaly of the area is the Great Kobuk Sand Dunes in which camel caravans rather than migrating caribou seem more fitting. Covering 25 square miles inland from the south bank of the Kobuk River within the wilderness-designated area of the park, the desertlike sands form concave dunes and crescent-shaped barchans, some up to 100 feet high, that are overrunning some sections of the boreal forest which encircles the dunes. Another smaller area of shifting sands, called the Little Kobuk Sand Dunes, lies near Onion Portage. Sandy soils underlying the vegetation that has stabilized a once more extensive dune topography furnish drier and less brushy landscape than is usual in permafrost areas.

Left: In the seemingly barren mass of the dunes, avens and other hardy plants find nourishment and brighten a gray landscape. (Mark McDermott)

Above: Kavet Creek borders on the large dune fields in the new park. (Manya Wik)

Left: More than 30 miles
above the Arctic Circle,
wind-sculpted sand dunes
cover 25 square miles of
the Kobuk Valley.
(John Nicholson)

Overleaf: An unnamed
creek flows through fields
still covered with several
inches of snow near
Great Kobuk Sand Dunes.
(Manya Wik)

79

Below: Caribou graze and rest south of the Kobuk River, waiting to begin spring migration north across the Kobuk and Noatak valleys to their calving grounds on the north slope. (Fred DeCicco)

Bottom: A bull moose wades through a narrow channel off the Kobuk River. (Fred DeCicco)

Fauna: Barren Ground caribou, part of the western Arctic herd of more than 200,000 animals, may winter in the Kobuk Valley. Caribou, among the most important mammal species in the area, constitute a key subsistence resource for Natives and the few whites who live along the Kobuk River. Other large resident mammals include moose, black and brown/grizzly bear, wolf, lynx, marten, wolverine and some Dall sheep in the Baird Mountains. Numerous ponds and oxbow lakes provide excellent waterfowl habitat. More than 100 species of birds have been recorded in the area. Fish —arctic grayling, lake trout, northern pike and five species of salmon — make up an important part of the Native diet and are found throughout the area.

Young birch grow in a stretch of open tundra bordered by a mixed spruce-hardwood forest in Kobuk Valley National Park. The northern border of the boreal forest and southern border of arctic tundra meet and overlap in the Kobuk Valley. (George Wuerthner)

Marestail *(Hippuris vulgaris)* is a common marsh plant growing in lakes of the Kobuk Valley. (Anore Jones)

Flora: The Kobuk Valley is unique botanically. During the ice age, an arctic-steppe biome of sagebrushlike plants and grasslands nourished woolly mammoths and other extinct mammals. Relics of this landscape still exist: species of flora found nowhere else in Alaska, lack of underbrush usually associated with a boreal forest, and extensive areas of sand dunes. The valley also forms a transition zone between the taiga and tundra in which one biome then the other dominates as the climate periodically becomes more severe, then moderates. This is what ecologists term an ecotone — the edge of interaction between two biotic zones.

Forests of white and black spruce,

paper birch, balsam poplar, quaking aspen and several species of willow mix with shrubs and tundra.

Labrador tea and cotton grass dominate tundra vegetation. Iris, daisies, asters, lupine, delphinium, moss campion, heathers and numerous other flowers brighten the landscape.

Cranberries, blueberries, salmonberries and crowberries add variety to the subsistence diet of nearby residents.

Accommodations: No accommodations are available within the park, and none are planned. Good campsites exist for primitive camping. Camping supplies — food and fuel — can be purchased in Kotzebue. Smaller Kobuk River villages nearer the park have limited supplies.

Recreational Opportunities: The Kobuk River furnishes an opportunity to float through the park by canoe, kayak, raft or small motorized river boats, camping along the way, fishing, visiting local villages, and taking side trips to explore the sand dunes and other areas away from the riverbank. For more skilled boat handlers, the Salmon River offers challenging, fast-flowing waters. Those wishing to travel exclusively overland by foot rather than by water can land at designated lakes and landing strips in the mountainous areas for extended backpacking trips. Kobuk Valley National Park abuts Noatak National Preserve on the north and Selawik National Wildlife Refuge on the south, each with designated wilderness areas adjoining the Kobuk Valley.

Human Use and Occupation:
Kobuk Valley National Park is a special unit of the National Park System because human settlement and use of the park is part of the park's heritage and an ongoing chapter in man's relation to nature. The park will be managed with subsistence use by Natives, who have hunted and fished in this area for centuries, as a major objective rather than tourism. Visitors and outdoor recreationists are welcome in the park, but are reminded that these lands are an Eskimo homeland. Courtesy and respect should be shown for their privacy and home life.

Suggested Reading:
►*Ancient Men Of The Arctic*, J. Louis Giddings, 1967
►*ALASKA GEOGRAPHIC®*, Vol. 8, No. 3, *KOTZEBUE BASIN*

Further Information:
►Superintendent, Kobuk Valley National Park
National Park Service
540 West Fifth Avenue
Anchorage, AK 99501

USGS Topographic Series:
Ambler River, Baird Mountains, Selawik

Left: The right trunk of this birch tree pair was stripped of its bark for basket-making many years ago. Eskimos of the Kobuk Valley traditionally used birch bark for making many items from canoes to baskets. (Manya Wik)

Above: Natives pick whitefish from their beach seine along the Kobuk. (Ken Alt)

Lake Clark National Park and Preserve

Location: Southcentral Alaska, west of Cook Inlet and north of Lake Iliamna; 100 miles west of Soldotna or Kenai and 150 miles southwest of Anchorage.

Size: 3,653,000 acres (2,439,000 acres in park; 1,214,000 acres in preserve), with 2,470,000 acres designated wilderness.

Access: Charter floatplanes are available from Anchorage or Soldotna or Kenai to Lake Clark or other lakes in the park and preserve. No road access.

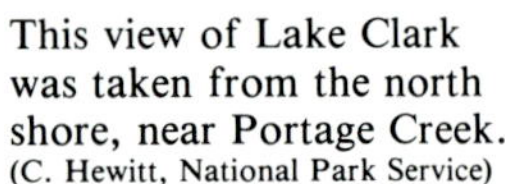

See detail map, page 221.

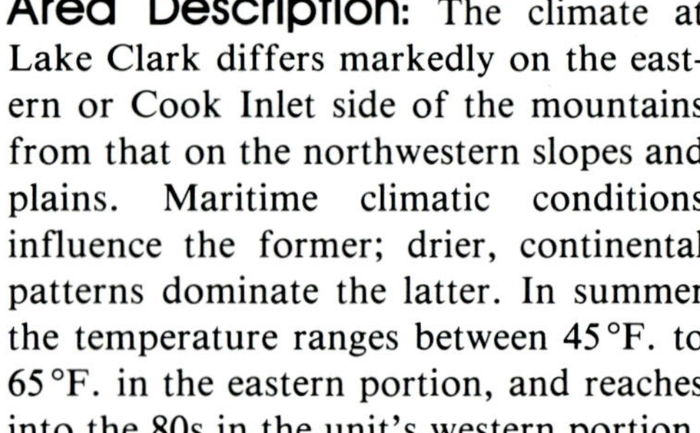

This view of Lake Clark was taken from the north shore, near Portage Creek.
(C. Hewitt, National Park Service)

Area Description: The climate at Lake Clark differs markedly on the eastern or Cook Inlet side of the mountains from that on the northwestern slopes and plains. Maritime climatic conditions influence the former; drier, continental patterns dominate the latter. In summer the temperature ranges between 45°F. to 65°F. in the eastern portion, and reaches into the 80s in the unit's western portion.

Precipitation along the coastal slopes reaches 60 inches annually while the interior gets only 20 inches.

Lake Clark National Park and Preserve seems to encompass every topographical feature one would choose as the most superlative for a national park. These features include a jumble of glacier-carved peaks ranging up to 10,000 feet; two steaming volcanoes; innumerable glaciers that are still sculpturing the landscape; many lakes from 50-mile-long Lake Clark with a densely forested shoreline to tundra ponds; deep U-shaped valleys with rushing streams; open, lichen-covered uplands where streams meander rather than rush; three wild and scenic rivers —the Tlikakila, Mulchatna and Chilikadrotna; and a coastline along Cook Inlet full of tidal bays and rocky

Above left: A coastal creek winds its way through a swampy area between Mount Redoubt and Cook Inlet. (John and Margaret Ibbotson)

Above: Iliamna Volcano (10,016 feet) towers over blue-green Crescent Lake. Tuxedni Glacier is visible in the top center portion of the photo. (John and Margaret Ibbotson)

Lake Clark Pass, a pass from
Cook Inlet to Lake Clark,
goes through the rugged
Chigmit Mountains.
(M. Woodbridge Williams,
National Park Service)

inlets. Then for good measure add a diversity of wildlife to an area almost devoid of human habitation — all this just an hour's bush flight from Alaska's largest city.

The park and preserve have four distinct physiographic regions: a coastal region along Cook Inlet; the rugged Chigmit Mountains where the Aleutian and Alaska ranges meet; a foothill-lake region; and a tundra plain. Many valleys are connected to each other by low passes.

Almost all lands designated as park rather than preserve are also classified as wilderness. Only a small area in the southeast along Cook Inlet is excluded from wilderness classification. A strip of land along the western boundary is designated preserve with sport hunting permitted in season.

Fauna: The Mulchatna caribou herd of up to 10,000 animals ranges in and out of the preserve. Moose are common in both the park and the preserve, and Dall sheep reach the southern limit of their range in the mountains of Lake Clark. Brown/ grizzly and black bear share the region with smaller mammals including wolf, wolverine, marten, mink, land otter, weasel, beaver, lynx and red fox. Whales and seals swim offshore along the coastal eastern boundary.

Waterfowl are abundant along Tuxedni Bay and in the ponds and marshes of the tundra plains. Bald eagles, peregrine falcons and numerous other raptors and smaller birds nest in the park.

Flora: Vegetation varies from fairly dense spruce-hardwood forests along low-lying valleys and lake shores to alpine tundra which covers most of the higher elevations. To the west and south moist tundra plant communities predominate.

Accommodations: At present facilities for visitors to the park and preserve are limited to a few specialized hunting and fishing lodges and camps on Lake Clark and other lakes. Several outfitters in the Anchorage area offer guided float and backpacking trips into the area. No developed campsites exist, but sites for primitive camping are abundant, especially along rivers and shorelines. Visitors should be prepared to be self-sufficient. Limited facilities may be established in the near future, but car access is not practical or probable.

Below: The Tusk, named for its unusual shape, rises 5,730 feet near Merrill Pass. (John and Margaret Ibbotson)

Right: A small lake provides a tranquil camping site, near Kontrashibuna Lake. (Connie Barlow)

Recreational Opportunities:

Large and numerous lakes plus several floatable rivers, including three wild and scenic rivers, invite water-oriented activities. Fish, including five species of salmon, lake trout and grayling, abound. Sport hunting under state fish and game regulations is permitted in the preserve to the west. High, snow-capped peaks and extensive glacier systems challenge the mountaineer. Although much of the terrain is very steep, very high or very brushy, other areas, especially to the northwest, offer good hiking. The backpacker will find much true wilderness to explore. For the less active, a base camp on a lonely lake to watch wildlife, storms and sunsets can be just as rewarding.

Human Use and Occupation:

Although little evidence of prehistoric use of the area has been found, several sites reveal occupation by the Tanaina Indians. Russian contact with Natives living or hunting in the area is established by the relics of European origin found at old villages and campsites. Russian Orthodox missionaries had contact with Natives around Lake Iliamna by the 1790s. In 1897 John W. Clark, an agent of the Alaska Commercial Company at Nushagak on Bristol Bay, made his way via river systems to the lake that now bears his name. Miners came into the area during the first part of this century, and a few patented claims still exist. A few year-round homesteads and some Native allotments are found around Lake Clark.

Suggested Reading:
▶ *ALASKA GEOGRAPHIC®*, Vol. 5, No. 3, *BRISTOL BAY BASIN*
▶ *ALASKA GEOGRAPHIC®* Vol. 1, No. 2, *ONE MAN'S WILDERNESS*

Further Information:
▶ Superintendent, Lake Clark National Park and Preserve
540 West 4th Avenue
Anchorage, AK 99501

USGS Topographic Series:
Lime Hills, Lake Clark, Iliamna, Kenai, Seldovia, Tyonek

Above: Throughout much of its meandering course the Noatak bisects a broad, interior valley. However, the river does cut through two canyons: Grand Canyon of the Noatak and farther downstream the much narrower Noatak Canyon. (John and Margaret Ibbotson)

Right: Cruising down the river, these rafters head for a bend in the Noatak just after its junction with the Cutler. (John and Margaret Ibbotson)

Noatak National Preserve

Location: Northwestern Alaska, 350 miles northwest of Fairbanks and only a few miles north of Kotzebue at its most southerly point. The preserve encompasses the major portion of the Noatak River Valley but excludes its headwaters in the central Brooks Range, which is part of Gates of the Arctic National Park and Preserve.

Size: Approximately 6,460,000 acres with 5,800,000 acres designated wilderness.

Access: No road access. Scheduled airlines fly to Kotzebue from both Anchorage and Fairbanks. From Kotzebue chartered light aircraft or chartered river boats provide access to the lower Noatak River. Access to the upper Noatak for float trips generally begins with a scheduled flight from Fairbanks to Bettles, and a charter floatplane flight to any of several lakes along the river's upper reaches.

Area Description: The northwestern Arctic is subject to both maritime and continental weather patterns. Summers provide almost continuous daylight from May to mid-August; conversely, in mid-winter the sun remains below the southern horizon for many weeks.

Precipitation is relatively light, but summer weather can be very wet with long periods of overcast skies. June generally has the most clear weather. Strong winds can produce a serious chill factor.

Summer temperatures may range between 40°F. and 85°F., with average daytime temperatures in the 60s and 70s. However, freezing can occur at night during the summer. Winter temperatures in the -50°F. range can be encountered, accentuated by winds, which have full sweep because of the lack of trees.

The Noatak flows westward from its source in the central Brooks Range for more than 400 miles to its delta in Kotzebue Sound. Only a single small settlement — Noatak (population 261) — lies along the river's entire route. Throughout its long, meandering trip to the sea, the dominant aspect of the Noatak River system is its remoteness. The river exists today much as it has through the ages, played upon by the elements, and sheltering great numbers of wildlife.

Six fairly well-defined regions of the river have been identified by those floating the full length of the Noatak. The first region consists of the mountainous terrain at the headwaters, deeply scored canyons with precipitous walls, with

River action has cut away this bank along the Noatak exposing layers of permafrost.
(John and Margaret Ibbotson)

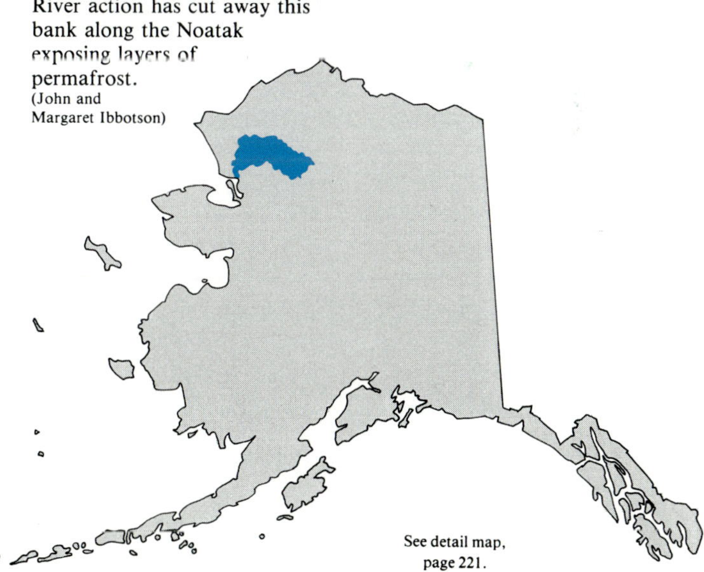

mountains close at hand but giving glimpses of great distance and openness.

The great Noatak basin forms the second region, an area in which the mountains become more rounded and more distant from the river. The basin, as much as 40 miles across and 75 miles long, is a major wildlife area. Its endless pothole lakes and wetlands shelter countless thousands of breeding and nesting birds, many of whom migrate the length of the Americas to reach this area.

Below the basin the Noatak canyons begin — the Grand Canyon of the Noatak is considered less spectacular than Noatak Canyon which is narrower with much steeper walls. Taken together, these canyons represent a third distinctive unit.

Beyond the canyons, another plains area appears, and as the river turns sharply south toward Kotzebue Sound, the woods become larger with both white and black spruce in addition to balsam poplar.

Although the river below Noatak village is outside the preserve, it is interesting to note that the last two regions consist of the Igichuk Hills and the coastal delta where tidal waters reach 40 miles upriver.

Fauna: Wildlife commonly found within the Noatak drainage includes the northwest Arctic caribou herd, numbering about 200,000 animals. This great herd migrates through the valley between its wintering haven in the taiga along the Kobuk River and its calving grounds in the Utukok drainage in National Petroleum Reserve-Alaska on the north slope. Moose, brown/grizzly and black bears, wolves, wolverines, foxes, Dall sheep and a varied array of birds, all found in a superb and unspoiled natural setting, are an integral part of the special appeal of this great waterway.

Left: Travelers in Noatak country need keep an eye on this critter, a Barren Ground brown/grizzly. Although smaller than their coastal cousins, interior and northern bears are just as quick and just as powerful. And on the open tundra there are no trees to climb to get out of harm's way. (John and Margaret Ibbotson)

Below: Outnumbered millions to one, visitors to Noatak National Preserve must be prepared to outwit the region's most numerous wildlife species, the mosquito. These pesky insects are at their worst just after the snow melts when the region is still covered with wet, boggy habitat. (John and Margaret Ibbotson)

Above: A walking pin cushion, the slow, prickly porcupine has an armor of hollow quills which detach easily and can penetrate deep into an attacker, piercing its vital organs. (John and Margaret Ibbotson)

Left: Seeking solitude, a young moose trots away up a bank of the Noatak. In times past moose were uncommon in northwestern Alaska, but in recent years these large mammals seem to be extending their range farther into the Kobuk and Noatak valleys. (John and Margaret Ibbotson)

Top: Colorful, edible and adaptable fireweed covers many slopes in the preserve, including the Grand Canyon of the Noatak, shown in left photo. (John and Margaret Ibbotson)

Above: Margaret Ibbotson picks blueberries, one of several kinds of berries that grow in the Noatak Valley. (John and Margaret Ibbotson)

Flora: Much of Noatak National Preserve is treeless with only willow and alder stands along stream beds as the river moves out of the mountains into the Noatak basin.

The canyon area coincides with the appearance of balsam poplar (cottonwood), which, with taller and denser stands of willow and alder, form thickets along stream beds. Spruce appear in the lower canyon area.

Accommodations: Within the preserve only primitive camping is available. No commercial accommodations exist, and to preserve the area's wilderness character this situation will probably continue. Visitors are on their own and should have enough supplies to be self-sufficient. If floaters or backpackers plan to be picked up by plane, they should be equipped to spend an extra few days in the wilderness since uncertain weather can delay flights.

Kotzebue has stores, hotel and eating facilities, as does Bettles.

Recreational Opportunities: Writers grow lyrical describing the experience of floating the Noatak and exploring its many side streams and tributaries. As one river explorer put it: ''Remoteness. That special quality seemed as endless and abundant as did these side valleys with their creeks and rivers pouring toward us from distant mountain passes to the south. In these valleys was the wilderness quality I never knew anywhere else before.''

Floating down the Noatak can be done by rubber raft, canoe or kayak. Hiking

Barry Santana brings in a fighting arctic char. More than 18 fish species, 12 of which are taken for subsistence, have been recorded in the Noatak drainage. (John and Margaret Ibbotson)

along the river and its tributaries ranges from easy to difficult to impossible, depending on the wetness or dryness of the tundra, the depth and force of side streams which must be forded and the steepness and nature of slopes. Mosquitoes can be a problem in early summer; whitesocks hatch in early August and are present until September frosts. Headnets and a good repellent are essential.

Wildlife observing and photographing are excellent. Since this is a National Park Service preserve, sport hunting and fishing are allowed in season under Alaska Department of Fish and Game regulations.

Human Use and Occupation:

Archaeological finds indicate primitive man may have been in this area 12,000 years ago, but little intensive work has been done to identify and research sites. The area's present-day inhabitants practice a subsistence lifestyle and depend upon the wildlife, fish, berries and other resources found here.

Suggested Reading:
►*ALASKA GEOGRAPHIC®*, Vol. 4, No. 2, *THE BROOKS RANGE*
►*ALASKA GEOGRAPHIC®*, Vol. 8, No. 3, *KOTZEBUE BASIN*

Further Information:
►Superintendent, Noatak National Preserve
National Park Service
540 West Fifth Avenue
Anchorage, AK 99501

USGS Topographic Series:
Survey Pass, Ambler River, Howard Pass, Baird Mountains, Misheguk Mountain

Wrangell-Saint Elias National Park and Preserve

Location: Eastern southcentral Alaska, extending from Glennallen on the Richardson Highway to the Canadian border (130 miles) and from Slana on the Tok Cutoff southward to the Gulf of Alaska (170 miles), and extending southeastward to Yakutat Bay.

Bounded on the east by Canada, Wrangell-Saint Elias National Park and Preserve adjoins Kluane National Park and Kluane Game Sanctuary in Yukon Territory, forming with its Canadian counterpart a World Heritage Area of 20 million acres.

Among the world's longest glaciers, 75-mile-long Nabesna Glacier originates on the slopes of Mount Wrangell.
(Steve McCutcheon)

Size: 12,318,000 acres (8,147,000 acres in park; 4,171,000 acres in preserve according to approximate federal acreage figures), with 8,700,000 acres designated wilderness.

Access: A major access is by road along the Richardson Highway and Edgerton Highway from Glennallen to Chitina. From Chitina the old Copper River & Northwestern Railway bed has been converted to a road terminating just west of the Kennicott River near the small town of McCarthy which can be reached by a primitive cable car across the river.

Along the northern boundary of the preserve, the Tok Cutoff runs through Slana where a graded secondary road leads to Nabesna, a tiny settlement within the preserve.

Air service is available from landing fields adjacent to the park/preserve, some of them served by scheduled air service such as Gulkana and Northway. Charter flights in small planes land

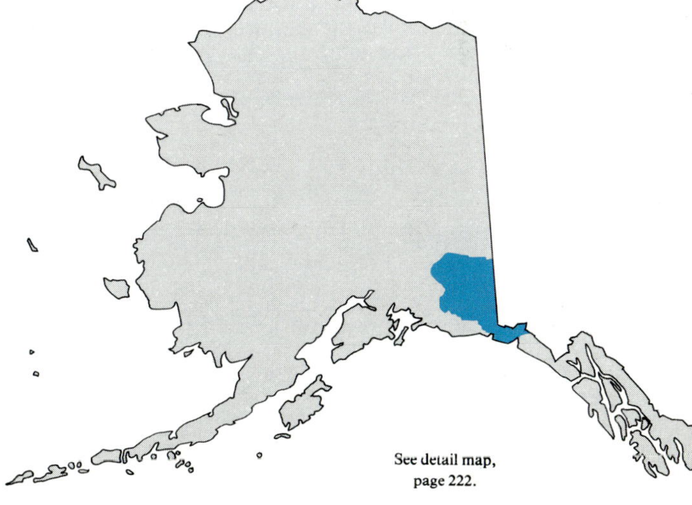

at well-maintained airstrips at McCarthy and May Creek, or on lakes within the park/preserve.

Area Description:

The enormous area of Wrangell-Saint Elias National Park and Preserve ensures a variety of climatic zones and weather. Coastal areas are subject to warm, moist air flowing from the west which condenses over the Chugach and Saint Elias mountains. Scientists estimate the Chugach peaks and Bagley Icefield may receive 600 inches of precipitation annually, heaviest known in the world. North of these mountains, a drier continental climate prevails.

The Copper River Valley experiences temperature variations of more than 150°, from winter lows of -60°F. to summer highs of 70°F. Precipitation averages 10 to 12 inches per year here; north of the Wrangells precipitation averages a scant eight inches annually.

Wrangell-Saint Elias National Park and Preserve, combined with its counterpart in Yukon Territory, Kluane National Park, comprise the largest glacial complex in North America. One glacier alone, Malaspina, is larger than the state of Rhode Island.

The Wrangell Mountains, which form the inner rampart of giant peaks and glaciers, has been sculptured by both fire and ice. The western peaks, Mount Drum (12,010 feet), Mount Sanford (16,237 feet) and Mount Wrangell (14,163 feet), are still considered active volcanoes with steam and ash issuing from the summit of Mount Wrangell, melting perpetual snows thereon, and warm mineral springs and mud volcanoes flowing from the foot of

Clockwise from upper left:
►Mount Wrangell, the central and most massive peak in the Wrangell Range, may be the largest volcano in North America. Its gradual dome-shaped profile is the result of eruptions of fluid lava.
►Within the active north crater, billowing fumaroles eat away at the snow and ice. In places, the sulphurous steam leaves bright yellow stains.
►Flowing glacial ice splits into gigantic sections as it slides over a prominence on the volcano's western flank.
►Fumaroles — holes created by the emerging columns of steam — contain poisonous gases.

Mount Wrangell: A Simmering Giant

Story and photos by Ransom Saltmarch

Mount Wrangell is a young volcano with a record of eruptive activity in present geological times. As recently as 70 years ago, observers in the booming mining town of Chitina reported fountains of lava shooting 2,000 to 3,000 feet above the volcano's summit and illuminating the night sky like bolts of lightning.

In 1953 the University of Alaska, working jointly with New York University, erected some crude huts on the rim of the mountain's north crater with logistical aid from the U.S. Air Force. Their interest was not in the volcano, but in the study of cosmic rays which the high-altitude station would facilitate. The crater rim seemed an ideal place as the heat venting from the rocky soil tended to keep part of the crater rim free of snow. However, the huts suffered wind damage and filled with snow during the first winter. Although they were dug out and repaired for the next year's operation, logistical problems proved to be too much and the station was abandoned after 1954.

In 1961 a new group from the Geophysical Institute of the University of Alaska, under the leadership of Carl S. Benson, was attracted to the mountain — this time to study its glaciers and its volcanism. They were especially interested in the interaction between glacier ice and the volcanic heat flow at the summit. Their interest has not been ill-rewarded. In 1964, with support from the U.S. Air Force's Arctic Aeromedical Laboratory, they built a hut specially designed to be heated by volcanic heat flow through its floor. The plan worked well for several years. However, the heat flow increased markedly after the 1964 earthquake and, together with corrosive volcanic gases, ruined the research station in 1970. The heat has continued to build to the present time. The geophysicists now carry out their research from tent camps, as before, and are using the melting glacier ice as a giant calorimeter in their determination of volcanic heat flux. At the summit this approach is simplified because volcanic heat is the only heat source for melting the ice. The north crater, barely visible beneath a cover of snow in the 1950s, is now a deep steaming bowl, three-quarters of a mile across.

Today the active north crater is a spectacular sight. Columns of steam billow from the central vents, and huge fragments of ice collapse from the walls of the bowl, forming a lake on the crater floor. Keels and terraces of streamlined ice rise a foot above the surface, carved by the gale-force winds that sweep the mountain's top. Changes in the crater can take place very quickly — a vent that begins as a funnel-shaped depression in the snow, for example, can become a large gaping hole in the space of a few days.

The enormous scale of the mountain is impressive. Crevasses that appear thread-thin from the air are in reality wide enough to easily swallow a small airplane, and some of the giant blocks of cascading ice are 600 to 800 feet across.

Signs of the fiery life stirring beneath the frozen cover are evident in a few spots. In places, the white snowy rims of the vents are tinged a bright yellow from the sulphur content of the steam. Large pockets of brightly colored rock, turned red, ochre and greenish-gray, indicate hydrothermal alteration—the possible remnants of earlier eruptions. High on Mount Wrangell's southwest side, a glacier approximately one mile square is riddled with fumaroles — holes created by the emerging columns of steam. Fumarole pits, which contain potentially poisonous gases, are often covered by a thin skin of fresh snow and thus pose a hazard to climbers, as a fall into one could prove fatal.

Relaxing in a roadside cafe far from the mountain, it is possible to recall the imaginary scenario described by one geologist: Mount Wrangell erupts, flowing lava and mudslides descend to dam the Copper River, and the entire Copper Valley is flooded. The little cafe and every human inhabitant for miles around would be swallowed in the disaster. Having experienced the volcano firsthand, having obtained some notion of its size and the fiery power lurking beneath it, the scenario is not so hard to believe.

Editor's note: Ransom Saltmarch was a member of an expedition that climbed to the north crater of Mount Wrangell, northernmost active volcano in the Pacific rim, and spent four days there exploring and observing.

Mount Drum. This is an area of high geothermal activity.

The area is extremely rugged with ice-clad mountains exceeding 18,000 feet: Mount Saint Elias at 18,008 feet is the second highest peak in the United States, and Mount Logan in Kluane National Park is the second highest peak in North America at 19,850 feet. Lowlands exist only in the central Chitina River Valley and along the western and northeastern fringes of the park/preserve.

The Totschunda Fault, one of the most active fault zones in Alaska, cuts through the northern section of the park/preserve. This entire region displays evidence of the mountain-building effects of tectonic plate collisions and volcanic activity associated with such collisions including major earthquakes. One of the most

recent earthquakes affecting this region occurred in 1964, and resulted in major uplifts of more than 40 feet in some areas.

The area of the headwaters of the Nizina, Chitistone and White rivers near Skolai Pass contains a particularly diverse and complete exposure of the geologic processes and features of eastern Alaska.

The junction of three mountain ranges, Chugach in the south, Wrangells in the north, and Saint Elias in the east, dominate this portion of Alaska. Two major rivers, the Copper, curving around the park/preserve's western boundary from north to south; and its major tributary, the Chitina, fed from glaciers in the Saint Elias Range and draining the southern Wrangells and north Chugach Mountains, serve as the region's major transportation corridors.

Draining Russell Glacier and other ice rivers along the northern flank of the Wrangells, the White River flows eastward through Yukon Territory to join the Yukon River on its way to the Bering Sea. Two other major streams in the northern Wrangells — Nabesna and Chisana — flow northward into the Tanana River.

Above right: The eastern Chugach Mountains cover much of Wrangell-Saint Elias National Park's southern boundary. Here the Chugach Mountains form a backdrop for Tebay Lake whose waters empty into the Hanagita River. (Gil Mull, reprinted from *ALASKA GEOGRAPHIC®*)

Right: Lobes of Malaspina Glacier, largest piedmont glacier in North America, reach toward the Gulf of Alaska north of Yakutat Bay. (Bruce Molnia, reprinted from *ALASKA GEOGRAPHIC®*)

Fauna: Thanks to a diversity of habitats, Wrangell-Saint Elias National Park and Preserve supports varied wildlife, although actual numbers of each species is limited. As in most of Alaska, much habitat is required to support each animal. On higher slopes range Dall sheep and mountain goats. The sheep favor the Wrangell Mountains and northern slopes of the Chugach Range, while the goats prefer more coastal mountains.

Caribou from three separate herds forage in the park/preserve: the Mentasta herd occupies the western and northern slopes of the Wrangells; the Chisana herd forages in the Beaver Creek and upper Chisana drainages; and the Nelchina herd occasionally strays out of its normal range in the Nelchina basin and Lake Louise area to winter on the northwestern flanks of the Wrangells where this herd mingles with the Mentasta herd.

Moose browse throughout the lowlands and river bottoms within the park/preserve, and two herds of introduced bison range along the Copper River and Chitina River.

Brown/grizzly and black bear share lower elevations with wolves, wolverines, coyotes, red foxes and a variety of small furbearers.

Sport fish, such as arctic grayling, ling cod and trout, thrive in lakes adjacent to the Chitina valley and on the northern slopes of the Wrangells, while the Copper River supports a major salmon run utilized by both commercial and subsistence fishermen.

Bird life is not outstanding within the park/preserve, although the nearby Copper River delta forms a heavily used nesting area just to the south of the park.

Marine species which can be observed in Yakutat Bay, where the park touches the sea, include seals, sea lions, sea otters and two species of dolphin as well as killer whales.

Flora: Three ecosystems are represented within the park/preserve: the northern coniferous, alpine tundra and coastal coniferous. Tree line in the park's interior occurs at about 3,000 to 4,000 feet. Below this the forest cover is composed of white spruce and balsam poplar at lower elevations, and a mixture of aspen, birch and balsam poplar higher on the slopes. Stream beds contain thick underbrush, usually alder, which also grows well on steep south-facing hillsides, and willow. Labrador tea and dwarf birch are major shrubs.

Above 3,000 feet moist sedges and grasses form open tundra meadows interlaced with blueberry and Labrador tea. The Bremner and Copper river valleys near their mouths exhibit vegetation typical of coastal areas: western and mountain hemlock and Sitka spruce form a rain forest whose understory may contain devil's club, blueberry and salmonberry.

Left: Bushy-tailed, stocky rodents, hoary marmots build complex tunnel communities on high mountain slopes. (Brad Ebel)

Above: The Wrangells are renowned for their Dall sheep habitat. About 10,000 of these sheep occupy slopes of the Wrangells; fewer are found in the northern slopes of the eastern Chugach Mountains. Much of the Wrangell area was given preserve status to allow continued hunting of these animals. (George Wuerthner)

Below: Chitina (population 50), a year-round community near the confluence of the Copper and Chitina rivers, serves as a major access point to McCarthy and the southern Wrangells. The 33-mile Edgerton Highway connects Chitina to the Richardson Highway. On the Edgerton 63 miles beyond Chitina visitors encounter the Kennicott River where travelers must park their cars and pull themselves across the river by cables to reach downtown McCarthy. (John and Margaret Ibbotson)

Right: Folks from throughout the Chitina Valley and Wrangell Mountain area gather at McCarthy Lodge in the settlement of McCarthy. (Gil Mull)

Accommodations:

McCarthy, once a thriving mining town of 4,000 during the heyday of Kennecott Mine operations, is now a small, congenial community of year-round residents. During the summer several of the old buildings, refurbished by the owners, serve as rustic hostelries with no modern frills such as inside plumbing or electricity, but with comfortable quarters and choice home-cooked meals.

At the old Kennecott Mine, a few miles up the glacier from McCarthy and accessible by road, some of the abandoned mine buildings have been converted to provide accommodations.

Several rustic lodges and fishing camps operate in the preserve at Tanada and Copper lakes in the north, Ptarmigan and Rock lakes in the northeast and Tebay and Hanagita lakes in the mountains south of the Chitina River. The town of Chitina has simple lodging facilities and primitive camping spots abound.

Modern motels and lodges are located in communities around the periphery of the park/preserve at Glennallen, Gulkana, Copper Center, Tok and Gakona.

Recreational Opportunities:

Every type of wilderness recreation is available in this huge park/preserve. Mountain climbing opportunities are challenging, especially when peaks in both the Wrangell-Saint Elias complex and Kluane National Park are included. These areas afford some of the highest, most rugged and most inaccessible peaks in North America.

Hiking, backpacking and wilderness exploring make use of the few historical trails, such as Goat Trail up Chitistone Canyon to Skolai Pass, in the region.

River running by raft, kayak, canoe and river boat is excellent on many of the streams.

Within the preserve hunting is allowed during regular seasons set by the Alaska Department of Fish and Game. The same organization oversees fishing regulations for the area.

Winter camping and cross-country ski touring are possible in accessible areas; those enjoying these activities should be reasonably self-sufficient.

Human Use and Occupation:

Native use of the Wrangell-Saint Elias area since prehistoric times probably occurred along the rivers. However, few permanent settlements predating the 20th century have been identified other than those at Taral on the Copper River and at Batzulnetas south of Nabesna Road.

White men's interest focused on mining, especially in the mountains on the north side of the Chitina valley. The most extensive workings occurred at Kennecott where rich copper finds along contact zones topping steep ridges resulted in con-

struction of the huge mill still existing at Kennecott and the now-abandoned Copper River & Northwestern Railway which ran between Cordova and McCarthy via Chitina. The old mill, and abandoned mine shafts at various locations on the mountainsides high above the mill, offer fascinating glimpses of this fabled era immortalized by author Rex Beach in *The Iron Trail* (1913).

Suggested Reading:
▶*ALASKA GEOGRAPHIC®*, Vol. 8, No. 1,
WRANGELL-SAINT ELIAS

Further Information:
▶Superintendent, Wrangell-Saint Elias National Park
and Preserve
National Park Service
Post Office Box 29
Glennallen, AK 99588

USGS Topographic Series:
Mount Saint Elias, Yakutat, Icy Bay, Bering Glacier,
McCarthy, Nabesna, Gulkana, Valdez

Top: Northwest access to the Wrangell-Saint Elias complex is along 51-mile Nabesna Road which runs from the Tok Cutoff to Nabesna. Ruins of Nabesna Mine, from which about $1.9 million in gold was extracted between 1931 and 1940, clutter the countryside at the end of Nabesna Road. (Jim Simmen)

Above: A fish wheel traps salmon swimming up the Copper River near Chitina. Controversy between subsistence and commercial fishermen has developed over declining Copper River stocks. (John and Margaret Ibbotson)

Yukon-Charley Rivers National Preserve

Location: Eastcentral Alaska, north and west of Eagle, Alaska. One side of the preserve borders Canada north of Eagle. The preserve includes a stretch of the Yukon River flowing northwest from just north of Eagle almost to Circle, and the Charley River drainage from its source to its confluence with the Yukon.

Size: 1,713,000 acres.

Access: Eagle and Circle, the two communities nearest the preserve, are reachable by road. From Eagle access to the preserve by boat is downstream, making it easy for canoes, kayaks or rafts; the water route from Circle is upstream and requires a power boat. At present only helicopters provide access for floaters wanting to run the Charley River.

Area Description: The area has a continental climate with extremes of temperature. Summer highs average in the low 70s and lows in the mid-40s, although freezing at night can occur any month of the year at higher elevations. Winter lows can reach -40°F. and lower for extended periods. Normal winter temperatures range from -5°F. to -25°F. Precipitation

is light, about eight to ten inches annually, mostly falling as rain in summer. Snow cover is light but continuous for about seven months of the year.

The preserve's landscape is not spectacular but is representative of the intermountain plateau region in parts of eastern Alaska lying between the Brooks Range and the Alaska Range. The hills are gentle and rounded, and forested on the lower slopes.

The Yukon River follows an old zone of instability known as the Tintina Valley, which separates the metamorphosed rocks of its southern banks from the unmetamorphosed sedimentary rocks to the north. This unmetamorphosed rock strata is rich in fossils, offering an almost uninterrupted sequence from the Precambrian era, when multi-celled organisms first appeared, to present time. These rocks constitute a geologic calendar important to researchers.

Numerous tributary streams flow into the Yukon within the preserve: Charley River; Woodchopper, Coal, Sam and Fourth of July creeks from the south; and Nation, Kandik and Tatonduk rivers from the north.

Left: The Charley River meanders through a wilderness setting of spruce and birch. (John Wise, reprinted from *ALASKA GEOGRAPHIC®*)

Above: Granitic spires, known as "tors," rise above the ground near Twin Mountain, west of the Charley River. (Robert Belous, National Park Service)

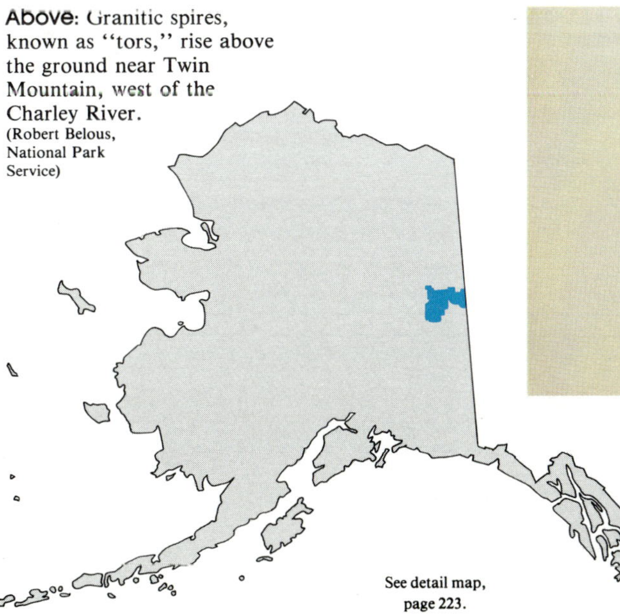

See detail map, page 223.

Above: A young Dall sheep ram climbs among the rocks above the Charley River. (Robert Belous, National Park Service)

Overleaf: The Yukon River, which has long been a highway for all types of watercraft, is shown near the mouth of the Tatonduk River. (George Wuerthner)

Fauna: Caribou from the Fortymile herd migrate from the preserve to Canada and back. A moderate number of moose browse along streams and lowland areas, while Dall sheep occupy heights above the Charley River. Principal predators are black bear and wolf.

More than 200 species of birds have been reported from the Yukon-Charley Rivers National Preserve. Of these, 20 species are raptors such as bald and golden eagles, rough-legged hawks and gyrfalcons. In its cliffs and rocky peaks the preserve contains some of North America's finest habitat for peregrine falcons, an endangered species. Yukon-Charley lies along a major flyway for waterfowl breeding on the Yukon Flats and wintering in the continental United States.

Flora: The Charley River watershed is among the few major drainages in Alaska relatively undisturbed by humans. The watershed's plant communities, dominated by spruce, aspen and birch, have remained relatively intact through the ages. Along the Yukon River vegetation is characterized more by bottomland spruce and poplar.

Accommodations: None are available in the preserve although good primitive camping sites exist. Suitable accommodations exist in Eagle and Circle.

Recreational Opportunities:

Hiking and canoeing opportunities abound along the many streams flowing into the Yukon; upland areas above timberline attract hikers. The Yukon River serves as a highway for all types of water craft. Sightseeing tours by river vessel operate out of Dawson City, Canada, to Fort Yukon with stops at Eagle and Circle. Alaska Raft Adventures offers float trips on the Charley River. Riverboat tours and raft rentals are also available in Eagle. Hunting and fishing, conducted under State of Alaska regulations, are popular in the preserve.

Top: Chip Bloomer and Pete Brown enjoy a canoe trip on the Tatonduk River, near its confluence with the Yukon River. (George Wuerthner)

Above: Fall colors brighten the Tatonduk River valley. (Gil Mull)

Human Use and Occupation:

The Yukon River has served as a highway for the movement of people and goods since prehistoric times. Human occupancy of the area probably began 10,000 years ago when ancestors of the present Athabascans moved along the river following game and fish. These tribes became known as the Kutchin.

White contact occurred as early as 1879, when the English coming overland through Canada floated down the Porcupine River to the Fort Yukon area. A Hudson's Bay Trading Post was established at Fort Yukon which served Natives up and down the river for many miles. Gold discoveries at Circle, Woodchopper Creek, Nation and other eastern Yukon localities preceded the Klondike gold rush and mining camps dotted the area. By 1899, 56 sternwheelers operated along the Yukon. Such traffic declined steadily as the gold was mined out and camps closed down. Today only a handful of mining operations are active within the preserve's boundaries.

Suggested Reading:
►*Coming Into The Country,* John McPhee, 1976

Further Information:
►Superintendent
 Yukon-Charley Rivers National Preserve
 National Park Service
 Eagle, AK 99738

USGS Topographic Series:
Eagle, Charley River, Big Delta, Circle

A visitor strolls on an August morning through the main thoroughfare in the village of Eagle. The mountain in the background is known as Eagle Bluff.
(Clinton Andrews, staff)

National Wildlife Refuges

National wildlife refuge acreage in Alaska increased nearly four-fold with the signing of the Alaska d-2 lands bill. Coincident with signing of the legislation, Alaska was given full regional status in Fish & Wildlife Service administration and the Anchorage office became a regional office.

Areas now included with the refuge system in Alaska contain a wide and nearly complete spectrum of ecosystems in Alaska. These lands are also large enough and diversified enough to maintain a representative sample of most of the various wildlife and habitats found here.

National wildlife refuges are designed to protect the habitats of representative populations of land and marine mammals, other marine animals and birds. Thus the sanctuaries vary widely in size, depending upon the life cycles and habitat requirements of a particular species. Some refuges include only a particular rocky cliff or an islet jutting out of the ocean, which furnishes a nesting site for one or several species of seabirds. Some smaller units protect hauling grounds and shoreline retreats of seals, sea lions or walrus. At the other end of the scale is the magnitude of the Arctic National Wildlife Refuge, whose 18 million acres encompass crucial habitat of the wide-ranging Porcupine caribou herd. This herd migrates thousands of miles between winter and summer locations. Even so, the Porcupine herd spends part of its time in Canada, outside of protected boundaries.

National wildlife refuges are not like national parks, although some of them enjoy similar status in terms of recreational use. National parks are created with a twofold mission: to protect unimpaired the natural values for which they were created, and to provide for the use and enjoyment of the people. Wildlife refuges consider the use and enjoyment of people also, but their primary purpose is to protect the

Below: A substantial population of moose browse on willows and other shrubs in Yukon Flats. (George Wuerthner)

Right: Monkey flower or wild snapdragon grows on moist, rocky slopes of the Alaska Peninsula National Wildlife Preserve. (John Sarvis)

habitat and wildlife within their boundaries. Use by people must be compatible with this primary goal.

National wildlife refuges do not provide visitor accommodations such as housing and meal service, but some of the more frequently visited refuges have interpretive centers to explain the area's ecology and to help visitors identify the refuge's wildlife.

Among the public recreational uses permitted within national wildlife refuges are sightseeing, nature observation and photography, sport hunting and fishing, boating, camping, hiking and picnicking. Trapping can be carried out under applicable state and federal laws. Commercial fishing, including the use of requisite campsites, cabins and motorized vehicles, is allowed.

Because refuges have expanded to include areas previously in the public domain, a number of privately built and owned cabins for recreational and subsistence uses are now within refuge boundaries. These cabins can continue to be occupied and used by the owners with special permits. Refuge visitors are permitted to possess, use and transport firearms for hunting and personal protection.

Subsistence living activities — hunting, fishing, berry-gathering, woodcutting, procuring logs for building and harvesting other plants — are all protected under the d-2 lands bill. Use of snowmobiles, motorboats and other means of surface transportation traditionally relied upon by local rural residents for subsistence is generally permitted under the new regulations.

Aircraft access to wildlife refuges is allowed, and off-road vehicles may be used on special routes and in areas designated by the refuge manager.

Portions of certain units of the refuge system are classified as wilderness, and will be included in the National Wilderness Preservation System.

National Wildlife Refuges (NWR) in Alaska

Before 1971*		As of December 2, 1980**		
Name	Acreage	Name (numbers refer to map)	Total Acreage (Includes acreage classified as Wilderness)	Wilderness Acreage (Lands within each NWR that are maintained as natural areas)
Aleutian Islands NWR	2,720,225	**1. Alaska Maritime NWR**	3,548,783†	2,460,000
Bering Sea NWR	81,340			
Bogoslof NWR	175			
Chamisso NWR	455			
Forrester Island NWR	2,832			
Hazy Islands NWR	32			
St. Lazaria NWR	65			
Semidi NWR	251,930			
Simeonof NWR	26,046			
Tuxedni NWR	5,683			
Total	3,088,783			
		2. Alaska Peninsula NWR	3,500,000	
Arctic National Wildlife Range Name later changed to Wm. O. Douglas NWR	8,894,624	**3. Arctic NWR**	18,054,624†	8,000,000
		4. Becharof NWR*	1,200,000	400,000
		5. Innoko NWR	3,850,000	1,240,000
Izembek NWR	320,893	**6. Izembek NWR**	320,893†	300,000
		7. Kanuti NWR	1,430,000	
Kenai National Moose Range	1,730,000	**8. Kenai NWR**	1,970,000†	1,350,000
Kodiak National Wildlife Range	1,815,000	**9. Kodiak NWR**	1,865,000†	
		10. Koyukuk NWR	3,550,000	400,000
		11. Nowitna NWR	1,560,000	
		12. Selawik NWR	2,150,000	240,000
		13. Tetlin NWR	700,000	
Cape Newenham NWR	265,000	**14. Togiak NWR**	4,105,000†	2,270,000
Clarence Rhode NWR	2,887,026	**15. Yukon Delta NWR**	19,624,458†	1,900,000
Hazen Bay NWR	6,800			
Nunivak NWR	3,330,632			
Total	6,224,458			
		16. Yukon Flats NWR*	8,630,000	
TOTAL ACREAGE	23,338,758		76,058,758	18,560,000

*1971 — Section 17(d)(2) of the Alaska Native Claims Settlement Act (ANCSA) authorized the withdrawal of unreserved public lands by December 1978. However, Congress failed to meet the deadline, so late in 1978 these lands were withdrawn under emergency authority prescribed by the Federal Land Policy and Management Act of 1976. Becharof Lake and Yukon Flats were established at that time as national monuments by the president.

**In December, 1980, The Alaska National Interest Lands Conservation Act established these lands as National Wildlife Refuges.

† Includes pre-1971 acreage

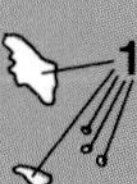
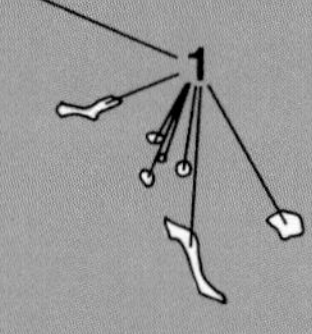
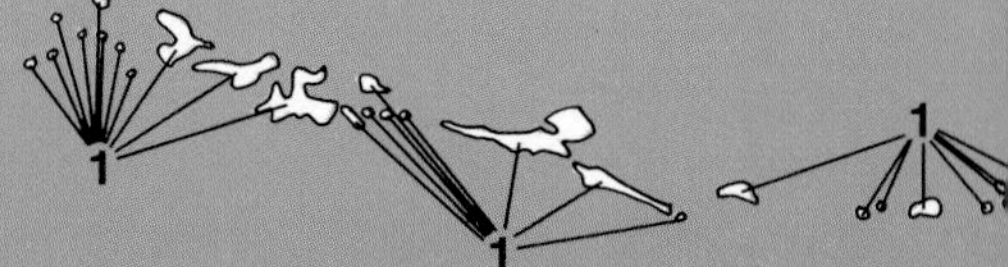

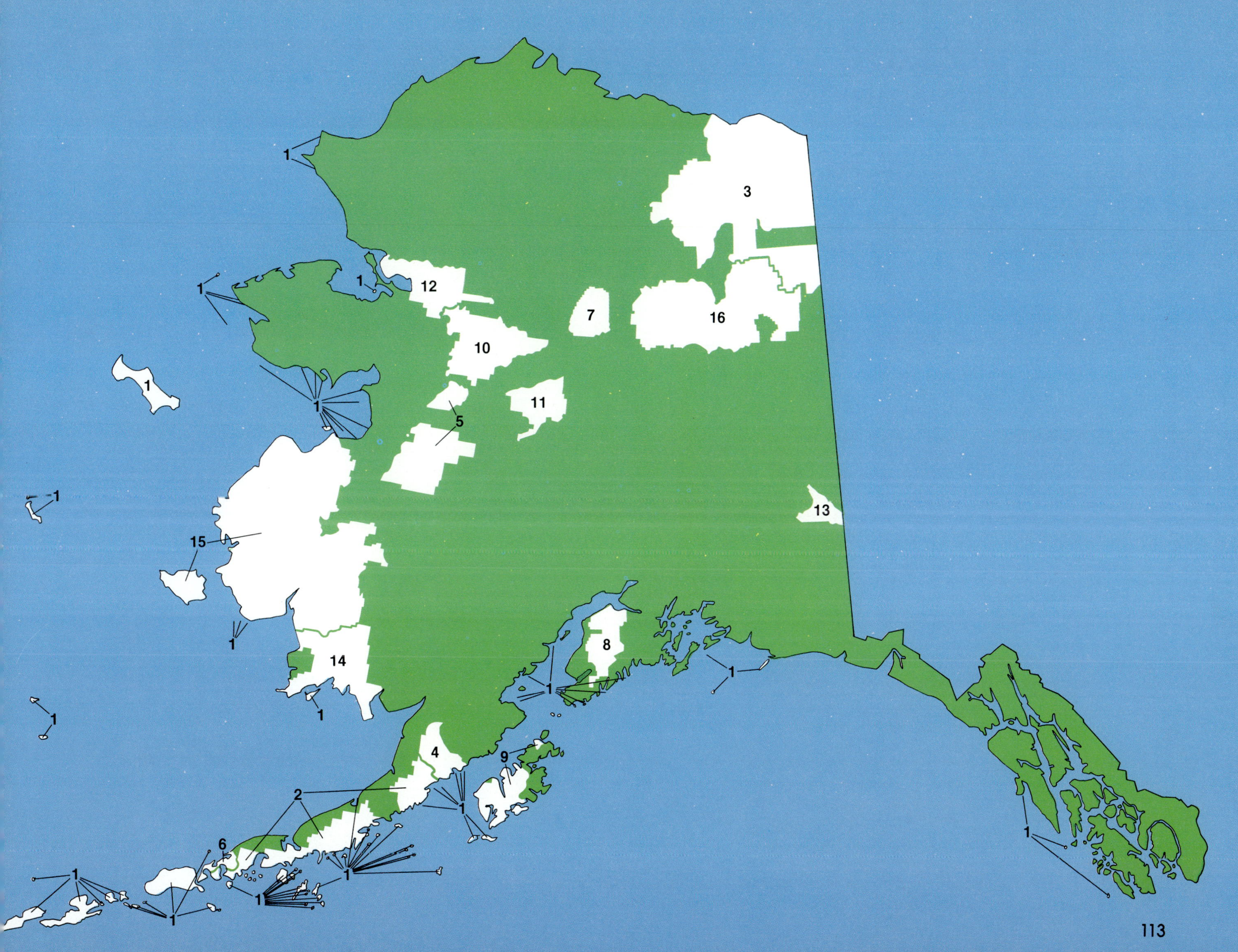

1
3
12
7
16
10
11
5
15
13
8
14
1
4
9
2
6
113

Alaska Maritime National Wildlife Refuge

Setting: Consists of more than 2,400 parcels of land on islands, islets, rocks, spires, reefs and headlands of Alaska coastal waters from Cape Lisburne in the Chukchi Sea to Forrester Island in southeast Alaska. Included in this new designation are 10 refuges created prior to the Alaska lands bill (see chart on page 112 for detailed listing). The act added 460,000 acres of new refuge land and the total acreage now amounts to about 4,500,000. The Aleutian Islands unit of the refuge accounts for the majority of this acreage.

Most lands involved in the Alaska Maritime National Wildlife Refuge are wild and lonely, extremely rugged and inaccessible. Several portions have been classified as wilderness.

Hundreds of sea lions gather on rocks near Lowrie Island, part of Forrester Island National Wildlife Refuge now incorporated into the Alaska Maritime refuge. The island group is about 20 miles west of Dall Island in extreme southeastern Alaska.
(Donald Grybeck, reprinted from *ALASKA GEOGRAPHIC®*)

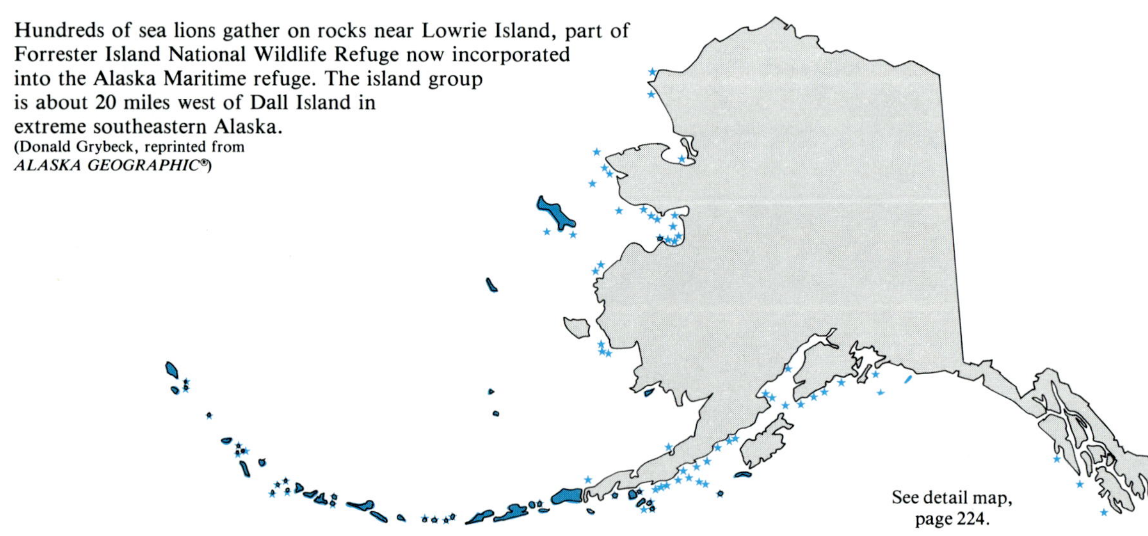

Clockwise from above:

►The Chiswell Islands, in the Gulf of Alaska south of the Kenai Peninsula, have been incorporated into the Alaska Maritime National Wildlife Refuge because of their marine mammal and seabird populations. One of the Chiswells, Beehive Island, a 530-foot monolith, has the largest tufted puffin colony on the Kenai Peninsula's outer coast. (David Miller, reprinted from *ALASKA*® magazine)

►One of the non-marine members of the bird community of Saint Lazaria National Wildlife Refuge, which has been absorbed into the Alaska Maritime refuge, is this immature northwestern crow. (Robert Armstrong, reprinted from *ALASKA*® magazine)

►Unimak Island at the tip of the Alaska Peninsula and the beginning of the Aleutians marks the farthest reach of many large continental mammals, such as this wolf, out into the Aleutian chain. (John Sarvis)

►Steller sea lions haul out on a steep rock at Cape Sarichef at the northwestern corner of Unimak Island. These animals are the most abundant marine mammal in the Aleutians today. (John Sarvis)

Right: Blue phase arctic foxes gather for a family meeting outside their den on Saint Paul Island in the Pribilofs. (Craig Hansen)

Above: Every spring about 1,500,000 northern fur seals migrate north to the rocky beaches of the Pribilofs. First to arrive, in May, are the adult males, followed in turn by adult females and older bachelors in June, the two-year-olds in July and some yearlings in late summer. More than half the yearlings do not come ashore during their second summer. (John and Margaret Ibbotson)

Right: A horned puffin pauses briefly along the rocky headland of Southwest Point on Saint Paul Island in the Pribilofs. The island is renowned for its wildlife populations, especially northern fur seals and seabirds. At the rookeries along Southwest Point live tufted and horned puffins; parakeet, least and crested auklets; northern fulmars, murres and a variety of gulls. (Penny Rennick)

Natural Resources: The major purpose of this refuge is to protect marine birds and mammals, and the habitats vital to their life cycles. Secondly, the refuge is intended to facilitate scientific research on Alaska's marine environment.

The refuge contains habitat for about 75% of the state's total marine bird population, between 15 and 30 million birds divided among some 55 species. Raptors — eagles, hawks and falcons —as well as other non-marine birds also use the refuge.

Sea lions, several species of seals, walrus, sea otters and polar bears seek shelter in the refuge. Sixteen species of whales swim in offshore waters, and a variety of land mammals including foxes, otters, mink, brown/grizzly bears, wolves and wolverines depend on the refuge's habitat.

Further Information:
►Alaska Maritime National Wildlife Refuge
U.S. Fish & Wildlife Service
Regional Office
1011 East Tudor Road
Anchorage, AK 99503

Birding Attu

Nudging the international dateline, Attu Island, at the end of the Aleutians directly north of New Zealand and directly south of Siberia's Anadyr River Valley, lies at the extreme eastern edge of the migration route for Asian birds heading north to summer breeding grounds. Each spring for the past several years birding groups have chartered flights to Attu where some of North America's most unusual bird sightings have been recorded. Birders come prepared with food and cooking equipment, foul-weather gear, binoculars and scopes, and bicycles . . . yes, bicycles . . . to cover as much of Attu as possible searching for migrants just in from an ocean flight.

In May 1980 birders were scoping the sea and rocky headland at Murder Point when a small brown bird flew in from the ocean, landed at the first rocky promontory and immediately went to sleep. Twenty minutes later the bird woke and began feeding. For many birders this was their first look at an Indian tree pipit.

Again at Murder Point, three birders, led by Daniel Gibson of the University of Alaska museum and one of the state's foremost bird authorities, reported the first North American record for the black-tailed gull. Bald and golden eagles are familiar to many birding enthusiasts, but Attu Island offers a chance to glimpse white-tailed eagles and Steller's sea eagles, both Asian species.

Birding Attu is strenuous and demands persistence and determination. When the report comes of a rare bunting at Henderson Marsh and a birder is several miles away searching the shores of Casco Cove for Polynesian tattlers and Mongolian plovers, a decision must be made. Does the birder pedal several miles uphill and upwind — and the Aleutians are known for their wind — in hopes that the bunting will remain long enough for the birder to come straggling up to see it.

Or worse yet, a call (group leaders carry radios and report at 30-minute intervals) comes that a falcated teal has been spotted at Alexai Point, more than seven miles one way from the end of the runway which serves as the main thoroughfare for bicycling birders. Quickly birders begin the trek to Alexai. After slogging through snow, crossing washouts and trudging through patches of nothing but mud, the birders reach Alexai Point and fan out to locate their quarry. Only then do they learn that the bird has been misidentified and is merely an ordinary wigeon. And in the meantime, a call

Below: Some of Attu's birds are difficult to see, but not this rock ptarmigan. Birders had a good look at this female even though she blended in with the gravel of this road near the Coast Guard Loran Station at Attu. (Lisa Oakley)

Right: Waves from Massacre Bay slide off the beach from which extend the remains of World War II docks. To the left of the docks is the beginning of Henderson Marsh, and behind rises Gilbert Ridge. (Penny Rennick)

has come through of another rare find . . . at Murder Point, miles away at the opposite end of the birders' normal range.

But for those who enjoy being on a remote island, searching for wildlife —arctic foxes, sea otters and whales as well as birds — among tundra, beaches, mountains and remains of World War II battles, Attu is just the place. For more information about bird excursions to the Aleutian Islands write Attours, 4529 Columbia, Lincolnwood, IL 60646; or Wings, Inc., Box 287, Seal Harbor, ME 04675.

Penny Rennick

Left: Elusive and mysterious, wolverines, such as this one crossing the ice of the Alaska Peninsula, range throughout mainland Alaska.
(John Sarvis)

Alaska Peninsula National Wildlife Refuge

Setting: Southwestern Alaska on the Alaska Peninsula. The 3,500,000-acre refuge extends southwest from Becharof National Wildlife Refuge along the Pacific coast side of the peninsula to False Pass but excludes lands designated as part of Aniakchak National Monument and Preserve. On the opposite side of the peninsula, the state of Alaska has selected lands along the Bristol Bay coastline extending southwest of Naknek to Izembek National Wildlife Refuge.

Above: A brilliantly plumaged male king eider swims along the shores of the Alaska Peninsula. These birds breed in the high Arctic and winter on inshore marine waters along the Alaska Peninsula and near Kodiak.
(John Sarvis)

Overleaf: Fresh snowfall glistens on the 4,800-foot Aghileen Pinnacles which straddle the Izembek-Alaska Peninsula refuges' boundary.
(John Sarvis)

Left: Surf tumbles onto the beach boulders of Beaver Bay, on the south coast of the Alaska Peninsula west of Cape Aliaksin.
(Roger Maier)

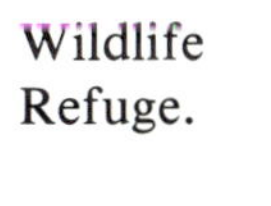

See detail map, page 226.

119

Natural Resources: Alaska Peninsula National Wildlife Refuge contains an unusual diversity of natural features: active volcanoes, lakes, rivers and a beautiful stretch of rugged, rocky Pacific Ocean coastline. Weather in this treeless area is often windy and overcast.

The peninsula's lakes and rivers support an extremely productive salmon fishery, and brown/grizzly bears swarm along salmon streams during the spawning season. Other large mammals found here are moose, caribou, wolves and wolverines.

The Pacific Ocean shores and offshore waters support large populations of sea lions, seals and sea otters. The entire refuge and the peninsula in general furnish habitat for many varieties of migratory birds, especially ducks, geese and shorebirds.

The Alaska Peninsula has been a major big game hunting area for many years, especially for the huge brown/grizzly bears found here. Beginning north of Katmai National Park and Preserve at the state game sanctuary at McNeil River, the big bears' habitat is protected, either as park, preserve or refuge, along the peninsula's entire Pacific coast to Unimak Island at the beginning of the Aleutian chain.

Further Information:
►Alaska Peninsula National Wildlife Refuge
U.S. Fish & Wildlife Service
Regional Office
1011 East Tudor Road
Anchorage, AK 99503

Clockwise from above:

►The village of King Cove sits on a small peninsula between King Cove Lagoon and King Cove which faces Deer Passage on the Alaska Peninsula's south coast. (Tom Doran)

►Rich waters off the Alaska Peninsula coast yield a valuable harvest of king crab and other species. Here fishermen work with their catch at King Cove, a cannery town with more than 400 inhabitants. (Lael Morgan, Staff, reprinted from *ALASKA GEOGRAPHIC*®)

►Portage Creek flows four miles through Portage Valley to the southeast arm of Herendeen Bay on the Alaska Peninsula. The valley takes its name from a portage route between the bay and Albatross Anchorage at Balboa Bay off Unga Strait in the Gulf of Alaska. (Dave Spencer, U.S. Fish & Wildlife Service)

Arctic National Wildlife Refuge

In the west central portion of Arctic National Wildlife Refuge, the Junjik River flows 65 miles southeast to join the East Fork, Chandalar River just north of Arctic Village.
(George Wuerthner)

Setting: Extreme northeastern Alaska, bordered on the north by the Beaufort Sea, on the east by Canada's Yukon Territory, and on the northwest by the Canning River. The original Arctic National Wildlife Range, created in 1960, extended south of the Brooks Range with its western limit the Canning River and Old Woman Creek. The new additions double the size of the refuge to about 18 million acres and extend the western boundary to the trans-Alaska pipeline corridor. The southern boundary follows a circuitous path eastward to where it shares a boundary with Yukon Flats National Wildlife Refuge.

The Arctic National Wildlife Refuge preserves a large portion of the migration routes of the Porcupine caribou herd, one of the two largest herds in Alaska, numbering about 120,000 animals. The refuge also encompasses a virtually undisturbed wilderness extending from the Porcupine River basin where it approaches the Canadian boundary north through the beautiful Sheenjek River Valley and across the eastern Brooks Range down to the Arctic Ocean.

For the most part this land is above tree line and offers rugged, snow-capped, glaciated peaks and countless streams, some quite large, draining both north into the Beaufort Sea and south into the Porcupine and Yukon drainages.

Tight folds showing the Sadlerochit (brown) and Lisburne (gray) formations are visible in this photo of the Franklin Mountains west of Lake Schrader.
(Gil Mull)

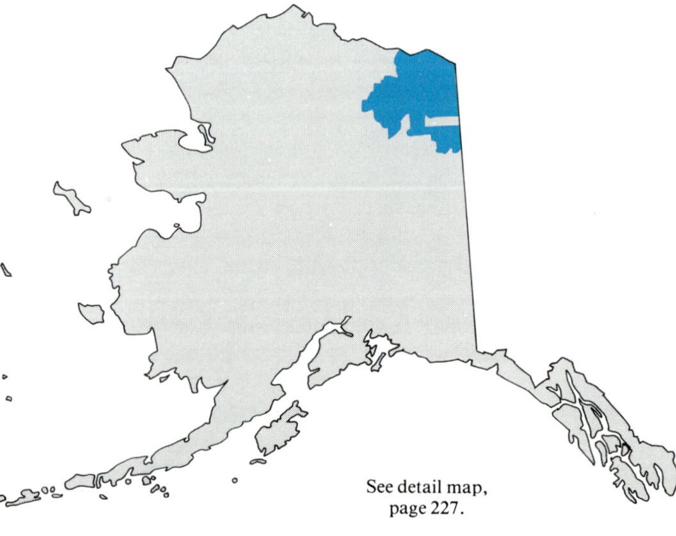

See detail map, page 227.

Natural Resources: Arctic National Wildlife Range (the unit's name has been changed twice; it is now officially designated a refuge) was set aside in 1960 to preserve an unspoiled area both north and south of the Brooks Range, a large enough region to contain a variety of ecosystems typical of its location. The refuge is rich in wildlife, particularly the Porcupine caribou herd, which has furnished the basis for subsistence living for both Eskimos along the northern coast and Athabascan Indians in the interior south of the Brooks Range.

Many other large mammals are found within the refuge. Polar bears den along the coast, and brown/grizzly bears roam the upland areas. Black bears can be found along the Porcupine River. Dall sheep frequent mountainous areas, while moose browse willow thickets in the streambeds. Wolves and wolverines, arctic foxes and smaller furbearers are numerous. On the north slope shaggy musk ox are gradually building up their numbers since reintroduction of the species in 1969.

Thousands of ducks, geese, swans and loons breed on coastal tundra and birds throng coastal migration routes all summer. Snowy owls and other predators can be seen along lagoons and river courses of the north slope. Raptors — two subspecies of peregrine falcons, gyrfalcons, rough-legged hawks, and golden eagles — nest inland.

The refuge's drainages harbor 17 species of fish. Arctic grayling are the most numerous sport fish, but arctic char are also present, as well as lake trout and whitefish. Northern pike are found in lakes on south-flowing drainages.

Left: Caribou cross the rotting ice of the Saviukviayak River in Arctic National Wildlife Refuge.
(Gil Mull, reprinted from *ALASKA GEOGRAPHIC®*)

Below: A semipalmated plover is right at home among the gravel beds of the Jago River in Arctic National Wildlife Refuge.
(Gil Mull)

Below: A long-tailed jaeger swoops above the tundra. Sometimes these predators feed on the eggs and young of other birds.
(Pat Powell)

Bottom: Arctic grayling, most numerous of the refuge's sport fish, gather in a refuge stream. The region's waterways also support arctic char, lake trout, whitefish and northern pike. (Jo Keller, U.S. Fish & Wildlife Service)

Above: A thunderstorm brings lowering clouds and gray skies to the Canning River Valley. (Gil Mull)

Right: A Baird's sandpiper keeps an eye on its chicks at Barter Island. (Jo Keller, U.S. Fish & Wildlife Service)

Backpackers set up camp in the Junjik River Valley. The original Arctic National Wildlife Range was set aside in 1960 to preserve an unspoiled area north and south of the Brooks Range. With the new additions, the refuge encompasses an undisturbed wilderness extending from the Porcupine River basin north to the Arctic Ocean. (George Wuerthner)

Recreational Opportunities: Arctic National Wildlife Refuge has seen rapidly increasing recreational use in the last few years. Major recreational activities include river kayaking and rafting on streams both north and south of the Brooks Range. Plane charters out of Kaktovik on Barter Island land parties on Peters or Schrader lakes, takeoff points to excellent hiking and backpacking possibilities. Mountaineering is becoming increasingly popular with Mount Chamberlin (9,020 feet) and Mount Michelson (8,855 feet), the two highest peaks, the usual destinations.

Coastal lagoons offer excellent fishing and kayaking opportunities, plus excellent wildlife observations.

Additions to the refuge include three wild and scenic rivers: the Ivishak, the Sheenjek and the Wind, as well as the superlative scenery and wildlife viewing opportunities found on the Marsh Fork of the Canning River.

Further Information:
▶Arctic National Wildlife Refuge
U.S. Fish & Wildlife Service
Federal Building & Courthouse
Room 226
101 - 12th Avenue
Fairbanks, AK 99701

Left: Practicing his technique, Don Ross does an Eskimo roll with his kayak on the Kongakut River. One of the state's most isolated watersheds, the river flows northeast for 100 miles from the Davidson Mountains to the Arctic Ocean. (Jo Keller, U.S. Fish & Wildlife Service)

Overleaf: Beaufort Sea ice still covers Camden Bay on the arctic coast in early July. (Gil Mull)

Becharof National Wildlife Refuge

Setting: Southwestern Alaska, sandwiched between Katmai National Park and Preserve to the north and Alaska Peninsula National Wildlife Refuge to the south. The 1,200,000-acre refuge has 400,000 acres classified as wilderness. The unit's landscape is dominated by Becharof Lake, and the surrounding low, rolling hills with tundra wetlands in the northwest and volcanic peaks to the southeast.

Natural Resources: Becharof is home of the great brown/grizzlies. The region's rich salmon-spawning streams attract perhaps the largest concentration of these bears in Alaska, and adjoining the lake are many bear denning sites. In addition to these great brownies, the area supports some moose and caribou, wolves and wolverines.

Nesting and migrant waterfowl can be found in the refuge's wetlands and lakes. Bald eagles nest near the mountains and gather at salmon-spawning streams.

Becharof Lake and its tributaries contribute great numbers of chinook, pink, red, coho and chum salmon to the Bristol Bay fishery. Sport fish include arctic grayling, Dolly Varden and rainbow trout.

Sea otters, sea lions and harbor seals inhabit the refuge's Pacific coast shoreline.

Top: A sow and cubs feed along a stream bed near Becharof Lake. The refuge's rich salmon-spawning streams attract perhaps the largest concentration of these bears in Alaska. (Jo Keller, U.S. Fish & Wildlife Service)

Above: A moose heads for shore after a swim in Becharof Lake. W.H. Dall of the U.S. Coast and Geodetic Survey named the lake in 1868 for a navigator in the Russian navy who was at Kodiak in the late 1700s. (Jo Keller, U.S. Fish & Wildlife Service)

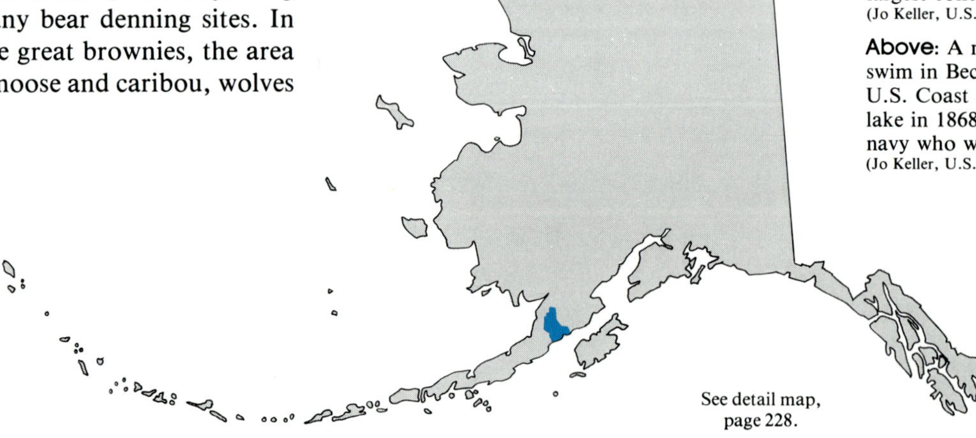

See detail map, page 228.

Further Information:
►Becharof National Wildlife Refuge
U.S. Fish & Wildlife Service
P.O. Box 211
King Salmon, AK 99613

Clockwise from below:

►The view from Cleo Creek shows Mount Peulik (4,835 feet) and Becharof Lake. (Jo Keller, U.S. Fish & Wildlife Service)

►A caribou herd grazes near Becharof Lake. Alaska has probably about 13 distinct caribou herds with some overlapping of ranges, and probably with transfers or intermingling between herds. These animals are from the Mulchatna herd. (James Faro, reprinted from *ALASKA GEOGRAPHIC®*)

►A major eruption belches ash from The Gas Rocks, on the shore of Becharof Lake, in April 1977. This form of eruption is known as *maar,* a release of pressure through cracks in the earth. (Lou Gwartney, reprinted from *ALASKA GEOGRAPHIC®*)

Izembek National Wildlife Refuge

Grant Point rises above the waters of Izembek Lagoon and Applegate Cove, eight miles northwest of Cold Bay. (John Sarvis, reprinted from *ALASKA®* magazine)

Setting: Southwestern Alaska, at the tip of the Alaska Peninsula. One of the older refuges, 320,893-acre Izembek faces on the Bering Sea side of the peninsula and adjoins Alaska Peninsula National Wildlife Refuge. Izembek is separated from Unimak Island in the Aleutians by Bechevin Bay which narrows to become False Pass.

Natural Resources: The rich eel grass beds, among the world's largest, of Izembek Lagoon form part of a large estuary which provides a haven for dense flocks of migratory birds passing through

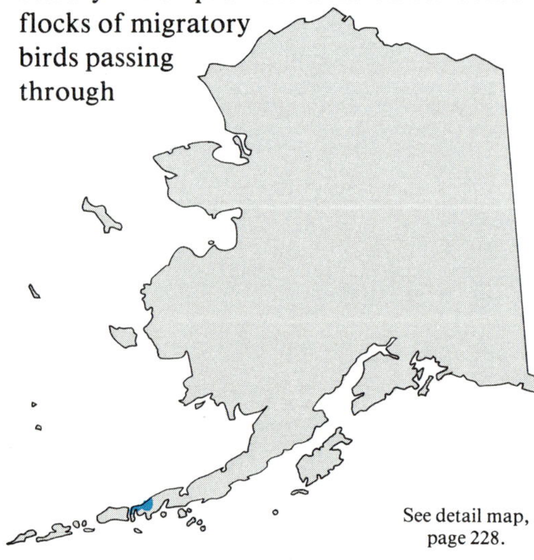

the area. Hundreds of thousands of ducks and geese use the lagoon in migration or for wintering habitat. North America's entire brant population assembles here before migrating en masse south across the Pacific.

The lagoon also supports a large number of fish of many varieties which form a food resource for migrating birds, as well as for bears, bald eagles, caribou and other wildlife in the refuge.

By fall these caribou at Moffett Point will have shed their old coat and scraped the velvet from their antlers in preparation for another round of breeding and winter survival. (John Sarvis, reprinted from *ALASKA GEOGRAPHIC®*)

Further Information:
►Refuge Manager
Izembek National Wildlife Refuge
Pouch 2
Cold Bay, AK 99571

See detail map, page 228.

Kenai National Wildlife Refuge

Setting: Southcentral Alaska across Turnagain Arm from Anchorage. The refuge bridges the Kenai Peninsula in a north-south direction. Its southern boundary adjoins Kenai Fjords National Park and abuts Kachemak Bay State Park, creating a system of protected land almost blanketing the peninsula. Nearly 2,000,000 acres are included in the refuge, of which 1,350,000 acres are designated wilderness. The refuge is close to Anchorage, Kenai and Homer and is situated on both sides of the Sterling Highway, an all-year, all-weather, paved road.

Natural Resources: A large part of this refuge was set aside in 1941 to provide habitat for the large Kenai moose population. Within its boundaries a variety of habitats and scenic and recreational resources are found, ranging from high mountains and glaciers to uplands, deep forests, lowland lakes, rivers and spreading wetlands. One-third of the salmon caught in Cook Inlet spawn in refuge streams, while the abundant waters also support large numbers of beaver, mink, muskrat and otter.

Dall sheep and mountain goat are found in mountainous areas, with lower

A common loon paddles among the lily pads and aquatic vegetation of Kenai National Wildlife Refuge. (Jo Keller, U.S. Fish & Wildlife Service)

foothill areas providing habitat for caribou, black and brown/grizzly bears, lynx, wolves and coyotes.

Recreational Opportunities:

Recreational use of the refuge is heavy because of its location only a few hours' drive from Anchorage and other population centers. The Swanson River Canoe Trail in the refuge's northern sector is a major attraction; other good-sized lakes also entice kayakers and canoeists. Hikers and backpackers find excellent walking in uplands of the southern part of the refuge, and horseback trips provide accessibility for hikers and hunters.

Further Information:
►Kenai National Wildlife Refuge
U.S. Fish & Wildlife Service
Box 2139
Soldotna, AK 99669

Above: A moose calf sleeps soundly amid lush vegetation of Kenai National Wildlife Refuge. Kenai National Moose Range, incorporated into the refuge, was set aside in 1941 to protect habitat and allow management of this important game species. (Jo Keller, U.S. Fish & Wildlife Service)

Left: A red-necked grebe inspects its nest on a marsh in the Kenai refuge. (Pat Powell)

See detail map, page 229.

Kodiak National Wildlife Refuge

Setting: On both Kodiak Island and Afognak Island in the western Gulf of Alaska across Shelikof Strait from Katmai National Park and Preserve. The refuge encompasses 1,865,000 acres.

Natural Resources: The Kodiak Island portion of the refuge, established many years ago, was set aside to protect the isolated Kodiak brown/grizzly bear population. On Afognak Island, an introduced band of elk share the refuge with the bears.

The islands support substantial fish populations, and their coastlines shelter waterfowl and marine mammals.

Further Information:
►Kodiak National Wildlife Refuge
U.S. Fish & Wildlife Service
Box 825
Kodiak, AK 99615

Right: Red salmon struggle to overcome Fraser Falls to reach their spawning grounds in western Kodiak. (Gerry Atwell, U.S. Fish & Wildlife Service; reprinted from *ALASKA GEOGRAPHIC®*)

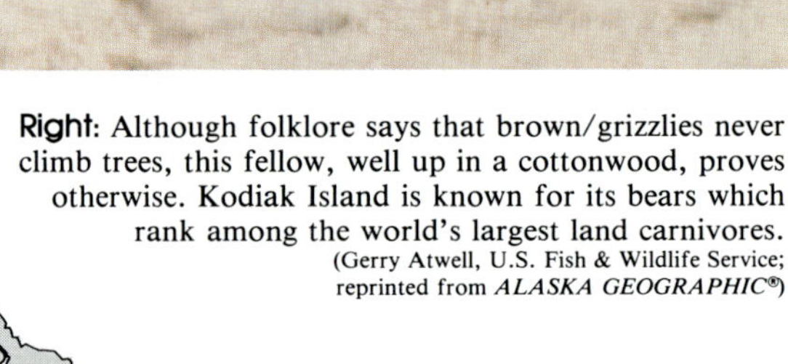

Right: Although folklore says that brown/grizzlies never climb trees, this fellow, well up in a cottonwood, proves otherwise. Kodiak Island is known for its bears which rank among the world's largest land carnivores. (Gerry Atwell, U.S. Fish & Wildlife Service; reprinted from *ALASKA GEOGRAPHIC®*)

See detail map, page 229.

Left: Even when they are not visible, Kodiak's bears make a definite impression. These tracks lead to a winter den near the center of a steep slope. (Gerry Atwell, U.S. Fish & Wildlife Service; reprinted from *ALASKA GEOGRAPHIC®*)

Below: A hiker pauses on the flank of Barometer Mountain (2,488 feet) to view Kodiak's interior valleys, many of which fall within the refuge. (W.E. Donaldson, reprinted from *ALASKA GEOGRAPHIC®*)

National Wildlife Refuges of Interior Alaska

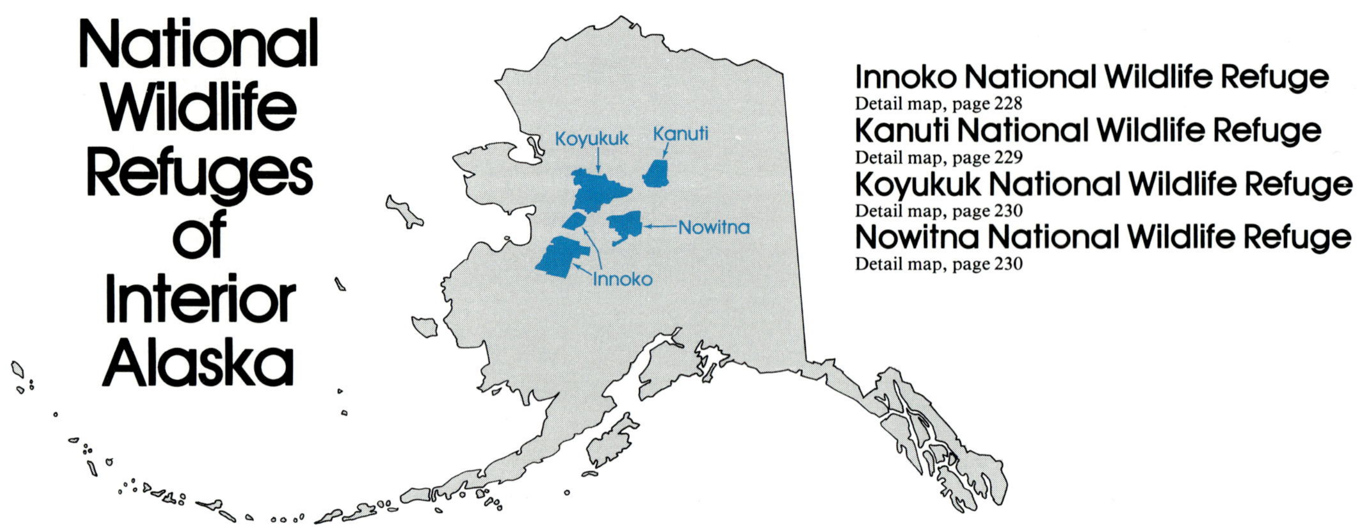

Innoko National Wildlife Refuge
Detail map, page 228
Kanuti National Wildlife Refuge
Detail map, page 229
Koyukuk National Wildlife Refuge
Detail map, page 230
Nowitna National Wildlife Refuge
Detail map, page 230

Setting: Western and central interior Alaska on major tributaries of the Yukon River.

Innoko National Wildlife Refuge, in the central Yukon River Valley, takes in lands within the Innoko River basin, certain Yukon River islands and the Kaiyuh Flats. The refuge's two separate sections total 3,850,000 acres, of which 80% is wetlands. More than 1,200,000 acres of the refuge are classified as wilderness.

Kanuti National Wildlife Refuge consists of the Kanuti Flats, just west of the trans-Alaska pipeline and south of Bettles, westward to the villages of Alatna and Allakaket. The 1,430,000-acre refuge is characterized by the broad, rolling plain of the Kanuti and Koyukuk rivers, interspersed with lakes, ponds and marshes.

Koyukuk National Wildlife Refuge, 3,550,000 acres, of which 400,000 are classified as wilderness, is north of the Innoko refuge and adjoins Selawik National Wildlife Refuge at its northwestern point. Lying in a circular floodplain formed by the lower Koyukuk River, the refuge is heavily forested, and contains much wetlands in the form of sloughs, ponds and lakes.

Nowitna National Wildlife Refuge, 1,560,000 acres, protects a lowland basin bordering the Nowitna and Yukon rivers. A portion of the upper Nowitna River is classified as a wild and scenic river.

Lou Mass weaves through tall grass fields between North Hather Creek and the Innoko River. The Innoko winds northeast and southwest on its 500-mile course to enter the Yukon River near Holy Cross. (Jo Keller, U.S. Fish & Wildlife Service)

Left: Late winter snow covers the
Mud River drainage in the Innoko refuge.
The Mud River runs southwest 100 miles
from the Tlatl Hills to join the Innoko
River northwest of Ophir.

Above: Aquatic vegetation and brilliant
green tundra surround this lake in
Innoko National Wildlife Refuge.
The refuge has two separate sections
totaling 3,850,000 acres. (Both by Jo Keller,
U.S. Fish & Wildlife Service)

Clockwise from upper left:
►This aerial shows the hills, crowned by rocky tors, and lowland ponds characteristic of Kanuti. (Gil Mull)
►A visitor inspects a beaver dam on the north fork of the Kanuti River. (U.S. Fish & Wildlife Service)
►A black bear, one of the species whose habitat is protected by the refuge, feeds on grass along a river bank. (Dave Patterson)
►A white-fronted goose flaps its wings while scooting along the Kanuti River. (Jo Keller, U.S. Fish & Wildlife Service)

142

Natural Resources:

The Innoko refuge is a major nesting area for waterfowl: pintails, wigeons and scaups breed here, as do white-fronted and Canada geese. Birds from the Innoko scatter through all the major continental flyways, some going as far as the Atlantic coast.

Moose are abundant, especially along the Kaiyuh River, and caribou from the Beaver Mountain herd winter in the area. The Innoko is famous for its high-quality beaver, and many other furbearers are present.

Kanuti National Wildlife Refuge furnishes subsistence resources for Natives throughout the area. Waterfowl breeding here include a variety of ducks and Canada and white-fronted geese, which contribute about 150,000 birds to the fall migrations. Portions of the large western Arctic caribou herd winter within the refuge. Black bears and brown/grizzly bears, wolves and wolverine are also found within the refuge.

Koyukuk National Wildlife Refuge includes the Nogahabara Sand Dunes, a 10,000-acre patch of shifting sand that looks like a misplaced southwestern United States landscape. Abundant wetlands attract great numbers of waterfowl including white-fronted geese, Canada geese and many ducks. Koyukuk is also

Overleaf: The Koyukuk refuge includes five-mile-wide Nogahabara Sand Dunes northwest of Roundabout Mountain, an approximately 10,000-acre active dune field related to the Great Kobuk Sand Dunes farther north. Nogahabara and Kobuk are the only two large, active dune fields in interior Alaska, and both were formed by deposition of wild-blown material during the mid to late Pleistocene period. (Jo Keller, U.S. Fish & Wildlife Service)

Left: Regular changes in the water level of the Nowitna River have caused erosion along its banks. (Bill Kirk)

Below: The forested lowlands of the Nowitna refuge provide a variety of habitats for both fish and waterfowl. (Dave Patterson)

Above: Well camouflaged among the rocks, this nest belongs to a semipalmated plover. (Dave Patterson)

the northwestern limit of the breeding range for North America's largest waterfowl, the trumpeter swan. In addition, the Koyukuk's wetlands support many nesting shorebirds.

The western Arctic caribou herd winters throughout the refuge, and moose are numerous. Wolves are common, and black bears are abundant in forested areas while brown/grizzly bears can be found in the open tundra. Many furbearers live here including beaver, muskrat, mink and marten.

Forested lowlands of Nowitna National Wildlife Refuge provide excellent wetland complexes with a diversity of habitats which support good populations of both fish and waterfowl. More than a quarter million birds, including the trumpeter swan, breed within the refuge.

Wildlife found here include a few small bands of caribou, black and brown/grizzly bears, and abundant moose. The Nowitna River contains important sheefish spawning grounds and nourishes several varieties of salmon.

All of these interior refuges are important links in the salmon fishery; whitefish, arctic grayling and northern pike reside in their lakes and rivers.

Further Information:
▶U.S. Fish & Wildlife Service
Regional Office
1011 East Tudor Road
Anchorage, AK 99503

Top: Fishing is a prime recreational use of the interior refuges which form an important link in the salmon fishery. In addition, whitefish, arctic grayling and northern pike inhabit lakes and rivers of these refuges. Here Lou Swenson lands his catch from the Kanuti River. (Jo Keller, U.S. Fish & Wildlife Service)

Above: Dave Patterson proudly displays the day's catch — two northern pike — taken from the Sulatna River. (Courtesy of Dave Patterson)

Clockwise from above:
►Geometrically shaped patches of tundra, active waterways, former stream beds and thousands of ponds characterize the wet country near Selawik. (Manya Wik)
►Huge Selawik Lake and the channels feeding the lake provide excellent waterfowl habitat. Here Mukuksok Channel, which branches off of Nazuruk Channel of the Kobuk River, enters Selawik Lake. (Fred DeCicco)
►Charley Smith pulls sheefish out of Selawik Lake. This species shares the refuge's waterways with whitefish, arctic grayling, northern pike and other species. (Ken Alt)

Selawik National Wildlife Refuge

Setting: Northwestern Alaska, 360 miles northwest of Fairbanks. Selawik refuge's northern boundary abuts Kobuk Valley National Park, and its southeastern corner joins Koyukuk National Wildlife Refuge. The refuge's northwestern edge lies along Hotham Inlet across from Baldwin Peninsula on which Kotzebue, the largest nearby town, is situated.

This refuge of more than two million acres includes an extensive system of estuaries and brackish lakes situated where the Kobuk and Selawik rivers form deltas. Inland to the east, lowlands — full of pothole lakes, ponds, marshes and streams — form a complex network of land and water. The Waring Mountains on the north and the Selawik Hills on the south add variety, and a tundra habitat, to the landscape.

Natural Resources: The major wildlife resource in this area is the western Arctic caribou herd which often winters in the refuge's upland taiga areas. Selawik is also a vital breeding and resting area for a multitude of migratory waterbirds, returning not only from North and South America, but from Asia, Africa and Australia as well.

One unique species is the Asiatic whooper swan, whose only reported nesting area in North America is found here. Waterfowl include ducks, geese and swans who return here via all continental flyways.

Fish occurring within the refuge include whitefish, sheefish, arctic grayling and northern pike.

A variety of mammals from black and brown/grizzly bears to moose, beaver, wolves and many smaller furbearers feed here.

The Selawik River is classified as a wild and scenic river.

A member of the saxifrage family, Alaska Boykinia is a hardy plant often seen in the Selawik area. (Stephen Talbot)

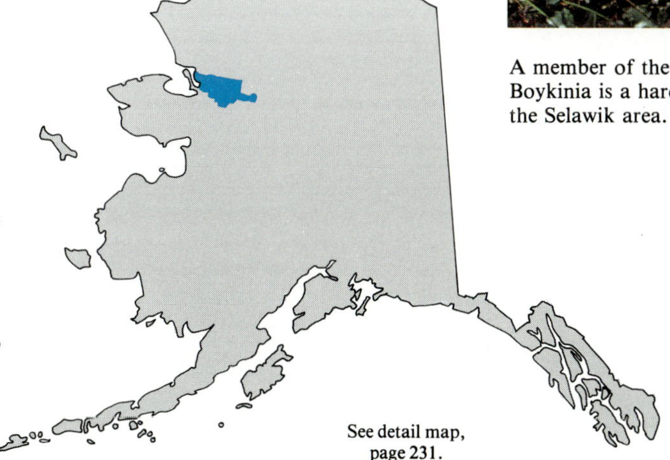

See detail map, page 231.

Further Information:
►Selawik National Wildlife Refuge
U.S. Fish & Wildlife Service
Regional Office
1011 East Tudor Road
Anchorage, AK 99503

Tetlin refuge supports both moose, such as this rain-drenched bull, and caribou, as well as black bear, some brown/grizzly bear, wolf, lynx, fox, muskrat, beaver and a host of smaller mammals. (George Wuerthner)

Tetlin National Wildlife Refuge

Setting: Eastern Alaska, adjacent to the Canadian border and south of the Alaska Highway. The major physical features of this 700,000-acre refuge are an undulating plain interspersed with hills, forest, ponds, lakes and extensive marshes. The Chisana and Nabesna rivers meander through the area, and the Tanana River is formed where they join. Tetlin reflects the influence of permafrost, wildfires and changing river channels, resulting in a mosaic of vegetation and habitats.

Natural Resources: This refuge's accessibility via the Alaska Highway makes it an easy one to visit. Tetlin has a high density of nesting waterfowl, and is capable of providing summer habitat for Canadian waterfowl displaced by drought in their usual breeding areas. Nesting densities of ducks here are second in Alaska only to the Yukon Flats; as many as 600 ducks per square mile have been counted here, and 17 different species have been

recorded. Redheads, ring-necked ducks and blue-winged teals, unusual species for Alaska, have been sighted here.

Sandhill cranes nest in the open wetlands, and as many as 300,000 cranes migrate through this refuge each fall. Loons and grebes, osprey, bald eagles and other raptors, and three varieties of both ptarmigan and grouse can be found here.

Caribou from the Chisana herd, quite a few moose, black bears and, in spring, brown/grizzly bears use the refuge. Wolves and wolverine, lynx, coyotes and red foxes are at Tetlin in moderate numbers. Smaller furbearers, too, make use of the refuge's habitat.

Arctic grayling, whitefish, lake trout and northern pike swim in the refuge's lakes and streams.

Further Information:
►Tetlin National Wildlife Refuge
U.S. Fish & Wildlife Service
Regional Office
1011 East Tudor Road
Anchorage, AK 99503

Above: Tetlin refuge is prime habitat for several species of birds. Only Yukon Flats has a higher density of nesting ducks; as many as 600 ducks per square mile have been counted at Tetlin. (Jo Keller, U.S. Fish & Wildlife Service)

Left: Snowshoe hares, abundant in the Tetlin refuge, are a major prey species and are crucial to the existence of a substantial lynx population. (Tom Walker)

151

Togiak National Wildlife Refuge

Setting: Southwestern Alaska, between Kuskokwim Bay on the west and Bristol Bay on the south and east. Togiak refuge is bordered on the north by Yukon Delta National Wildlife Refuge and on the east by Wood-Tikchik State Park.

Togiak National Wildlife Refuge absorbs the former Cape Newenham National Wildlife Refuge and, with additional acreage allotted the new refuge under the d-2 bill, now comprises more than four million acres. Of this acreage, 2,270,000 acres in the refuge's northern half are designated as wilderness.

The refuge is roadless. Eighty percent of it is in the Ahklun Mountains where large expanses of tundra uplands are cut by several broad glacial valleys opening onto a coastal plain. Off the coast, Hagemeister Island is part of Alaska Maritime National Wildlife Refuge, primarily because of its use as a hauling grounds for walrus.

Togiak village overlooks Togiak Bay on the north side of Bristol Bay. On the horizon is High Island in the Walrus Islands group. (Steve Westfall, reprinted from *ALASKA GEOGRAPHIC*®)

The image caption:

Cape Newenham, photographed after a snowfall in November, juts into the Bering Sea between Kuskokwim and Bristol bays. The former Cape Newenham National Wildlife Refuge has been incorporated into the new Togiak refuge. (Bill Crocker, reprinted from *ALASKA GEOGRAPHIC®*)

Natural Resources:

Togiak National Wildlife Refuge forms a continuous chain of protected land which, with Yukon Delta National Wildlife Refuge, extends from Bristol Bay to Norton Sound. Togiak is a breeding and resting area for such birds as oldsquaw, common scoters, greater scaup and pintails. Millions of seabirds, including large numbers of murres and kittiwakes, frequent the refuge's offshore waters and Cape Pierce and Cape Newenham.

Major land-based wildlife are brown/grizzly bear and moose, while marine wildlife includes sea lions, walrus and four species of seals.

Six Native villages are found in the vicinity and use the refuge for subsistence activities.

Further Information:

►Togiak National
Wildlife Refuge
U.S. Fish &
Wildlife Service
Regional Office
1011 East Tudor Road
Anchorage, AK 99503

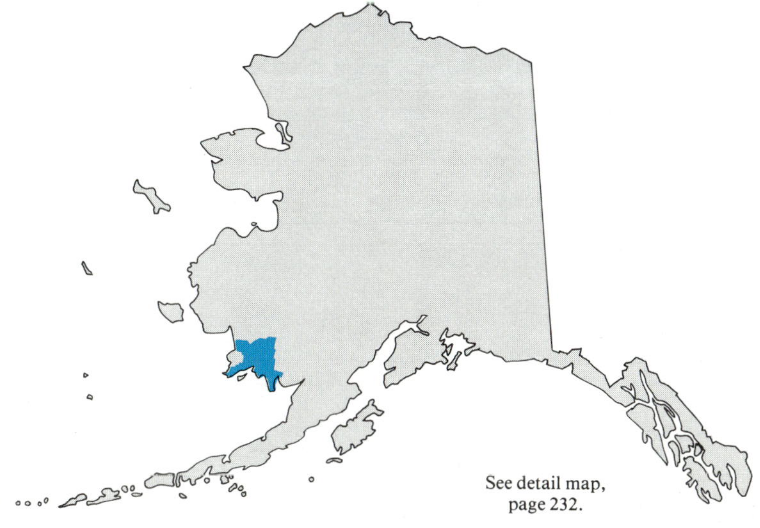

See detail map,
page 232.

153

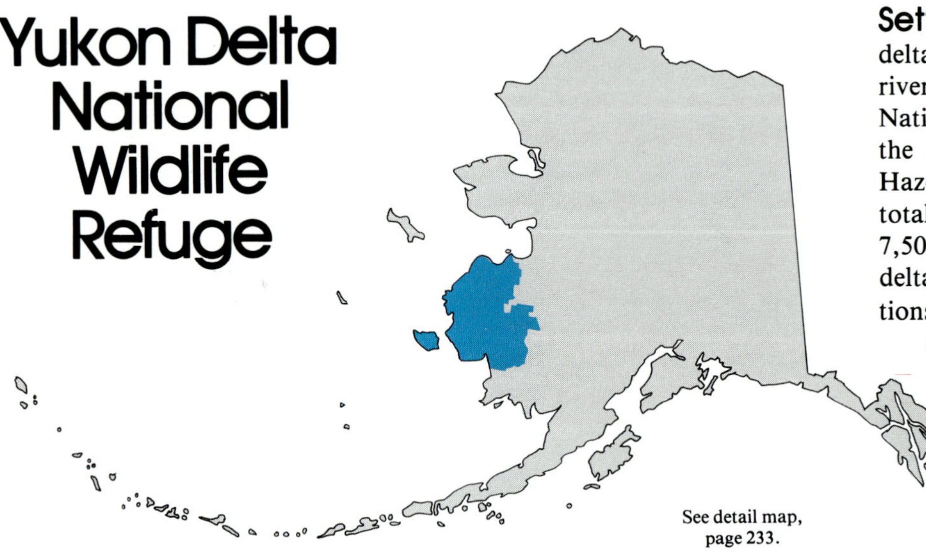

Yukon Delta National Wildlife Refuge

Setting: Western Alaska, on the great deltas of the Yukon and Kuskokwim rivers. Included within Yukon Delta National Wildlife Refuge's borders are the earlier refuges of Clarence Rhode, Hazen Bay and Nunivak. The refuge totals 19,624,458 acres. Approximately 7,500,000 acres of additional land on the delta will be owned by Native corporations. At least 56 villages, many within the refuge's boundaries, rely on this area for subsistence resources.

The great delta is treeless, and apart from uplands of the Andreafsky and Kilbuck hills, is a seemingly limitless

See detail map, page 233.

The deltas of the Yukon and Kuskokwim rivers form an immense, water-logged plain stretching 250 miles from Norton Sound to Kuskokwim Bay and inland for 200 miles to the Kuskokwim Mountains. Most of this huge delta area is part of Yukon Delta National Wildlife Refuge.
(Jerry Hout, reprinted from *ALASKA GEOGRAPHIC®*)

expanse of wetlands. On Nunivak Island the terrain consists of volcanic craters, sand dunes, sea cliffs and rolling tundra. Extensive permafrost and pothole lakes combined with the very low elevations make this a prime habitat for waterfowl and shorebirds.

Natural Resources:
Wetlands of the Yukon Delta refuge are one of the most significant waterfowl breeding areas in North America. A total of 170 species of birds have been observed, and upwards of 136 species nest here. The refuge provides summer habitat for almost all white-fronted geese following the Pacific Flyway, more than half of the continent's

Clockwise from above:
►In March the thick cloak of winter still covers Toksook Bay (also spelled Tooksook Bay) on Nelson Island in the delta. The village was established in the mid-1960s when most of the population of Nightmute moved to this location. Approximately 7,500,000 acres of the 19,624,458-acre Yukon Delta refuge will be owned by Native corporations. (Alissa Crandall)
►A brown/grizzly cub wrestles with a willow while its mother and sibling feed. Moose and caribou also roam mainland portions of the refuge. (Steve McCutcheon)
►In addition to huge numbers of waterfowl, the refuge supports shorebirds, perching birds and seabirds. This Sabine's gull, the only gull with a forked tail, is quite at home on the delta's wet tundra and tidal flats. (Will Troyer)

brant population and 80% of the world's emperor and cackling Canada geese. The fall migration of waterfowl averages more than two million birds.

Nunivak Island shelters a transplanted musk ox herd, and a reindeer herd. On the mainland occur many large mammals such as moose, brown/grizzly bear and caribou.

Five species of salmon spawn in the refuge, and resident fish include pike, blackfish, sheefish and whitefish.

The Andreafsky River and its east fork are designated wild and scenic rivers. These clear-water streams flow about 120 miles through a narrow mountain valley to enter the Yukon River at Saint Marys.

Yukon Delta National Wildlife Refuge protects a global migratory bird resource affecting six continents, as well as a host of other wildlife resources, and is a storehouse of cultural values relating to the Yup'ik Eskimo culture dating from prehistoric times.

Further Information:
►Yukon Delta National Wildlife Refuge
U.S. Fish & Wildlife Service
Box 346
Bethel, AK 99559

Above: Designated a wildlife refuge in 1937, Hazen Bay is now part of the Yukon Delta refuge.
(Dave Spencer, U.S. Fish & Wildlife Service)

Left: A television cameraman prepares to photograph Nanwaksjiak Crater, 15 miles north of Cape Mendenhall on Nunivak Island. The former Nunivak Island refuge has also been absorbed into Yukon Delta refuge. (Alissa Crandall)

Right: Carrying his compass with him, Peter Smith of Mekoryuk on Nunivak Island is all set to go seal hunting.
(Alissa Crandall)

Moving The Musk Ox

In March 1981 officials from Point Defiance Zoo in Tacoma, Washington, arranged for the capture of six musk ox on Nunivak Island. Wien Air Alaska agreed to transport the shaggy mammals to their new home in the Lower 48, thus expanding the opportunity for viewing these once-abundant northern animals.

Eskimo hunters killed the last surviving herd of Alaska's original musk ox about 1865. About 1930, 34 musk ox from Greenland were transported to the University of Alaska in Fairbanks. In 1935-1936, the 31 musk ox still at the university were moved to 1,100,000-acre Nunivak Island in the Bering Sea.

Clockwise from above:
►Riding snow machines, Eskimo herders from Mekoryuk round up
musk ox south of the village.
►Its feet tied together, this shaggy beast awaits its fate.
►Native herders keep an eye on a musk ox securely tied to a sled.
►When disturbed, musk ox make protective circles with young in the middle
and adult bulls in the outer ring. Enclosed in a compound in Mekoryuk,
the animals backed up against a fence in a version of their traditional circle.
►Steer wrestling, musk ox style. These hefty herders tried to corral their charges,
which can weigh up to 900 pounds in adult bulls and to 500 pounds in adult cows,
for loading into crates for the Wien flight.
(All photos by Alissa Crandall, Wien Air Alaska)

Yukon Flats National Wildlife Refuge

Setting: Eastcentral Alaska, about 100 miles north of Fairbanks. This refuge contains 8,630,000 acres in the vast interior basin commonly known as the Yukon Flats, primarily a complex wetlands which includes more than 40,000 lakes, ponds and sloughs. The flats are nearly surrounded by low hills which form the rim of the basin. Here a continental climate features extremes of temperatures: higher than 90°F. in the summer and to -60°F. in the winter.

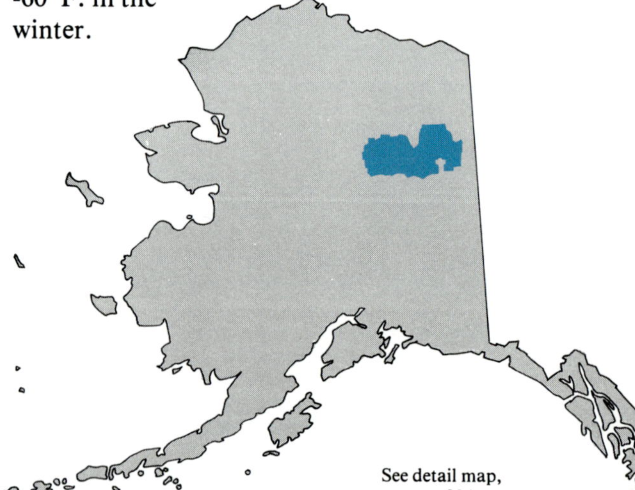

See detail map, page 234.

Top: The warm, rich, lake-filled valley of the Sheenjek River is wild, and fine for canoeing, camping and general looking around. The Sheenjek heads in the Brooks Range and cuts through the northern flats to enter the Porcupine River, which flows into the Yukon near Fort Yukon. The Yukon Flats lie at the most northerly point reached by the Yukon River, and make up the largest and most productive warm basin in Alaska's Arctic. (Ave Thayer, reprinted from *ALASKA*® magazine)

Above: A host of Canada geese and other waterfowl nest and feed in Yukon Flats. Changing water levels alter water channels throughout the lowlands causing build-up of mud layers in some areas and washing away of cut banks in others. (Penny Rennick)

Natural Resources:

Nesting densities for ducks is greater here than in any other large area in Alaska and one of the highest densities on the continent. The flats contribute more than two million ducks to all flyways of North America. It is estimated that 15% of all canvasback ducks breed here, and more than 16,000 geese migrate from here each fall. Sandhill cranes, loons, grebes and gulls inhabit the refuge in lesser numbers.

A substantial population of moose browse here, and a few caribou graze the upland areas around the edge of the basin. Wolves, black and brown/grizzly bears and a host of furbearers inhabit the flats and have been harvested by humans since the Ice Ages.

Further Information:
►Yukon Flats National Wildlife Refuge
U.S. Fish & Wildlife Service
Federal Building & Courthouse, Room 226
101 - 12th Avenue
Fairbanks, AK 99701

Clockwise from left:
►Rock ptarmigan and other non-waterfowl game species forage in uplands of the Yukon Flats refuge. Rock ptarmigan must eat the equivalent of 1/10th to 1/5th of their body weight each day. (Pat Powell)
►Chalkyitsik, on the Black River, is one of the Athabascan villages lying within the boundaries of the Yukon Flats refuge. (Gil Mull)
►Sharing the flats with the waterfowl are beaver, such as this one trying to maneuver some willow, and muskrat as well as many other small furbearers. A large percentage of Alaska's muskrat skins come from 11,000-square-mile Yukon Flats basin. (Steve McCutcheon)

National Forests

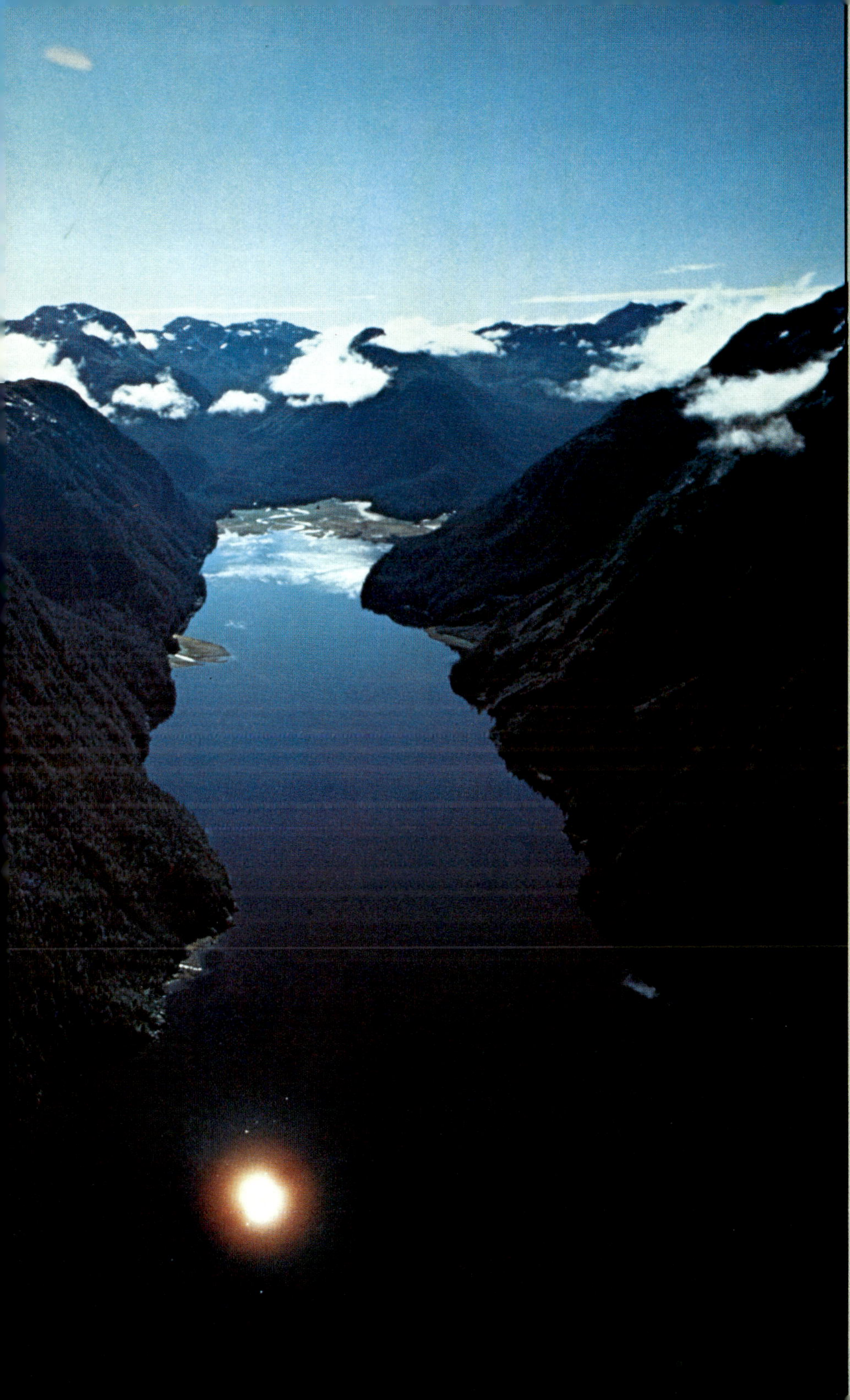

Below: The unusually rich tidal zone of Prince of Wales Island supports much colorful sea life, such as this green anemone and red sea urchin. (Tom Kogut)

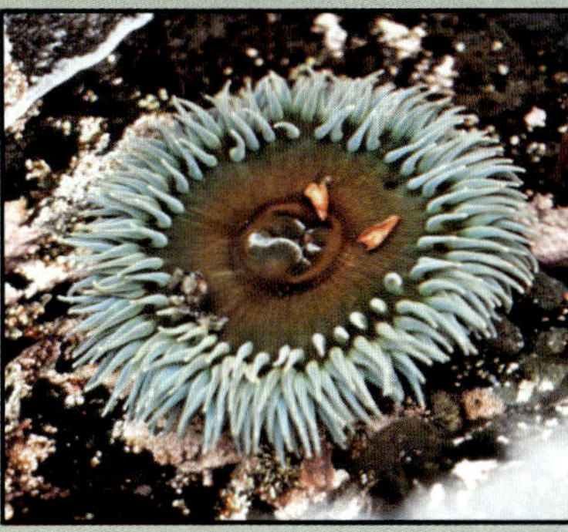

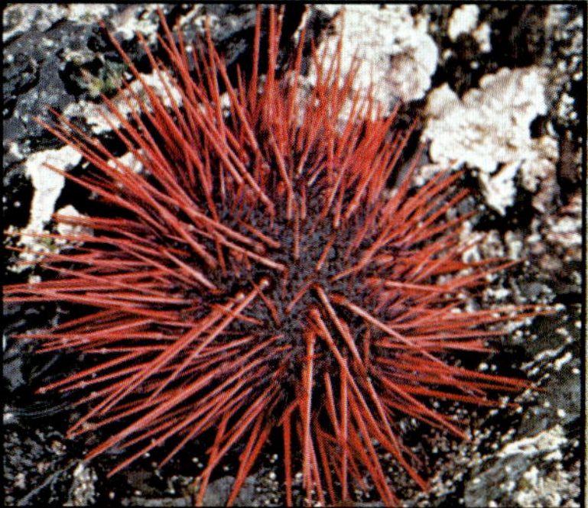

In Alaska the U.S. Forest Service, Department of Agriculture, administers the nation's largest, Tongass, and second largest, Chugach, national forests. Among the first areas to be withdrawn when the national forest system was established in 1891 was Afognak Island near Kodiak. President Benjamin Harrison set aside the island as a Forest and Fish Culture Reserve early in 1892. In 1907 portions of land bordering Prince William Sound on the west and north and extending east to the Copper River Delta and south to the southern tip of Montague Island were the first areas to be officially designated Chugach National Forest. In 1908 the Afognak reserve was included in this withdrawal. Chugach National Forest now stretches from Chugach State Park near Girdwood and the eastern Kenai Peninsula to beyond the Bering River east of Cordova and south to include Afognak Island. State and Native land selections, however, are likely to affect these boundaries.

Left: The tranquil waters of Stag Bay, off Lisianski Strait on Chichagof Island, provide a direct contrast to the island's stormy Pacific coast. (Staff)

Additions to the Chugach National Forest

The massive ice front of Columbia Glacier, now entirely encompassed within Chugach National Forest, rises above Columbia Bay west of Valdez. (Jon Nickles)

The Alaska d-2 lands bill provided for extensive additions to Chugach National Forest of lands previously in the public domain and managed by the Bureau of Land Management. These additions, totaling about two million acres, include the Nellie Juan area east of Seward, the College Fiord extension, the Copper/Rude rivers addition and a small extension at Controller Bay.

The Nellie Juan addition, in western Prince William Sound, takes in the eastern portion of the Resurrection Peninsula along the coast to Puget Bay. The portion of the Sargent Icefield previously not part of the national forest, and Nellie Juan Lake and Nellie Juan River drainage become a part of Chugach National Forest with this addition.

The College Fiord addition in northwestern Prince William Sound takes in all of the College Fiord drainage and Barry Glacier. The addition extends north to include Mount Marcus Baker (13,176 feet), tallest peak in the Chugach Range. All of Harvard and Columbia glaciers join the forest under this act.

In addition to transferring jurisdiction over this area to the U.S. Forest Service, Congress directed that the area be part of a two-million-acre wilderness study unit, to be known as "The Nellie Juan-College Fiord Wilderness Study Area," which will be investigated for possible addition to the National Wilderness Preservation System. Congress allowed three years for the study, after which they will act on the recommendations.

The Copper/Rude rivers addition extends the forest's boundary north and east of Cordova. The new boundary follows the Copper River to its confluence with

See detail map, page 235.

Right: The Copper/Rude rivers extension constitutes a major addition to Chugach National Forest. Here Miles Glacier and Mount Tom White (10,630 feet) dominate the background as the Copper River flows past the Million Dollar Bridge on its way to the Gulf of Alaska. (Gil Mull)

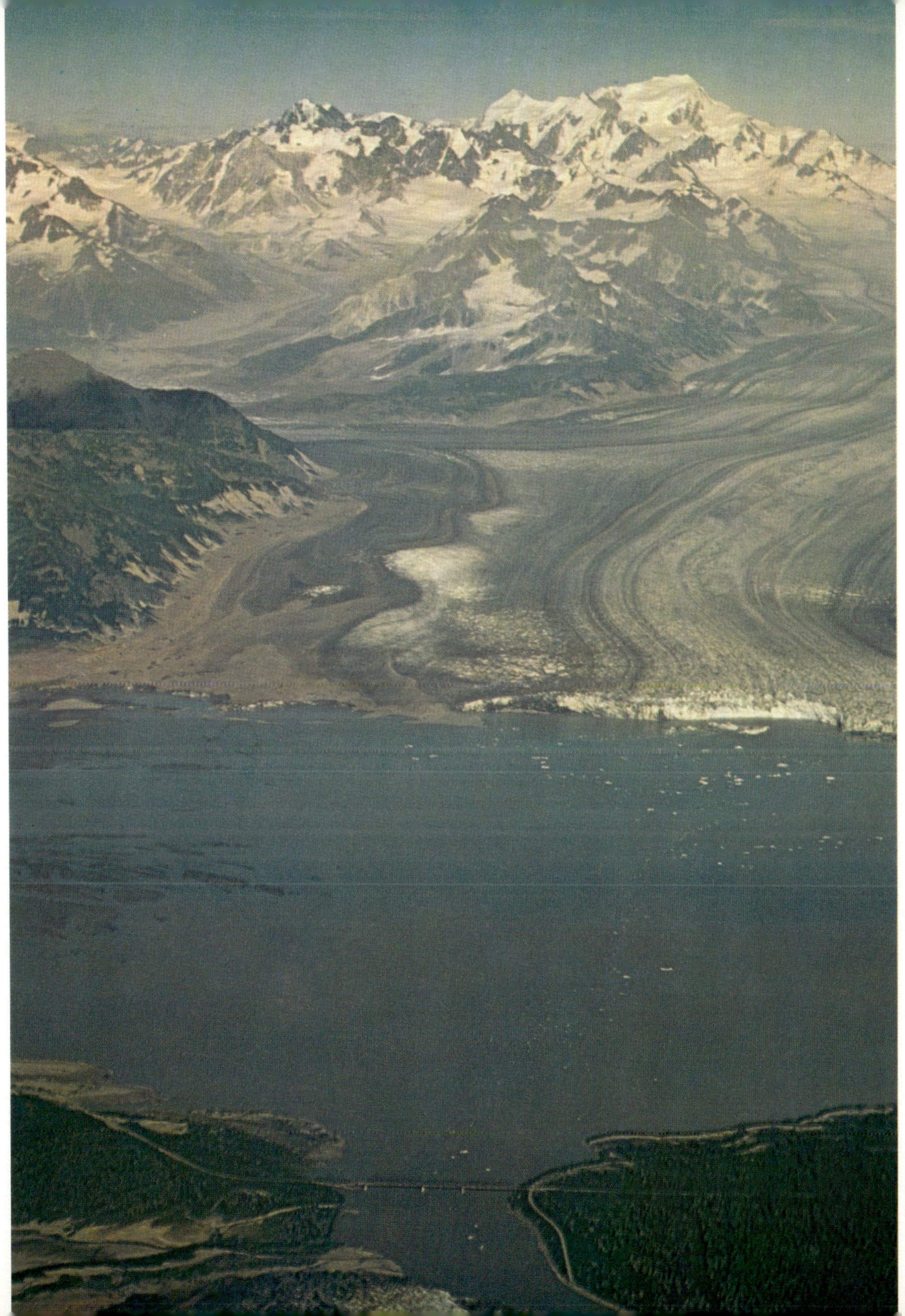

the Wernicke River. From this point the
boundary turns east to encompass the
Wernicke River drainage and Wernicke
Glacier. The addition's eastern boundary
runs from Wernicke Glacier south to
Martin River Glacier and includes Miles
Glacier. The Copper/Rude river area will
be managed for "the conservation of fish
and wildlife and their habitat. . . ."
Minerals in public lands within the
Copper River addition are withdrawn
from location, entry and patent under the
mining laws. The Secretary of Agriculture, under reasonable regulations, may
permit the removal of nonleasable
minerals.

A small addition at Controller Bay is a
triangle-shaped area at the outlet of the
Bering River north of Kayak Island.

Wilderness Units and National Monuments in Tongass National Forest

A forest service trail cuts through the lush rain forest in Misty Fiords National Monument creating a spectacular setting for hikers.
(R. Romei, U.S. Forest Service)

The Alaska d-2 lands bill created approximately 5.3 million acres of wilderness within the 16-million-acre Tongass National Forest, in southeastern Alaska, the largest national forest in the United States. It also added three new areas to that forest: the Juneau Icefield, Kates Needle and parts of the Brabazon Range, totaling more than one million acres.

As part of this wilderness designation, two new national monuments were created, to be managed primarily as wilderness by the forest service: Admiralty Island National Monument and Misty Fiords National Monument.

The 5,300,000 acres of wilderness consist of 14 units, ranging in size from 4,000 acres to more than two million acres.

The Wilderness areas will be managed as directed by the 1964 Wilderness Act as amended by the Alaska Lands Act. The primary objective of a wilderness area is to maintain the wilderness character of the land.

Wilderness classification directs that management of these lands shall emphasize retaining their natural qualities, unmarked by the works of man and where man himself is a visitor who does not remain. However, in Alaska, with its great distances and difficult terrain, certain exceptions were specified in the legislation.

Mechanized vehicles, such as airplanes and motorboats, may be used to gain access to and within wilderness areas where such use is traditional. Also, because of the climate, shelter cabins now existing were permitted to remain and provisions were included for building other cabins for public safety. The Alaska Lands Act specificallly authorizes the following uses for Alaska wilderness areas:

1. Fishing, Hunting & Trapping

Fishing, hunting and trapping will continue as on other national forest land. They are subject to state fish and game regulations.

2. Subsistence

Subsistence uses, including sport hunting and fishing, will be given special attention on all national forest lands including wilderness. The State of Alaska prescribes hunting, fishing and trapping regulations.

Tongass National Forest Wilderness Areas

	Acres
Monuments*	
Admiralty Island National Monument	900,000
Misty Fiords National Monument	2,136,000
Wilderness	
Coronation Island	19,122
Endicott River	94,000
Maurelle Islands	4,424
Petersburg Creek-Duncan Salt Chuck	50,000
Russell Fiord	307,000
South Baranof	314,000
South Prince of Wales	97,000
Stikine-LeConte	443,000
Tebenkof Bay	65,000
Tracy Arm-Fords Terror	656,000
Warren Island	11,353
West Chichagof-Yakobi	265,000
TOTAL ACREAGE	5,361,899**

*Admiralty Island and Misty Fiords were designated monuments under the d-2 bill, the first areas so designated in the National Forest system. Within each monument is a non-wilderness area, indicated by shading.

**The final acreage of wilderness areas may vary from these figures as official boundary maps are completed and State and Native selection acreages are deleted from these totals.

A powerboat cruises through the still waters of Chaik Bay. (Robert Henning, staff)

See detail map,
page 236.

Admiralty Island National Monument

Location: Southeastern Alaska, approximately 15 miles southwest of Juneau, bounded by the mainland and Stephens Passage to the east, Frederick Sound to the south and Chatham Strait to the west.

Size: Approximately 900,000 acres.

Access: Boats or floatplanes from Juneau provide primary access to the area. Wheeled planes are permitted to land on beaches.

Area Description: Annual precipitation is 100 inches over most of the island, although Angoon is drier because it is in the rain shadow of snow-capped Baranof Island to the southwest.

A ridge of mountains runs up the northern portion of the island, with alpine meadows visible above the dark tree line. South of the ridge of peaks, a strong geologic contact zone breaks the continuity of the mountain complex. The middle of the island embraces a myriad of lakes and streams. South of the lake area, the terrain is studded with lofty peaks.

Above: A brown/grizzly bear relaxes with his dinner along Pack Creek, on the east side of the island. (John S. Crawford, reprinted from *ALASKA GEOGRAPHIC®*)

Left: Casting a cautious look at the photographer, this Sitka black-tailed deer stands at the head of Mitchell Bay. (George Wuerthner)

Fauna: Giant brown/grizzly bears dominate all other animals. There are no black bears or wolves on Admiralty. The only other large mammal is the Sitka black-tailed deer.

Bald eagles form an outstanding feature on the island; where hundreds of nesting sites have been identified.

Marine life includes several varieties of salmon, whales, sea otters, harbor seals, sea lions, crabs and clams.

Flora: The majority of Admiralty Island is spruce-hemlock rain forest, interspersed with small areas of muskeg. Timberline is typically 1,500 to 2,000 feet. Above timberline, the forest gradually changes to alpine-tundra with rocky outcrops and semipermanent to permanent ice fields.

Accommodations: One commercial establishment, Thayer Lake Lodge, provides housekeeping and American plan accommodations. There are two small motels in Angoon. The forest service maintains seven trail cabins and 12 public recreation cabins.

Above: This climax forest along the banks of Lake Florence Creek is typical of Amiralty Island. (George Wuerthner)

Overleaf: Mitchell Bay at sunset creates an atmosphere of absolute serenity. (George Wuerthner)

167

Recreational Opportunities: Mit-

chell Bay and Admiralty Lakes Recreational Area are the two major recreational attractions within the monument. A 25-mile trail system links the eight major lakes on the island, and is part of the Cross-Admiralty Canoe Trail, which consists of a series of lakes, streams and portages across the island from Mole Harbor on the east to Mitchell Bay, near Angoon, on the west.

Kayaking and canoeing around the island is a popular holiday journey.

Hunting and fishing in season draw visitors, as does bird-watching, nature study and photography.

Above: The small Tlingit village of Angoon, with about 500 inhabitants, is the principle community on the island. (Lael Morgan, staff)

Right: A Tlingit fisherman in Angoon cleans his halibut before selling them to the fish buyer. (Shelley Schneider)

Human Use and Occupation:

Tlingit Indians have occupied Admiralty Island for countless generations. Today the small Tlingit village of Angoon is the principal community on the island, with about 500 inhabitants. There are about 20 private recreational cabins scattered along the beaches, and a few whites occupy homesteaded land around Angoon.

Mining on Admiralty

The only coal mine in Southeast is at Kanalku Bay at the end of Kootznahoo Inlet to the east of Angoon. This mine of low-grade coal deposits has been operated on a small scale sporadically and is currently overgrown and almost invisible.

High-grade gold was mined off and on at the north end of the island. Developmental work on a large scale is now proceeding on a low-grade nickel deposit between Funter Bay and Hawk Inlet.

Several base ore prospects as far south as Pybus Bay show evidence of a well-recognized mineral zone of complex zinc, copper, lead and silver running relatively southeast to northwest.

A major base ore prospect was recently drilled extensively near Hawk Inlet at Greens Creek. This area is specifically excluded from the monument.

During historic times, Capt. George Vancouver probably made the first recorded observation of Admiralty Island, naming it in honor of his branch of service, and mapping the shoreline. Russians followed, intent on pursuit of the sea otter, which they hunted to virtual extinction in Admiralty's waters.

Later a whaling station and herring saltery were built and operated at Killisnoo. Some mining developed, but the major industries were the operation of fish traps and salmon canneries. Logging occurred mostly in connection with providing facilities for the fishing industry. Following statehood, fish traps were outlawed and the fishing business declined. The outstanding wildlife and scenic attributes of Admiralty Island brought about many earlier attempts to preserve the land in its natural condition, including proposals for national park status made by the Secretary of the Interior in 1931, and again in 1938.

Suggested Reading:

►*ALASKA GEOGRAPHIC®*, Vol. 1, No. 3, *ADMIRALTY . . . ISLAND IN CONTENTION*
►*ALASKA GEOGRAPHIC®*, Vol. 5, No. 2, *SOUTHEAST: ALASKA'S PANHANDLE*
►*Discover Southeast With Pack and Paddle*, Margaret Piggott, 1974

Further Information:

►Admiralty Island National Monument
U.S.D.A. Forest Service
P.O. Box 1980
Sitka, Alaska 99835

USGS Topographic Series:

Juneau, Sitka, Sumdum

A couple strolls on the rocky beach near Angoon. The rock in the foreground shows the effects of years of tidal action. (Lael Morgan, staff)

Misty Fiords National Monument

Location: Southeastern Alaska, at the southern end of Tongass National Forest, adjacent to the Canadian border on the east and south, extending northward from Dixon Entrance to beyond the Unuk River. Its western boundary lies about 22 air miles east of Ketchikan.

Size: 2,285,000 acres, with 2,136,000 classified wilderness.

Access: Primary access is by floatplane or boat. Floatplanes can be chartered out of Ketchikan, which is on the Alaska ferry route. A small cruise boat offers two-day all-expense trips through the fiords of the monument.

Area Description: Taking its name from the almost constant precipitation characteristic of the area, Misty Fiords is covered with thick forests which grow on nearly vertical slopes from sea level to mountain tops. Dramatic waterfalls plunge into the salt water through narrow clefts or course over great rounded granite shoulders, fed by lakes and streams which absorb the annual rainfall of more than 14 feet.

The major waterway cutting through

the monument, Behm Canal, is more than 100 miles long and unusually deep.

About 10,000 years ago, massive ice bodies probably covered much of this land, and active glaciers still abound along the Canadian border, which forms the northern and eastern edges of the monument. Botanists can study the succession of plants springing up in the wake of this recent glaciation.

Periodic lava flows have occurred over several thousand years close to the Blue River near the northern edge of the monument, the most recent eruption taking place in the 1920s.

Fauna: Wildlife within the monument is unusually varied and plentiful: mountain goat, brown/grizzly bear, black bear, moose, marten, wolf, wolverine and river otter are well represented.

The coasts and salt-water bays contain sea lions, harbor seals, killer whales and Dall porpoises. Bird life is fantastic, ranging from tiny hummingbirds to trumpeter swans and herons, with great numbers of eagle nesting sites.

Flora: The forests, typical of southern Tongass National Forest, consist of Sitka spruce, western hemlock and cedar. Some Pacific silver fir, sub-alpine fir and black cottonwood are found. A thick understory consisting of huckleberry, alder, willow and other brushy vegetation create impenetrable thickets.

Accommodations: Commercial establishments in the vicinity of the monument are at Bell Island and at Yes Bay.

The forest service maintains 12 recreational cabins on fresh-water lakes, and three on salt water. Access to the cabins is primarily by floatplane, since hiking is impossible without trails. There are only about 15 miles of maintained trails within the monument.

Left: A waterfall cascades down through the rain forest surrounding Punchbowl Cove. (Shelley Schneider)

Above: A layer of mist hangs over the end of Bakewell Arm. (Connie Barlow)

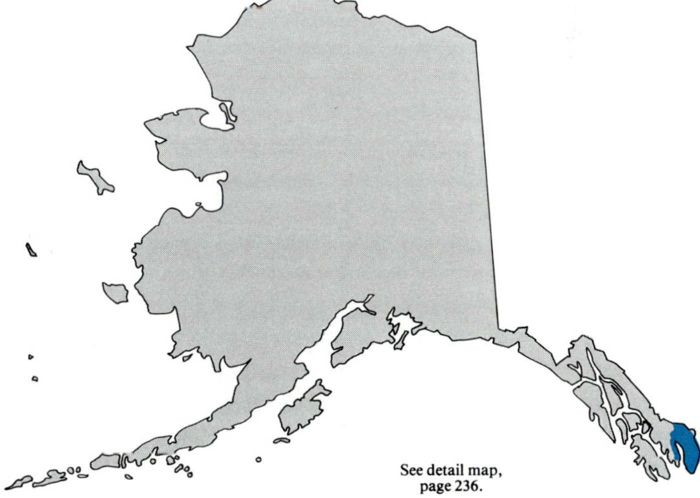

See detail map, page 236.

173

Recreational Opportunities: The scenic qualities of the monument are unparalleled. Inlets, bays, arms and coves are variations on the fiords for which the area is named. Some are long, narrow fingers winding between spectacular peaks and great gaunt granite crags and rounded ridges. Others are short and broad, blunt and windswept. Each is unique. The highlands are dotted with thousands of small and large lakes, feeding innumerable streams that rush down to salt water.

The Walker Cove-Rudyerd Bay Scenic Area has been protected for many years, and has always been a favorite playground for boaters from Ketchikan. Vertical granite faces topped by snowy peaks give an impression of boating through Yosemite Valley.

The most comfortable way to visit Misty Fiords is by cabin cruiser or some other sleep-aboard boat. Good moorages can be found, fresh water is available ashore, and crabs, clams and fish can be readily added to the menu.

Kayak trips are popular, despite the weather. Campsites are difficult. Tides of up to 18 feet may be encountered; often the only safe camping spot is up among the trees above the high tide line. Firewood is plentiful but usually wet. Behm Canal has few suitable camping sites.

Two kayakers unpack their gear on the shore of Punchbowl Cove, off Rudyerd Bay. (Connie Barlow)

Left: The Walker Cove-Rudyerd Bay Scenic Area has long been popular with area boaters. This scene shows the entrance of Walker Cove, off Behm Canal. (Stephen Hilson, reprinted from *ALASKA GEOGRAPHIC*®)

Above: Bright green vegetation adds color to this scene on the shore of Behm Canal, near Walker Cove. (Connie Barlow)

Suggested Reading:
►*ALASKA GEOGRAPHIC*®, Vol. 5, No. 2, *SOUTHEAST: ALASKA'S PANHANDLE*

Additional Information:
►Misty Fiords National Monument
U.S.D.A. Forest Service
Federal Building
Ketchikan, AK 99901

USGS Topographic Series:
Prince Rupert, Ketchikan, Bradfield Canal

Coronation Island Wilderness
Maurelle Islands Wilderness
Warren Island Wilderness

A dark cloud hangs over Chatham Strait just after sunrise. On the horizon is Coronation Island, with the tip of Kuiu Island visible on the left. (Matt Donohoe)

Location: Southeastern Alaska, off the west coast of Prince of Wales Island, south of the southern tip of Kuiu Island and north of Noyes Island.

Size: Coronation Island Wilderness: 19,122 acres; Maurelle Islands Wilderness: 4,424 acres; Warren Island Wilderness: 11,353 acres.

Access: The islands are accessible by boat or floatplane. Air mileage from Ketchikan is 73 miles to Maurelle Islands, 75 miles to Warren Island and 110 miles to Coronation Island. Craig and Klawock on Prince of Wales Island are the nearest communities. Access to many of the islands is difficult, either by boat or floatplane, as sheltered landing places are not available. Warren Island is so exposed to the prevailing southeast winds that it is inaccessible much of the year. Some of the islands do have protected coves and beaches on their leeward sides.

Area Description: These islands lie fully exposed to the Pacific Ocean, and bear the full brunt of the wind and the seas. Coronation and Warren islands rise nearly 2,000 feet above sea level, and form prominent landmarks, while the nearly 30 small islands of the Maurelle group are low (under 400 feet), with numerous rocky shoals in nearby waters. Beaches are windswept and rock-strewn shorelines rise to steep cliffs.

Fauna: Wolves, black bears and Sitka black-tailed deer are found on many of the islands. Bald eagles and seabirds share the rocky cliffs. Sea otters, seals and sea lions inhabit the coastal waters. Some of the streams contain trout and salmon.

Flora: Vegetation consists of some thick stands of spruce and hemlock, with other typical rain forest vegetation.

Accommodations: None.

Recreational Opportunities: Kayaking among the Maurelle Islands would be possible although rugged. On the two larger islands, principal activities would be beachcombing and observing wildlife.

Further Information:
►U.S.D.A. Forest Service
Ketchikan Area
Tongass National Forest
Federal Building
Ketchikan, AK 99801

USGS Topographic Series:
Craig

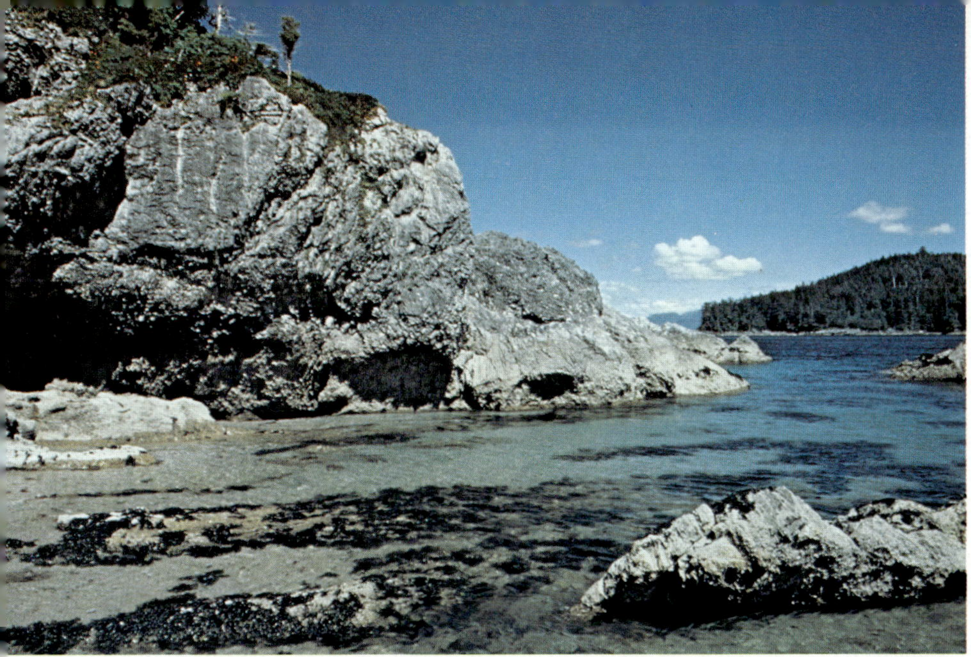

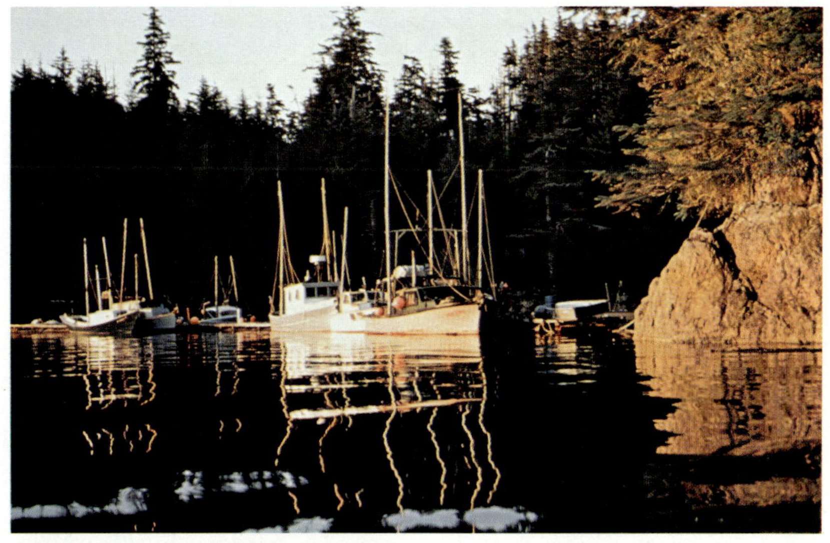

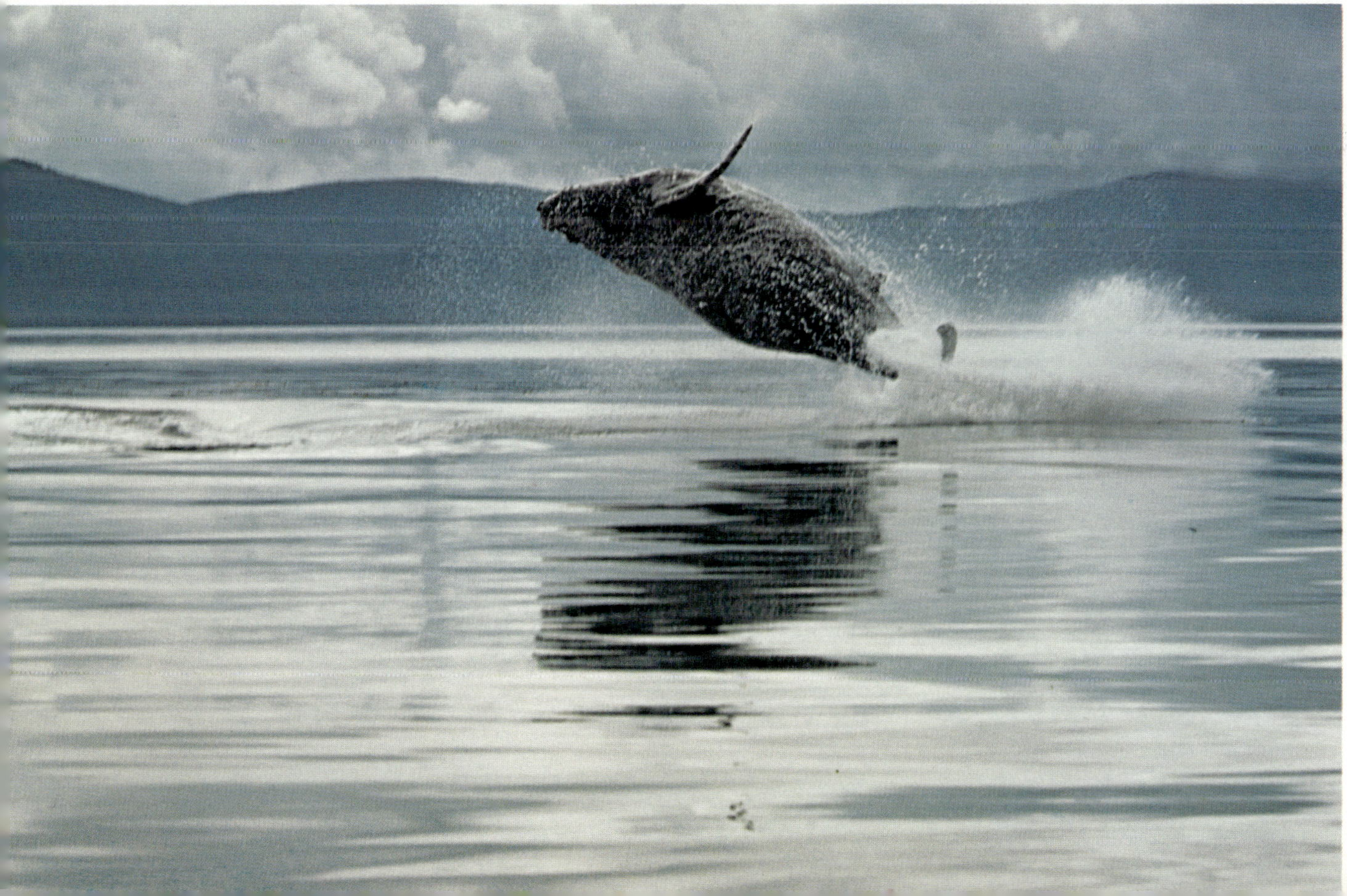

Clockwise from left:
►The humpback whale, easily identified by its huge flippers and ventral grooves, is a common sight in the waters of southeast Alaska. (Jack Beedle)
►Rock-strewn beaches such as this one at Egg Harbor surround much of Coronation Island. (Matt Donohoe)
►Hand trollers anchor at Hole-in-the-wall, a mecca for fishermen when the coho salmon are running. Hole-in-the-wall is part of the San Lorenzo Islands which form the southern point of the Maurelle group. (Matt Donohoe)

Endicott River Wilderness

Location: Southeastern Alaska, on the Chilkat Peninsula, on the west side of Lynn Canal, approximately 45 miles northwest of Juneau and 30 miles south of Haines. The western portion of the area bounds Glacier Bay National Park for about 40 miles.

Size: About 94,000 acres.

Access: The area can best be reached by boat, where the Endicott River meets Lynn Canal. Travel within the wilderness is by foot. Spring and summer months are the best times to visit; Lynn Canal is extremely stormy in fall and winter.

Area Description: The area is rugged, extending from sea level to elevations of more than 5,000 feet. Mount Young, in the northwest portion of the area, rises 5,700 feet. The river canyon is large, formed by glacial action. Glaciers cover the highlands of the upper valley, adjoining those in the park. Rainfall is around 92 inches per year, lowest in April through June and highest in September through December.

Fauna: Both black and brown/grizzly bear are found here, as well as moose, mountain goat and deer. Bald eagle nesting density is high. The Endicott River has several varieties of salmon.

Flora: The vegetation is typical of southeast rain forest, containing spruce and hemlock. Higher elevations support brush, small trees and alpine vegetation.

Accommodations: No commercial lodgings or forest service recreational cabins are found in the area.

Recreational Opportunities: This wilderness provides a chance to explore a primitive, unspoiled, rugged and untracked wilderness area. Hunting during open season attracts some visitors.

Further Information:
►U.S.D.A. Forest Service
Chatham Area
Tongass National Forest
Sitka, AK 99835

USGS Topographic Series:
Juneau

Above: Much of the wilderness area is covered with rugged mountains, reaching heights of more than 5,000 feet. (Lael Morgan, staff)

Right: The wilderness area is a popular nesting site for the bald eagle. (Jo Keller, U.S. Fish & Wildlife Service)

Left: Mosses, ferns and other shade-loving plants cover the floor of the typical southeastern rain forest. (Pete Martin, reprinted from *ALASKA GEOGRAPHIC*®)

Above: Mountain goats are frequent inhabitants of southeastern Alaska. This animal was photographed just west of the wilderness area. (William Boehm, reprinted from *ALASKA GEOGRAPHIC*®)

Petersburg Creek-Duncan Salt Chuck Wilderness

Location: Southeastern Alaska, on the Lindenberg Peninsula of Kupreanof Island. The eastern boundary is near the small community of Kupreanof, directly across Wrangell Narrows from the city of Petersburg, continuing west through the Petersburg Creek drainage to the Salt Chuck at the north end of Duncan Canal.

Size: Approximately 50,000 acres.

Access: Petersburg is the usual access point. The eastern boundary is easily reached by boat via Petersburg Creek, which flows into Wrangell Narrows. The western side is reached by boat via Duncan Canal and the Salt Chuck. Safe negotiation of these bodies of water requires high tides. Floatplanes can land in Duncan Canal, on the Salt Chuck (at higher tides) and on Petersburg Lake. Petersburg Lake National Recreation Trail leads from salt water to Petersburg Lake, where the forest service recreational cabin is located.

A stand of lodgepole pine grows out of the muskeg. (Ernest Manewal)

Area Description: Petersburg Creek flows through a typical U-shaped glacial valley, very steep in some places with rock outcroppings.

Fauna: Wildlife found within the wilderness area include black bear, deer, wolves, other furbearers and a variety of waterfowl.

All species of salmon (except king salmon), Dolly Varden and cutthroat trout are found in Petersburg Creek and Lake and their tributaries.

Flora: The thick forest cover consists mainly of spruce and hemlock, with some muskeg in the lower areas.

Accommodations: The forest service maintains three recreational cabins: two in the vicinity of Duncan Canal and Salt Chuck; and one at Petersburg Lake.

Recreational Opportunities: Activities include hiking, backpacking, kayaking, fishing, wildlife observation and photography. Hunting in season is permitted.

Human Use and Occupation: Petersburg Creek and Lake and the Duncan Salt Chuck have long been the back-door playground of Petersburg residents, and they have worked very hard to protect these areas.

Suggested Reading:
▶*Discover Southeast Alaska With Pack and Paddle,* Margaret Piggott, 1974

Further Information:
▶U.S.D.A. Forest Service
Stikine Area
Tongass National Forest
P.O. Box 309
Petersburg, AK 99833

USGS Topographic Series:
Petersburg

Russell Fiord Wilderness

Location: Southeastern Alaska, 25 miles northeast of Yakutat, which can be reached by commercial airline. The wilderness encompasses Russell Fiord, lying between the rugged Fairweather Range to the northeast and the Brabazon Range to the southeast.

Size: Approximately 307,000 acres.

Access: The most common form of access is by floatplane from Juneau or Yakutat, or by boat from Yakutat. Much of the area is too rugged for easy access, since it is mostly mountains, glaciers and ice fields.

Area Description: Russell Fiord is heavily glaciated. It extends inland 35 miles from Disenchantment Bay. Nunatak Fiord takes off from Russell Fiord about midway, extending 15 miles to the east. Active glaciers abound. Russell Fiord has great scientific interest because of its record of catastrophic geologic events.

Fauna: The area has a great variety of wildlife, which has attracted hunters over the years: brown/grizzly and black bears, glacier bears (a color phase of black bears), mountain goats, wolves and many furbearers. Marine life, such as harbor seals and sea lions are numerous. Bald eagles, shorebirds and waterfowl can be found. Fish are scarce in the wilderness area.

Left: Shorebirds crowd the waters of Yakutat Bay. Here a wandering tattler pokes among the rocks for small worms and other treats. (Penny Rennick, reprinted from *ALASKA GEOGRAPHIC®*)

Above: One of the characteristics of Art Lewis Glacier is its contorted medial moraines. The glacier heads near the Alaska-Canada boundary and trends southeast 15 miles to East Nunatak Glacier, three miles east of the head of Nunatak Fiord.
(Gil Mull, reprinted from *ALASKA GEOGRAPHIC®*)

Large icebergs calved off of Yakutat Glacier fill Harlequin Lake.
(K.W. Tarr)

Flora: Lower elevations have typical spruce-hemlock forest, changing to alpine vegetation at higher altitudes.

Accommodations: No commercial lodges are found, except in Yakutat. The forest service maintains one recreational cabin at Situk Lake.

Recreational Opportunities: Possible outdoor activities in this area include hiking and backpacking, kayaking in the fiords and kayaking or rafting down the Situk River out of Situk Lake. Hunting is permitted in season.

Human Use and Occupation: Yakutat is the only settlement left of many which existed prior to the coming of the white man. The Gulf Coast was settled by interior people migrating to the coast, coming along the shore from the mouth of the Copper River, and Tlingits coming by foot and canoe from southeastern Alaska. Later, many of the best known early Alaska explorers came this way — Bering, Cook, LaPerouse and Dixon.

A section of Hubbard Glacier is shown as it calves into Disenchantment Bay. Scientists are studying the glacier, to see if its forward thrust might cut off Russell Fiord from the bay.
(Steve McCutcheon, reprinted from *ALASKA GEOGRAPHIC*®)

Suggested Reading:

►*Under Mt. St. Elias: The History and Culture of the Yakutat Tlingit,* Dr. Frederica de Laguna, 1972
►*ALASKA GEOGRAPHIC®*, Vol. 2, No. 4, *YAKUTAT: THE TURBULENT CRESCENT*

Further Information:

►U.S.D.A. Forest Service
Chatham Area
Tongass National Forest
P.O. Box 1980
Sitka, AK 99835

USGS Topographic Series:

Yakutat, Mount Saint Elias

South Baranof Wilderness

Left: The wilderness area is characterized by high mountains, rising to more than 4,000 feet, and permanent glaciers. (Jeffrey S. Johnson)

Below: This view of Sitka Sound was taken from Sitka, the largest community on Baranof Island, located 50 miles north of the wilderness area. (Rollo Pool, staff)

Location: Southeastern Alaska on the southern portion of Baranof Island. Bounded by the Gulf of Alaska on the west and Chatham Strait on the east, the wilderness lies about 50 miles south of Sitka, and several miles north of Port Alexander.

Size: Approximately 314,000 acres.

Access: The area can be reached by floatplane or boat, from Sitka or Port Alexander. Sitka is on the Alaska ferry route. Many sheltered bays and fiords provide safe boat anchorages and sheltered floatplane landings.

Area Description: The typical weather pattern is inclement. Little Port Walter, just south of the wilderness area, receives more than 200 inches of precipitation annually. Prevailing winds from the southeast can reach gale velocity of more than 100 mph, usually between September and December.

This portion of Baranof Island is characterized by high mountains which rise from sea level to above 4,000 feet. These higher elevations have permanent glaciers, with many cirques and hanging valley lakes spilling out in numerous waterfalls near the coast. The coastline is broken by long, narrow fiords.

Fauna: Wildlife found here include brown/grizzly bear, Sitka black-tailed deer and furbearers such as mink, marten and land otter. Seals frequent coastal waters. Bald eagles are numerous and waterfowl pause in migratory flights.

The area contains some of Baranof

Further Information:
►U.S.D.A. Forest Service
Chatham Area
Tongass National Forest
Sitka, AK 99835

USGS Topographic Series:
Port Alexander

Above: Old rooming houses and other buildings line the shore of the small community of Port Alexander, one of the access points to the area. (Charlie Ott, reprinted from *ALASKA GEOGRAPHIC®*)

Right: An old clear cut, an area where loggers have removed the trees, has left its mark despite new growth along the shore of Baranof Island. (Staff)

Island's best steelhead-producing streams. Salmon, trout, Dolly Varden and char can be found in lakes and streams. Crabs, shrimp, herring and halibut are plentiful in the coastal waters.

Accommodations: The forest service maintains five recreational cabins in the area.

Recreational Opportunities: Fishing, kayaking and canoeing, as well as cruising in sleep-aboard motorboats or sailboats are possible in the area.

South Prince of Wales Wilderness

Location: Southeastern Alaska, at the southern tip of Prince of Wales Island, approximately 40 air miles southwest of Ketchikan. The wilderness fronts on Dixon Entrance and partly on Cordova Bay, extending north to take in all of Klakas Inlet and including approximately the western third of this southeastern peninsula of Prince of Wales Island.

Size: Approximately 97,000 acres.

Access: Floatplanes and boats provide the primary access to the area. Small boats can negotiate the area during the summer; however, Dixon Entrance is exposed to the ocean and can be stormy and rough during other seasons.

Area Description: The seacoast is deeply indented with numerous bays and inlets. The Barrier Islands, a collection of more than 75 islets ranging in size from a few acres up to 500 acres, jut out into Cordova Bay. Topography on the main island ranges from lowlands containing many streams, lakes and wetlands, to the walls of Klakas Inlet, sheer rock rising 2,000 feet out of the sea.

Fauna: Large animals include black bear, wolf and Sitka black-tailed deer. Coastal areas and wetlands support large populations of bald eagles, shorebirds and waterfowl.

Several kinds of salmon, trout and Dolly Varden can be found in lakes and streams. The unusually rich tidal zone contains abalone, giant barnacles, clams, large mussels, octopus, sea urchins, sea anemones and starfish. It is also one of the better sea otter habitats.

Flora: Vegetation in the area consists of hemlock and Sitka spruce; however, the area is exposed to the sweep of Pacific winds and storms, and what trees there are appear stunted and windswept.

Accommodations: No commercial lodges or forest service recreational cabins are available.

Human Use and Occupation: Klinkwan, the first Haida village in Southeast Alaska, is located within the wilderness area. The village was established in the 19th century and abandoned in 1911.

Below: A glaucous-winged gull proudly displays its freshly-caught starfish. (Tom Kogut)

Bottom: A lesser yellowlegs rests along the rocky shore. Coastal areas and wetlands support large populations of shorebirds. (Tom Kogut)

Further Information:
►U.S.D.A. Forest Service
Ketchikan Area
Tongass National Forest
Federal Building
Ketchikan, AK 99901

USGS Topographic Series:
Dixon Entrance, Craig

Waves lap over the rocks on the shore of Moira Sound, just east of the wilderness area. (Mary Henrikson, reprinted from *ALASKA GEOGRAPHIC®*)

Stikine-LeConte Wilderness

Location: Southeastern Alaska, covering much of the mainland between Petersburg, opposite its northern tip, and Wrangell, a few miles south of its southern boundary. The region extends from Frederick Arm on the west to the Canadian border on the east, including part of the Kates Needle addition to Tongass National Forest.

Size: Approximately 443,000 acres.

Access: Boats are the most frequently used means of access into the wilderness area, especially for negotiating the Stikine River. Former freight boat service up the river from Wrangell to Telegraph Creek, British Columbia, has been discontinued. The most common access is by chartered floatplane out of Wrangell to Telegraph Creek, where kayaks or rafts are readied for the trip downriver. Some motorboats will haul rafts and rafters upriver, and limited small boat service is available.

The Stikine River braids out between Mud Glacier and Flood Glacier in the Boundary Range of the Coast Mountains, just across the Canadian border.
(Staff, reprinted from *ALASKA GEOGRAPHIC®*)

Area Description: A major feature of this wilderness area is the powerful Stikine River, which heads in the Cassiar Mountains of northcentral British Columbia, in Spatsizi Wilderness Park, and finally empties into tidewater a few miles from the town of Wrangell. The river valley is narrow, surrounded by steep, rugged peaks, many of them glaciated. One person described the river trip, "like kayaking through the Swiss Alps." The river is heavily laden with silt from the numerous glaciers emptying into it. Springs, two warm and one hot, are found along the river. The Stikine delta is about 17 miles wide, an expanse of grass flats, tidal marshes and sand bars. LeConte Glacier is the southernmost glacier in North America to empty directly into salt water. The vicinity of LeConte Glacier is mountainous, with steep peaks, glacier-filled valleys and numerous ice fields to the east toward Canada.

Left: Incredibly sheer, this unnamed peak juts skyward above the Stikine Icecap, which extends north about 80 miles along the backbone of the Coast Mountains. (Daniel Kulin, reprinted from *ALASKA GEOGRAPHIC®*)

Below: Meeting salt water (in the distance), the Stikine River becomes a shallow and confusing jumble of sandy islands and mud flats — almost impossible to navigate except at high tide. (Staff, reprinted from *ALASKA®* magazine)

Fauna: The Stikine River drainage is an important fish, waterfowl and wildlife area. Large mammals found here include moose, mountain goat, brown/grizzly bear, black bear, deer and wolf. The delta of the Stikine River forms a major nesting and resting area for migratory birds. Several varieties of salmon are found in the area.

Flora: Vegetation along the Stikine River reflects the changing climatic zones through which the river travels. Close to the Canadian border rainfall diminishes and stands of cottonwood are found; they also grow on many of the islands in the river. The lower valley floor contains many muskeg bogs, and dense alder and willow thickets. The mountains on their lower levels support dense spruce-hemlock rain forest.

Above: A black bear feeds on sedge grass in the Stikine River delta — a rich estuary which supports a wide variety of mammals, birds and fish. (George Weurthner, reprinted from *ALASKA GEOGRAPHIC®*)

Right: The steel-hulled tour boat *Blue Star* makes its way through the mass of ice in front of LeConte Glacier. (Tim Thompson, reprinted from *ALASKA GEOGRAPHIC®*)

Accommodations: No commercial lodges. The forest service maintains at least 13 recreational cabins in this area, and an enclosed bathing structure at Chief Shakes Hot Springs.

Recreational Opportunities:

Fishing and hunting, especially waterfowl on the Stikine Flats, is permitted in season.

Kayaking and rafting trips down the Stikine River from Telegraph Creek are available, both private and commercial trips. Hiking is difficult along the river due to thick brush.

Human Use and Occupation:

The Stikine River has been a highway from prehistoric times for Athabascan Indians from British Columbia's Interior and for people from the Tahltans and the Cascas, groups belonging to the Déné branch originating in the Nahanni division of the Athabascan linguistic family. They occupied the upper portions of the Stikine drainage, while Tlingits dominated the Alaska portion, and maintained a trading relationship all along the river.

The fur trade drew white men up the Stikine River as early as 1790, but it was the gold rushes of the late 1800s that brought about steamboat travel up the river.

Suggested Reading:
►*ALASKA GEOGRAPHIC®*, Vol. 6, No. 4, *THE STIKINE RIVER*
►*Trail to the Interior,* Raymond M. Patterson, 1966
►*Travels in Alaska,* John Muir, 1915

Further Information:
►U.S.D.A. Forest Service
Stikine Area
Tongass National Forest
P.O. Box 309
Petersburg, AK 99833

USGS Topographic Series:
Petersburg, Bradfield Canal, Sumdum

Devils Thumb (9,077 feet), the northernmost tip of the wilderness area, is the second highest peak in the Stikine region. The tallest is Kates Needle (10,023 feet) to the southeast. (Paul Starr, reprinted from *ALASKA GEOGRAPHIC®*)

Tebenkof Bay Wilderness

A common sight in the area, gulls congregate in large numbers when salmon are spawning. (Rollo Pool, staff)

Location: Southeastern Alaska, on the west side of Kuiu Island, approximately 50 miles west of Petersburg, and bordered on the west by Chatham Strait.

Size: Approximately 65,000 acres.

Access: Main access is by boat or floatplane. Many of the area's coves are protected and provide good anchorage. Access across Chatham Strait is hazardous at times because of swells and strong winds off the Pacific Ocean.

Area Description: Tebenkof Bay Wilderness is an expansive and complex bay system which includes many small islands and numerous bays and coves. There is some muskeg, and many small lakes and creeks.

Fauna: Wildlife consists of black bears, wolves and some smaller furbearers on land. Marine mammals are abundant. The area is on the migration route of many waterfowl. Some trumpeter swans are found, as are many bald eagle nesting sites.

The area is rich in fish and shellfish, including several varieties of salmon, trout, Dungeness and tanner crab, shrimp and halibut.

Flora:
Spruce-hemlock forests tower above a lush understory typical of the southeastern Alaska rain forest.

Accommodations:
No commercial accommodations or forest service recreational cabins are available.

Recreational Opportunities:
Kayaking and exploring along the many streams, bays and coves are possible activities.

Human Use and Occupation:
An early Tlingit Indian village site has been found in this area.

Further Information:
►U.S.D.A. Forest Service
Tongass National Forest
P.O. Box 309
Petersburg, AK 99833

USGS Topographic Series:
Port Alexander

Clockwise from left:
►The waters of Chatham Strait, which make up the western edge of the wilderness area, are rich in fish and shellfish, such as these Dungeness crabs. (Richard Billings, reprinted from *ALASKA GEOGRAPHIC®*)
►Judy Erickson lends scale to an ancient Tlingit pictograph, painted on a rock wall near Saginaw Bay, north of the wilderness area. (Jay West, reprinted from *ALASKA GEOGRAPHIC®*)
►Spray rising in its wake, a killer whale speeds through the water. Whales abound in the coastal waters of the wilderness. (Craig Harrison, reprinted from *ALASKA GEOGRAPHIC®*)
►Although absent from many of the islands in southeastern Alaska, black bears inhabit Kuiu Island, the site of the wilderness area. (Drew Welsh)

Tracy Arm–
Fords Terror
Wilderness

Left: Carved over centuries, a classic round-sided glacial valley leads to Tracy Arm, barely visible in the distance. (Donald Grybeck, USGS, reprinted from *ALASKA GEOGRAPHIC®*)

Above: Sheer rock walls climb almost vertically to heights of 3,000 to 4,000 feet along Tracy Arm. (Courtesy of U.S. Forest Service)

Location: Southeastern Alaska, off the end of Holkham Bay, between Tracy Arm and Endicott Arm, and bordered on the east by Canada. The area is about 50 miles southeast of Juneau, and 70 miles north of Petersburg.

Size: Approximately 656,000 acres, of which approximately 148,000 acres lie in the Kates Needle addition to Tongass National Forest.

Access: The usual means of reaching this wilderness is by boat via Stephens Passage and Holkham Bay to Tracy Arm, or via Endicott Arm into Fords Terror. Floatplanes from either Juneau or Petersburg offer another means of entering the area. Large cruise ships and small charter boats include Tracy and Endicott arms on their itineraries.

Area Description: Major features of the area are the two main fiords, Tracy Arm and Endicott Arm, both long, narrow, deep and penetrating more than 30 miles into the Coast Range. Both arms have active tidewater glaciers at their upper ends, which calve icebergs, and contain much floating ice during the summer, with some chunks as large as a three-story building. Active glaciers filled both arms solid during the recent glacial epoch. Fords Terror is an area of sheer rock walls enclosing a narrow entrance into a small fiord. Its name comes from a navy crew-man who rowed into the entrance at slack water and was caught in the surging tidal currents for six hours when the tides changed.

Fauna: Upland areas are inhabited by mountain goats, Sitka black-tailed deer, wolverines and brown/grizzly and black bears. Bald eagles and shorebirds use the coastal areas. Marine mammals include harbor seals, sea lions and whales. Harbor seals are thought to use the floating ice near the calving glaciers as protected areas for raising young.

Flora: Vegetation consists of some thick stands of spruce and hemlock, with other typical rain forest vegetation.

Accommodations: No accommodations are available. Camping may be difficult because of lack of suitable areas.

Recreational Opportunities: Motor cruisers with sleep-aboard facilities offer the best means of visiting this isolated area. Some kayaking opportunities are available in the lower fiords.

Further Information:
►U.S.D.A. Forest Service
Chatham Area
Tongass National Forest
P.O. Box 1980
Sitka, AK 99835

USGS Topographic Series:
Sumdum, Taku River

Misty conditions enhance the beauty of Fords Terror. (Stephen Hilson, reprinted from *ALASKA®* magazine)

West Chichagof-Yakobi Wilderness

Location: Southeastern Alaska, covering the western portions of Chichagof and Yakobi islands in the extreme northwestern portion of the Alexander Archipelago.

Size: Approximately 265,000 acres.

Access: Pelican is a few miles east of the area, on Lisianski Inlet. Sitka lies about 30 miles south of the area's southern boundary. The coastal area of the wilderness has excellent moorage and landing sites for boats and floatplanes. Charter flights are available from Sitka and charter boats can be hired there.

Area Description: The major feature of this wilderness is the 65-mile stretch of rugged Pacific Ocean coastline, with exposed offshore islands and rocky highlands. The quiet waters of a scenic inside passage, protected by the barrier islands and rocks and reefs of the outer coast, are honeycombed with bays, inlets and lagoons. Steep mountains rise directly out of the ocean, with peaks more than 3,000 feet high.

Above: The outer coast of Chichagof Island is often battered by strong winds and storms off the Pacific Ocean, evidenced by windblown trees and rocky shores. (Staff)

Right: Low clouds hang over Lisianski Strait, which separates Chichagof and Yakobi islands. (Staff)

Fauna: Deer and brown/grizzly bear inhabit the area. Offshore islands, notably White Sister Island, Cape Cross and Cape Bingham, provide hauling grounds for sea lions. Sea otters have been re-established at Surge and Khaz bays. Seals abound in coastal waters.

An old building, once part of the Kimshan Gold Mine, still stands at Kimshan Cove, on the west coast of Chichagof Island. The mine operated from 1905 to 1938. (Staff)

Flora: About a third of the area is covered by forests of western hemlock and Sitka spruce, with some lodgepole pine and Alaska cedar. The grassy meadows of higher elevations are deceiving — downed logs, unexpected holes and hidden streams make them unsuitable for hiking.

Accommodations: Goulding Lake, White Sulphur Springs and Lake Suloia are sites of the area's three forest service recreational cabins. At White Sulphur Springs, a bath house has been built to house the hot water pool, with panels which can be opened to permit bathers to look out into Bertha Bay.

Recreational Opportunities: The area is a paradise for power boat, sailboat and kayak enthusiasts. The coast offers excellent cruising and kayaking, with its thousands of islands, reefs, intricate bays, lagoons and passages. Picturesque ruins of early day mining camps attract adventuresome visitors.

Strong winds and storms coming in off the Pacific Ocean can be dangerous in exposed stretches.

Human Use and Occupation: Tlingit Indians occupied the area because it is hospitable and rich in resources.

Further Information:
►U.S.D.A. Forest Service
Chatham Area
Tongass National Forest
P.O. Box 1980
Sitka, AK 99835

USGS Topographic Series:
Sitka, Mount Fairweather

Wild
and
Scenic
Rivers

Left: A hillside directly opposite Bombardment Creek offers this view of the North Fork Koyukuk in late summer. (Stuart Pechek)

Right: Birch Creek winds back and forth along this section south of the Steese Highway. (Jo Keller, U.S. Fish & Wildlife Service)

The Alaska National Interest Lands Conservation Act of December 2, 1980, gave wild and scenic river classification to 13 streams within the National Park System, six in the National Wildlife Refuge System, and two in Bureau of Land Management Conservation and Recreation areas. The remaining five rivers are located outside designated preservation units. Twelve more rivers were designated for further study and possible wild and scenic classification.

The criteria for wild and scenic river classification is not just for float trip possibilities. Scenic features, wilderness characteristics and other recreational opportunities that would be impaired by alteration, development or impoundment are also considered.

Rivers are classified into three categories under the Wild and Scenic Rivers Act. The wild classification is most restrictive of development or incompatible uses — it stresses the wilderness aspect of the rivers. The scenic classification permits somewhat more intrusions upon the natural landscape, and recreational classification is the least restrictive category. A specified amount of land back from the river's banks is also put in protected status to insure access, use and the preservation of aesthetic values for the public.

For those desiring to float these rivers, special consideration must be given to put-in and take-out points as most of the new wild and scenic rivers listed here are not accessible by road. This means that voyagers and their crafts have to be flown in and picked up by charter bush planes, so plan float trips accordingly. Because Federal Aviation Administration regulations prohibit the lashing of canoes and kayaks on pontoons of floatplanes when carrying passengers, inflatable rafts and folding canvas or rubber kayaks are often more convenient and less expensive to transport.

Breakup on northern Alaska rivers sometimes does not occur until early June or even later. Check with the agency within whose lands a particular river lies for the names of bush plane operators in the area, and for advice on river conditions.

Water level in rivers can fluctuate in a few hours because of rain storms — which can occur upriver in headwater areas even though the area where voyagers camp may be cloudless. Always carry the boat high up on the bank and tie it overnight. An extra paddle is a must, as well as extra rope for lining around rapids or shallows.

As temperatures of Alaska rivers are usually only a little above freezing and the water is often glacier-fed, wearing of a life preserver at all times when in a small boat is advised. A small emergency kit containing a knife, mosquito repellent and waterproof matches and strapped to the traveler is advisable in case of capsizing — especially if the expedition consists of only one boat.

Further information on rivers and river running can be obtained from offices of the National Park Service, U.S. Fish & Wildlife Service, and Bureau of Land Management, listed elsewhere in this volume.

Wild and Scenic River System in Alaska

(numbers refer to the map)

Within National Park Units:

1.	*Alagnak*	Katmai National Preserve
2.	*Alatna*	Gates of the Arctic National Park and Preserve
3.	*Aniakchak*	Aniakchak National Monument and Preserve
4.	*Charley*	Yukon-Charley Rivers National Preserve
5.	*Chilikadrotna*	Lake Clark National Park and Preserve
6.	*John*	Gates of the Arctic National Park and Preserve
7.	*Kobuk*	Gates of the Arctic National Park and Preserve
8.	*Mulchatna*	Lake Clark National Park and Preserve
9.	*Noatak*	Gates of the Arctic National Park and Noatak National Preserve
10.	*North Fork Koyukuk*	Gates of the Arctic National Park and Preserve
11.	*Salmon*	Kobuk Valley National Park
12.	*Tinayguk*	Gates of the Arctic National Park and Preserve
13.	*Tlikakila*	Lake Clark National Park

Within National Wildlife Refuges:

14.	*Andreafsky*	Yukon Delta National Wildlife Refuge
15.	*Ivishak*	Arctic National Wildlife Refuge
16.	*Nowitna*	Nowitna National Wildlife Refuge
17.	*Selawik*	Selawik National Wildlife Refuge
18.	*Sheenjek*	Arctic National Wildlife Refuge
19.	*Wind*	Arctic National Wildlife Refuge

Within Bureau of Land Management Units:

20.	*Beaver Creek*	The segment of the main stem from confluence of Bear and Champion creeks within White Mountain National Recreation Area and Yukon Flats National Wildlife Refuge
21.	*Birch Creek*	The segment of the main stem from the south side of Steese Highway downstream to approximately Twelve-mile House on Steese Highway, within Steese National Conservation Area

Rivers outside of designated preservation units:

22.	*Alagnak*	Those segments or portions of the main stem and Nonvianuk tributary lying outside and westward of Katmai National Park and Preserve
23.	*Delta*	The segment from and including all of the Tangle Lakes to a point one-half mile north of Black Rapids
24.	*Fortymile*	The main stem within the State of Alaska plus tributaries
25.	*Gulkana*	The main stem from the outlet of Paxson Lake to the confluence with Sourdough Creek; various segments of the west fork and middle fork
26.	*Unalakleet*	Approximately 65 miles of the main stem.

Designated for study for inclusion in Wild and Scenic River System:

Colville River	Koyuk River	Situk River
Etivluk-Nigu Rivers	Melozitna River	Squirrel River
Kanektok River	Porcupine River	Utukok River
Kisaralik River	Sheenjek River (lower segment)	Yukon River (Ramparts section)

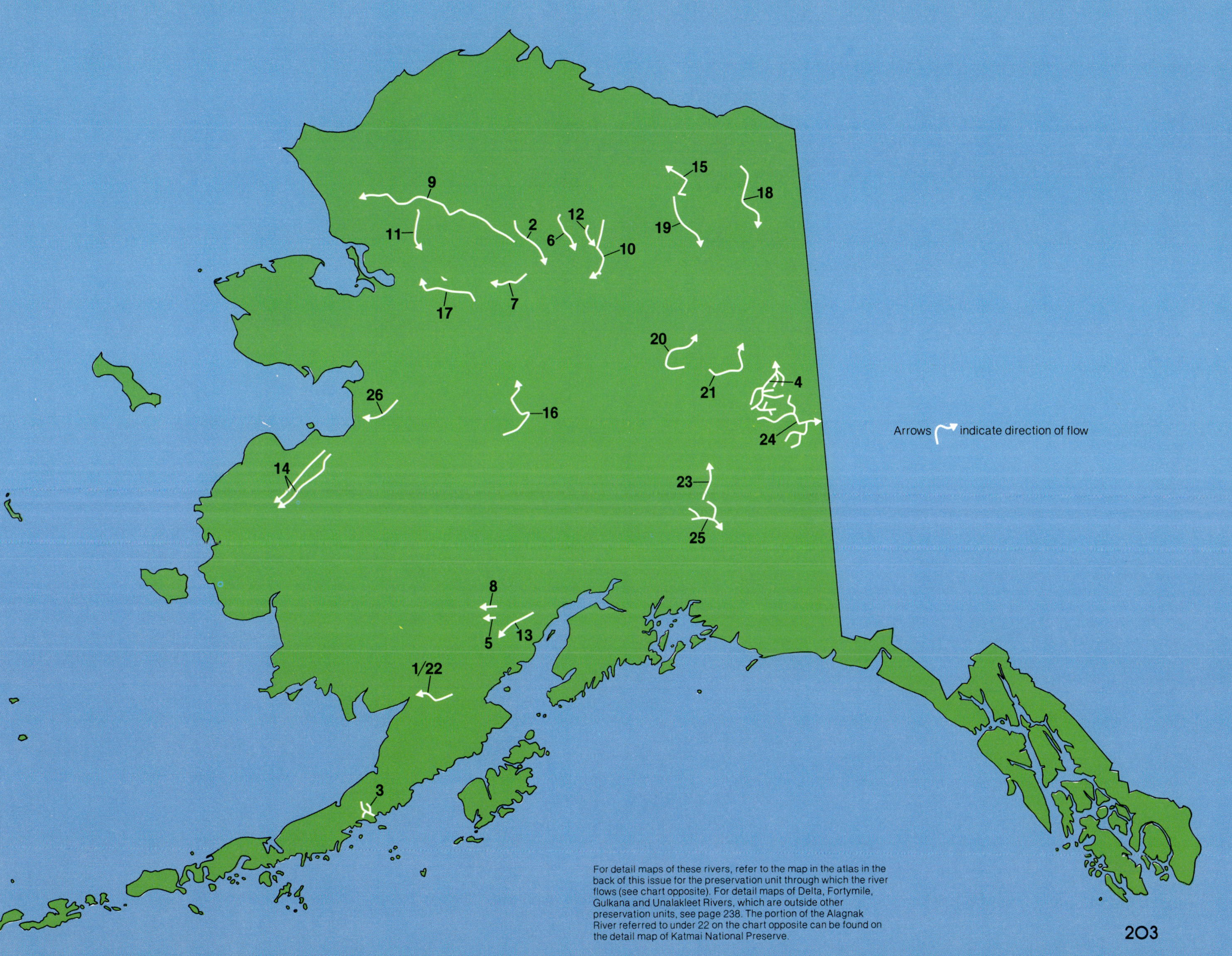

For detail maps of these rivers, refer to the map in the atlas in the back of this issue for the preservation unit through which the river flows (see chart opposite). For detail maps of Delta, Fortymile, Gulkana and Unalakleet Rivers, which are outside other preservation units, see page 238. The portion of the Alagnak River referred to under 22 on the chart opposite can be found on the detail map of Katmai National Preserve.

Top: Brilliant fall colors surround the Alagnak River, near Katmai National Park and Preserve. (Doug Hunt)

Above: Beaver Creek flows through the White Mountains National Recreation Area. (Jo Keller, U.S. Fish & Wildlife Service)

Right: The Alatna River, in Gates of the Arctic National Park and Preserve, weaves its way south from the Arrigetch Peaks to the Koyukuk River. (John & Margaret Ibbotson)

Left: This aerial view shows the Situk River entering the Pacific Ocean, near Yakutat. (K.W. Tarr)

Below: The Nowitna River, shown here at its confluence with the Big Mud River, has been designated a Wild and Scenic River. (Dave Patterson)

Left: The Unalakleet River winds through a flat marshy area to its delta at the village of Unalakleet, on Norton Sound. (George Wuerthner)

Overleaf: The Noatak River flows westward from its headwaters in the central Brooks Range, shown here, more than 400 miles to its delta in Kotzebue Sound. (Walt Quade)

Bureau
of
Land
Management

White Mountains National Recreation Area and Steese National Conservation Area

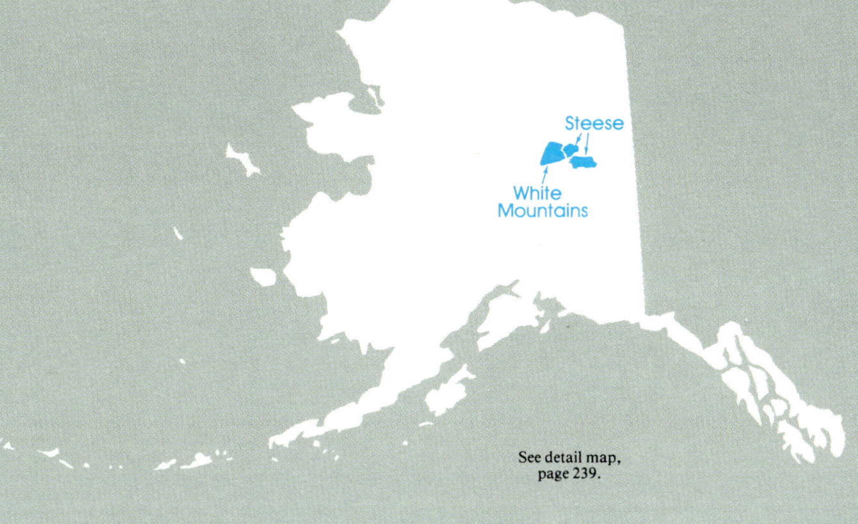

See detail map, page 239.

Setting: Adjacent to the Steese Highway about 100 miles north of Fairbanks. The Steese Conservation Area consists of two portions, which total 1,220,000 acres. One area is situated on the northern side of the Steese Highway, adjacent to the White Mountains National Recreation Area; the other lies south and east within the drainage of Birch Creek.

The one-million-acre White Mountains National Recreation Area is located on the northern side of the Steese Highway, enclosing the Beaver Creek drainage and some high peaks of the White Mountains.

Left: Spruce and birch create a colorful mosaic in the Steese National Conservation Area. This unit is separated into two parts, one on each side of the Steese Highway. (Robert Langlotz)

Purpose: Both of these areas were given special classification and protection because they include representative land forms, wildlife habitat and vegetation complexes peculiar to the interior Alaska uplands, ranging from spruce and birch, to willow and alder and finally to alpine tundra, with accompanying species.

These classifications still permit mining of valid existing claims, and access thereto, but in the recreation area, no additional mining claims may be staked. In both areas, patenting of mining claims is limited to minerals and not to surface rights to the land.

Two wild and scenic rivers are included in these units. Major portions of Beaver Creek are located in the White Mountains National Recreation Area and Birch Creek is classified as wild and scenic on that portion within Steese National Conservation Area. In both cases a small portion of the classified streams are outside the protected classification on public domain land.

Wilderness Travel in Alaska

Below: Even cross-country travelers with day packs, like this adventurer, have to contend with snow and ice when exploring the Alaska Range. (George Wuerthner)

Right: A pack string crosses a swift-flowing stream in Denali. (Ginny Wood)

Remoteness, vastness, topography and latitude dictate that access, tourist facilities and management policies for the new parks, refuges, and monuments in Alaska will differ in many ways from those in the lower states. Visitors expecting the same type of accommodations, amenities and regulations that they find in Yosemite, Yellowstone or the Great Smokies will be surprised at the lack of them in Alaska's national interest lands. Whether or not they are officially classified as wilderness, most of the lands in almost all of the units described in this book are essentially undeveloped and probably will remain so for years to come. And therein lies their uniqueness and appeal.

Those who will want to visit and experience these crown jewels of the North should be forewarned and forearmed. Proper clothing and equipment specific for the activity and area involved are essential, not only for maximum enjoyment, but sometimes for survival. This does not mean that unless one has the stamina and experience needed to climb Mount McKinley, one is excluded from Alaska's wild lands. Families with youngsters can be set down by plane on a secluded lake to camp or to stay at a U.S. Forest Service cabin for a few days or a week, then be picked up again — a vacation that requires little more preparation or experience than needed to car camp in a national park or forest in Washington State. However, there is no handy grocery store or friendly ranger nearby.

Backpackers of both sexes in their fifties and sixties are not uncommon on guided expeditions into the rugged Brooks Range. Experienced outfitters and guides operate raft, cross-country ski, hiking and dog team trips down wild rivers and into remote wilderness areas of

Alaska for a wide range of clients for whom adventure and close encounters with pristine nature on its own terms are more important than luxury hotels, gourmet cuisine or improved campgrounds for motor homes.

For those who wish to go it on their own by foot or hand-propelled watercraft in back country, here are a few points of information and tips on Alaska wilderness travel.

Access: Except for Denali (formerly Mount McKinley National Park) and the periphery of the Wrangell-Saint Elias National Park and Preserves; and the Kenai and Tetlin national wildlife refuges, there is no improved connecting highway access to the parks, preserves, monuments and refuges in Alaska. Transportation is limited to small chartered aircraft and boats. Landing areas for the former are usually lakes or sand bars. For the U.S. Forest Service monuments and wilderness areas in Southeastern, access is generally by small boat or floatplane from transportation centers served by the Alaska ferry system or commercial, scheduled airlines.

Routes: Within the units, a visitor will find few man-made trails or signposts. Knowledge of the use of topographical maps and a compass is imperative. No foot bridges or cable cars will carry the traveler over streams and rivers that cross his path. A heavy downpour of rain or melting glaciers from high summer temperatures can cause a stream that is ankle deep in the early morning to be a hip-deep torrent in the afternoon. Streams will be the most shallow and usually have less cur-

Above: Hardy hikers climb a rocky slope in the Tinayguk River Valley. Robert Marshall, early explorer in the Gates of the Arctic, recommended that this valley be named for the Eskimo word for moose because of the abundance of these large mammals here. (George Wuerthner)

Overleaf: River runners set up camp on a sandy beach at the junction of the Noatak and Cutler rivers in Noatak National Preserve. The Cutler heads in the eastern Baird Mountains and flows 45 miles north to the Noatak, 45 miles southwest of Howard Pass. Lt. George Stoney, one of the first explorers in the region, named this river the Caribou, but delay in publishing his report led to acceptance of the name Cutler. (John and Margaret Ibbotson)

rent where they are the broadest or most braided. Always wear shoes when fording streams as most of them are excruciatingly cold and a rock rolled on a bare foot can result in a bad bruise or fracture.

Fuel and Fires: The tree line in Alaska is erratic. All of the Aleutian Islands, the greater part of the Alaska Peninsula in the southwest, the Bering Sea coastal plain as well as the north slope of the Brooks Range are devoid of trees. Timberline ranges from 1,500 to 2,500 feet in interior Alaska, and above that altitude is tundra.

Beyond tree line, firewood is limited to clumps of willows and alders, and cannot sustain heavy backcountry use. Primus stoves using gasoline or kerosene (not butane or propane because the empty containers must be packed out) are a necessity. Primus fuel is not allowed on scheduled airlines, so make arrangements with your bush pilot, who can transport it, to have a supply available when you are flown in.

Where dead wood is plentiful (never cut a slow-growing green tree), campfires should be kindled only on gravel bars or where there is mineral soil. The tundra, although damp to the touch, is a veritable peat bog, that, once ignited, can burn underground, even under the snow, for several years. And the lichens, essential for caribou sustenance, can take up to 100 years to regrow. Eradicate all evidence of your campfire when you leave, so others may experience the feeling of "I'm the first here."

Beasts and Bugs: Wildlife, especially species such as the brown/grizzly bear, the wolf and caribou, which are vanishing or are not found elsewhere, gives added dimensions to the Alaska wilderness. Only the bears and moose can be life-threatening, and then very seldom. Others like the red squirrel and the arctic ground squirrel can be more of a nuisance if they chew into a tent and get at the grub. In contrast to regulations in parks and monuments in the continental United States, guns for protection are allowed in new Alaska parks and preserves except where expressly prohibited, such as within the former boundaries of Mount McKinley National Park (now included in Denali National Park).

The odds of meeting a malicious bear, as long as it is not provoked, are slight. Guns are heavy and can be dangerous in themselves. If a gun is taken along, be sure it is of the right caliber for thick bear skulls and that the shooter knows how to use it skillfully. More important, make noise when in brush or thick forest, do not get between a mother and a cub or moose calf or provoke by getting too close with a camera. Do not carry odoriferous food such as bacon or leave garbage around.

Mosquitoes are thickest just after the snow and the ice on ponds melt, dwindling off towards mid-summer and fall. Gnats and noseeums come after the mosquitoes are no longer a problem. Carry a good bug repellent and a head net. Be sure to have a screened tent that can keep out the smallest of bugs.

Weather: Always expect the unexpected, as far as weather is concerned. Be equipped with good lightweight raingear and hope that it won't be needed too often. Hypothermia can strike even in temperatures above freezing with wind, exhaustion, and damp clothing. Don't forget sunglasses and lotion.

Tents should be of good quality and able to withstand strong winds, especially above timberline. As frozen ground is quite often found a few feet below the surface, especially in the Interior and Arctic, take a foam pad to insulate under a sleeping bag.

Be prepared to have to wait out the weather when depending on small bush plane transportation. The terrain is rugged and there are no navigational aids to facilitate landing in remote areas. Plan food and on-going schedules accordingly. In interior and northern Alaska a flashlight is unneccessary from May to mid-August.

Impact: The boreal and tundra environment is fragile. Trampled plants take much longer to recover than in temperate climates; tin cans, plastics and tinfoil become embalmed rather than decaying. Frost will heave up any refuse that is buried, so pack out anything except paper, which can be burned. Plan menus accordingly. Fishing can vary from mediocre to fantastic, but do not plan to live off the land. When traveling through Native-owned lands and villages, remember that you are an intruder and their guest. Treat Natives and their lands with courtesy and respect.

Further information and details about routes, plane charters and outfitters and guides in any particular area can be obtained by contacting offices of the National Park Service, U.S. Fish & Wildlife Service, and the U.S. Forest Service. Addresses for particular units will be found where descriptions of those units appear.

For information about guided trips, contact The Alaska Association of Mountain and Wilderness Guides, Box 3685, Anchorage, Alaska 99510, as one source. This is a non-profit organization representing many of the guides and outfitters working in Alaska.

Atlas
Alaska National Interest Lands

*Detailed color maps follow for the areas listed below. Some of
those maps include areas of gray diagonal shading to illustrate
the abuttal of other national interest lands to the specific area.*

National Park System

Aniakchak National
Monument and Preserve

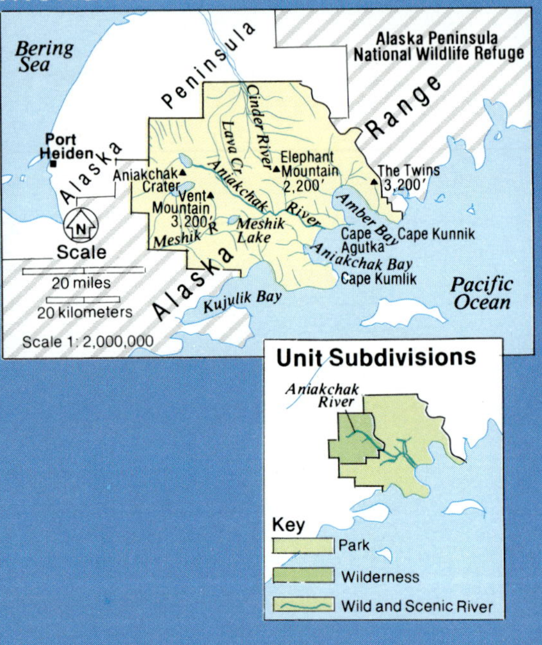
Bering
Sea
Peninsula
Alaska Peninsula
National Wildlife Refuge
Range
Port
Heiden
Cinder River
Alaska
Aniakchak
Crater
Vent
Mountain
3,200'
Lava Cr.
Elephant
Mountain
2,200'
The Twins
3,200'
Aniakchak River
Amber Bay
Meshik
Cape Kunnik
Meshik
Lake
Cape Bay
Agutka
Aniakchak Bay
Alaska
Cape Kumlik
Kujulik Bay
Pacific
Ocean
N
Scale
20 miles
20 kilometers
Scale 1: 2,000,000

Unit Subdivisions
Aniakchak
River
Key
Park
Wilderness
Wild and Scenic River

Bering Land Bridge National Preserve

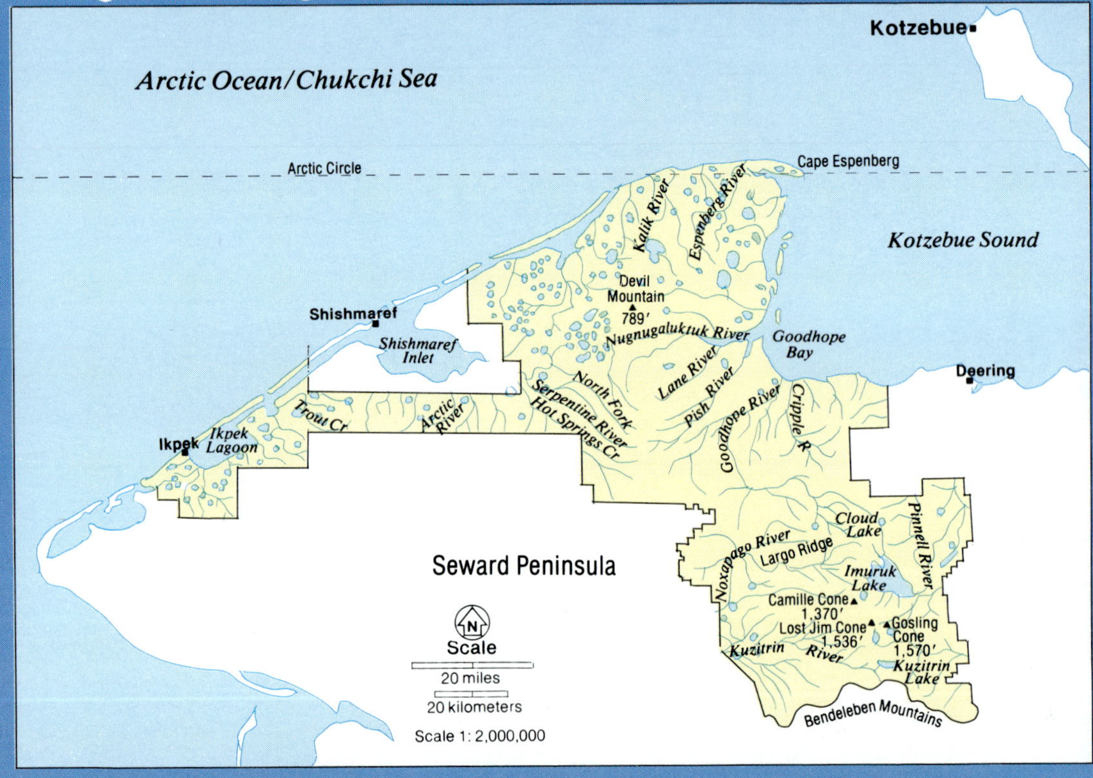
Kotzebue
Arctic Ocean/Chukchi Sea
Arctic Circle
Cape Espenberg
Kotzebue Sound
Kalik River
Espenberg River
Devil
Mountain
789'
Goodhope
Bay
Shishmaref
Nugnugaluktuk River
Deering
Shishmaref
Inlet
Lane River
North Fork
Pish River
Goodhope River
Cripple R.
Trout Cr.
Arctic River
Serpentine River
Hot Springs Cr.
Ikpek
Ikpek
Lagoon
Cloud
Lake
Pinnell River
Noxapaga River
Largo Ridge
Imuruk
Lake
Seward Peninsula
Camille Cone
1,370'
Lost Jim Cone
1,536'
Gosling
Cone
1,570'
N
Scale
Kuzitrin
Kuzitrin
River
Kuzitrin
Lake
20 miles
20 kilometers
Bendeleben Mountains
Scale 1: 2,000,000

Cape Krusenstern National Monument

Denali National Park and Preserve

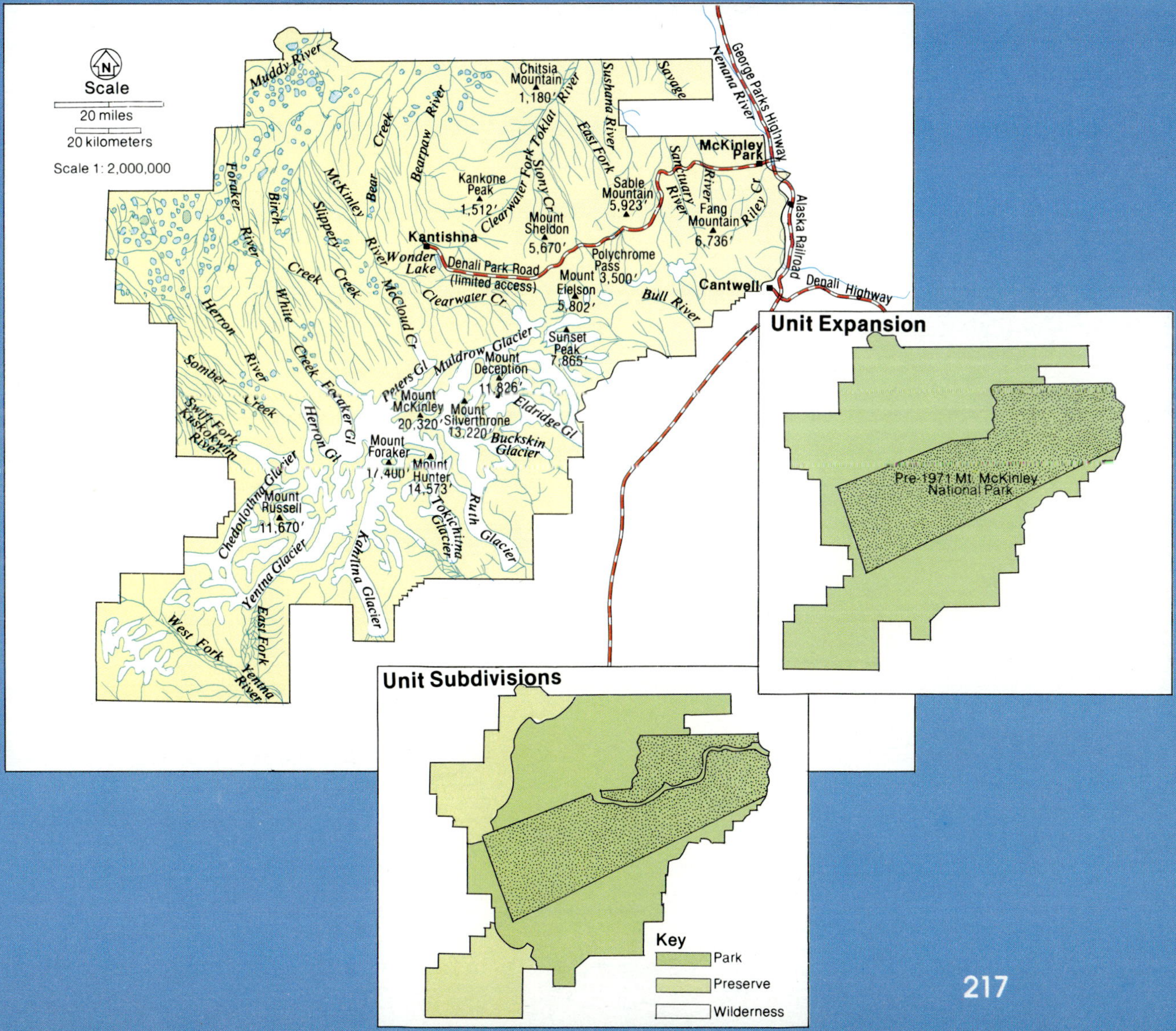

Unit Expansion

Unit Subdivisions

Gates of the Arctic National Park and Preserve

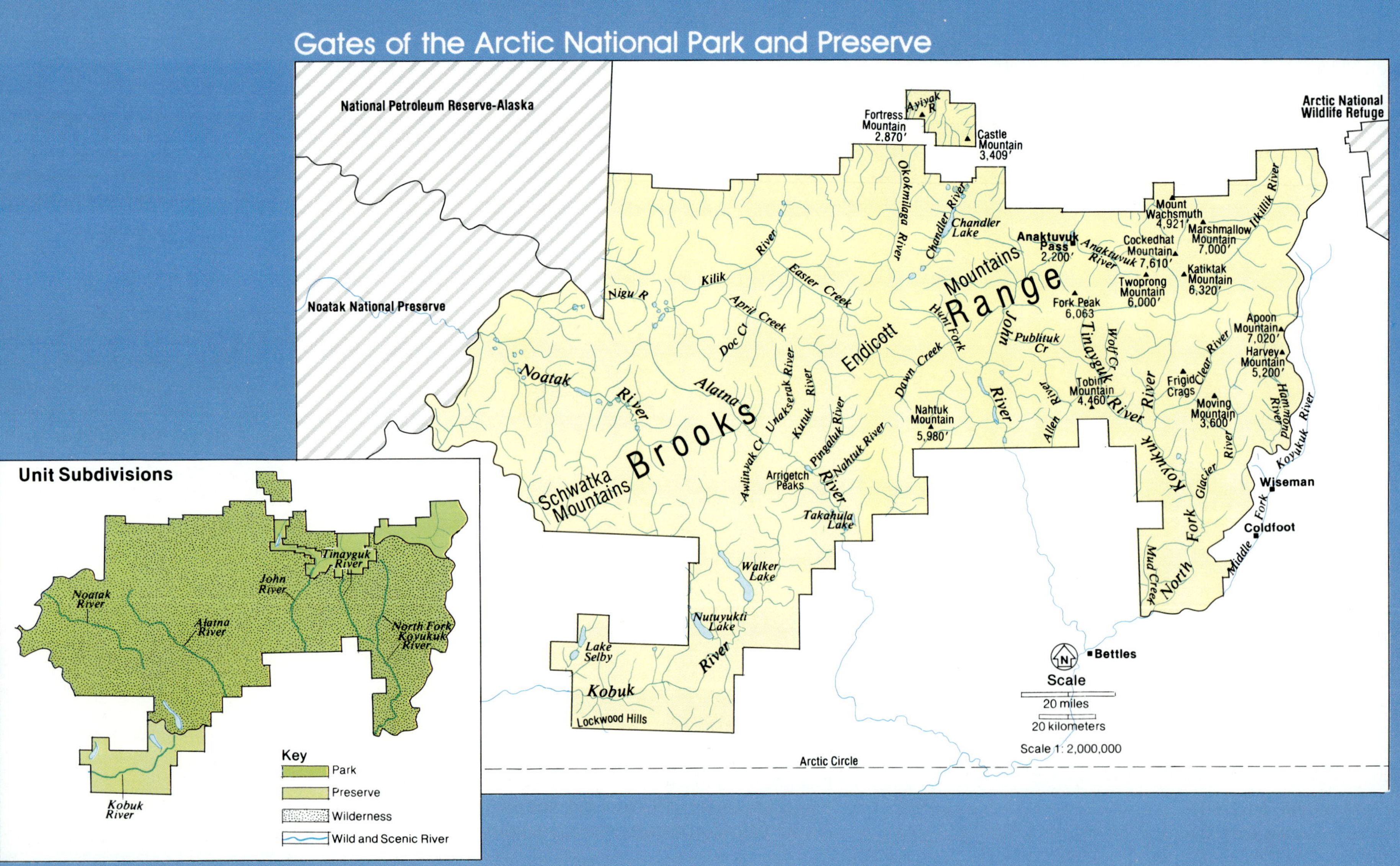

Unit Subdivisions

Glacier Bay National Park and Preserve

Unit Expansion

Unit Subdivisions

Katmai National Park and Preserve

Unit Expansion

Unit Subdivisions

Kenai Fjords National Park

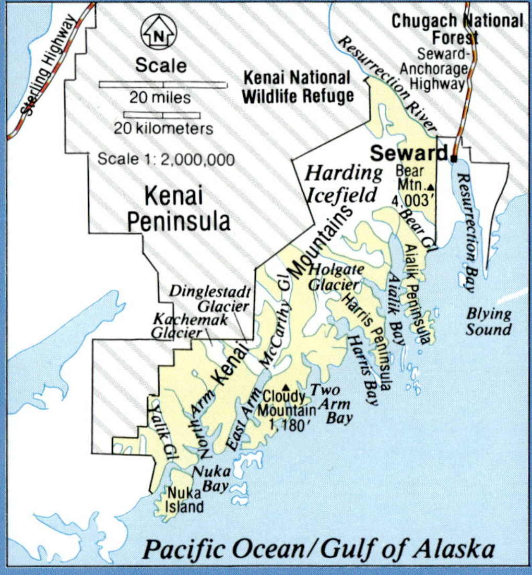

Kobuk Valley National Park

Unit Subdivisions

Lake Clark National Park and Preserve

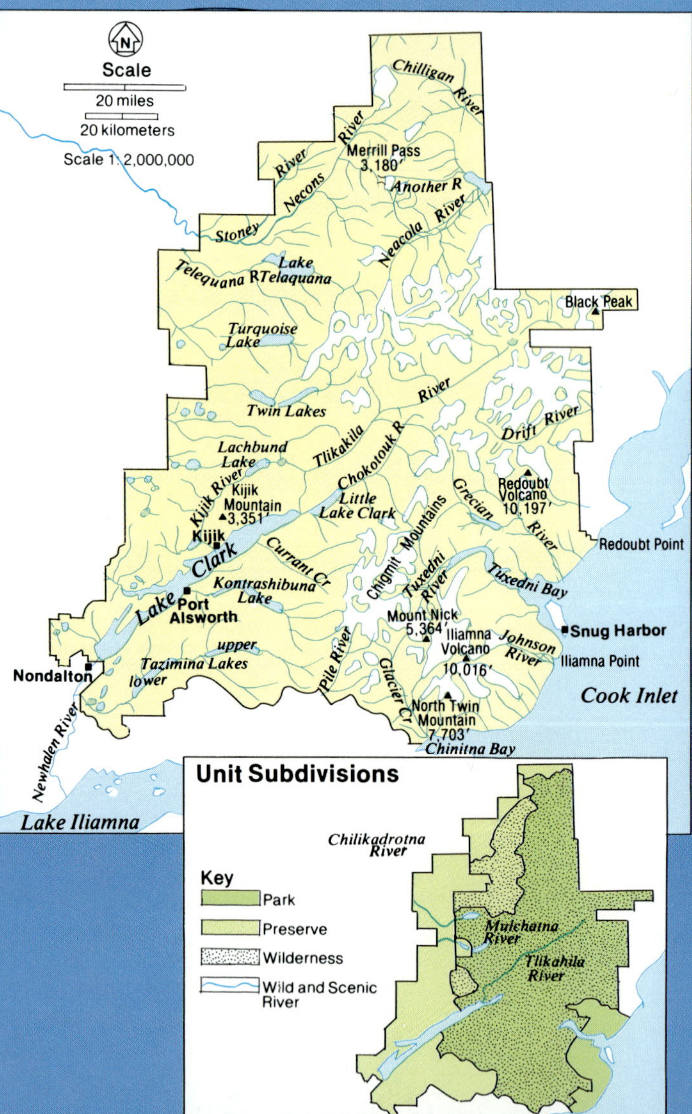

Unit Subdivisions

Noatak National Preserve

Unit Subdivisions

Wrangell-St. Elias National Park and Preserve

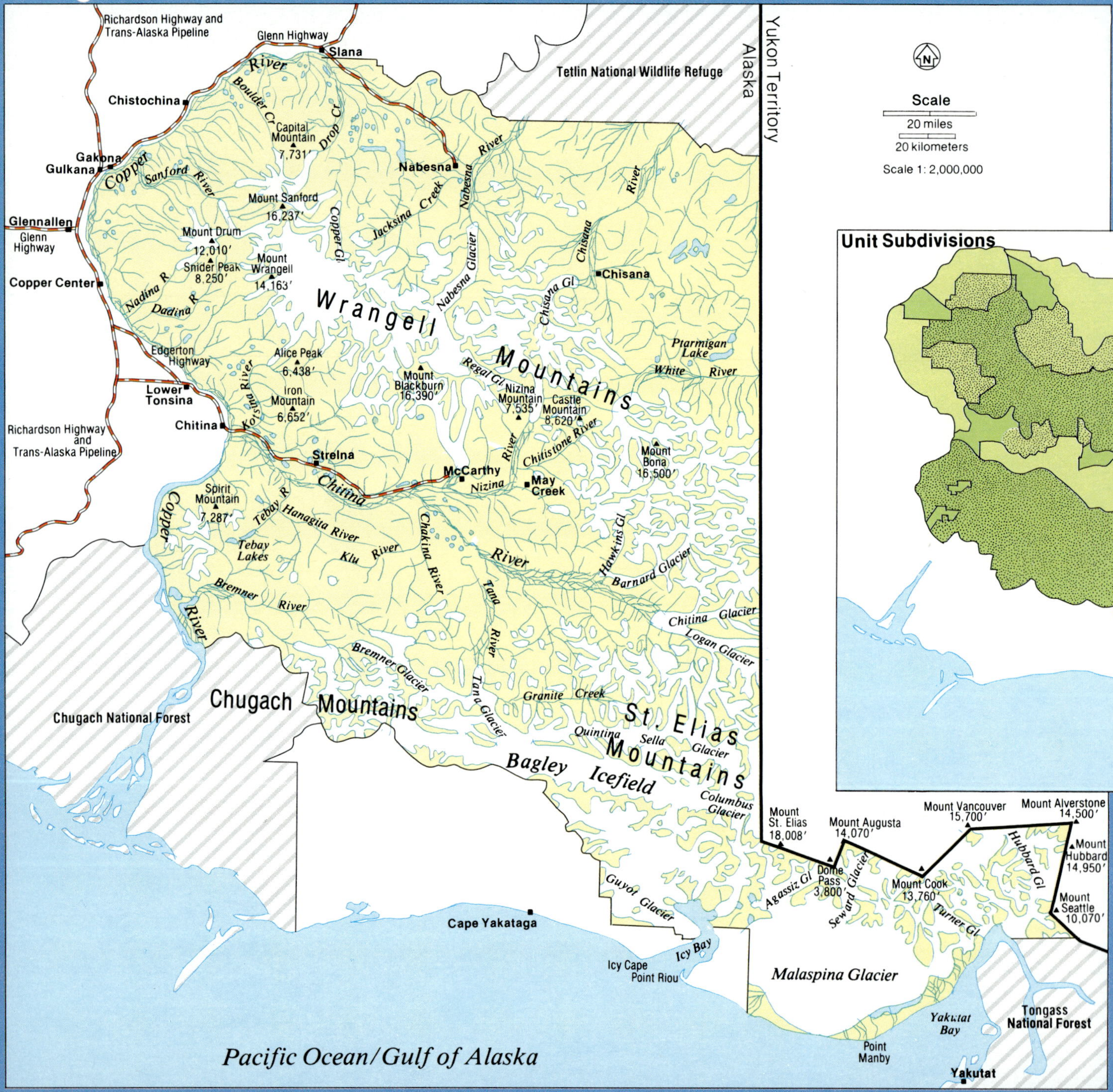

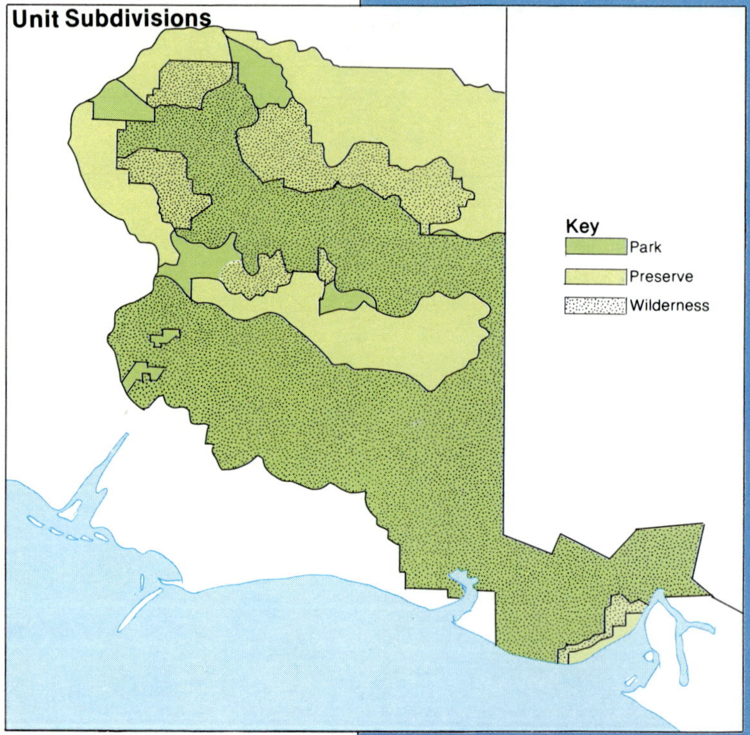

Yukon-Charley Rivers National Preserve

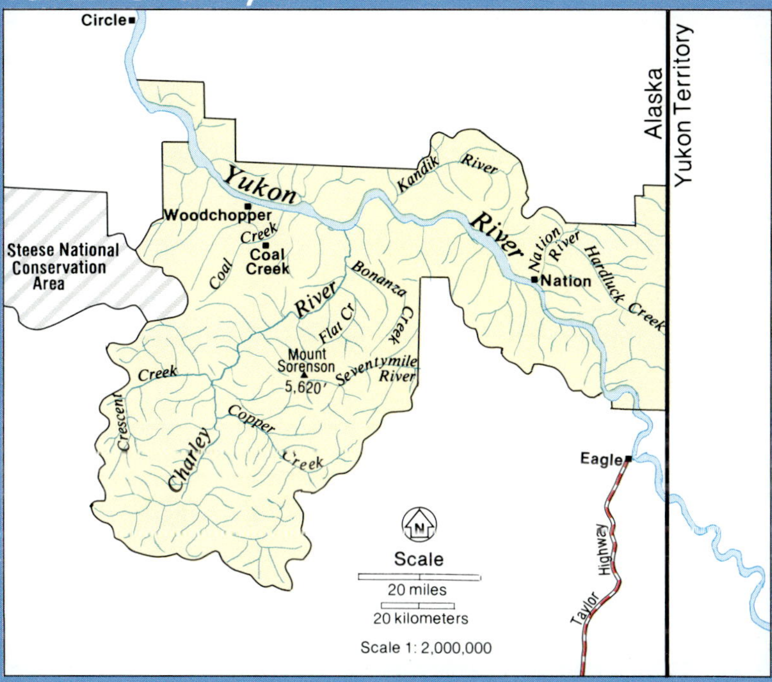

National Wildlife Refuge System

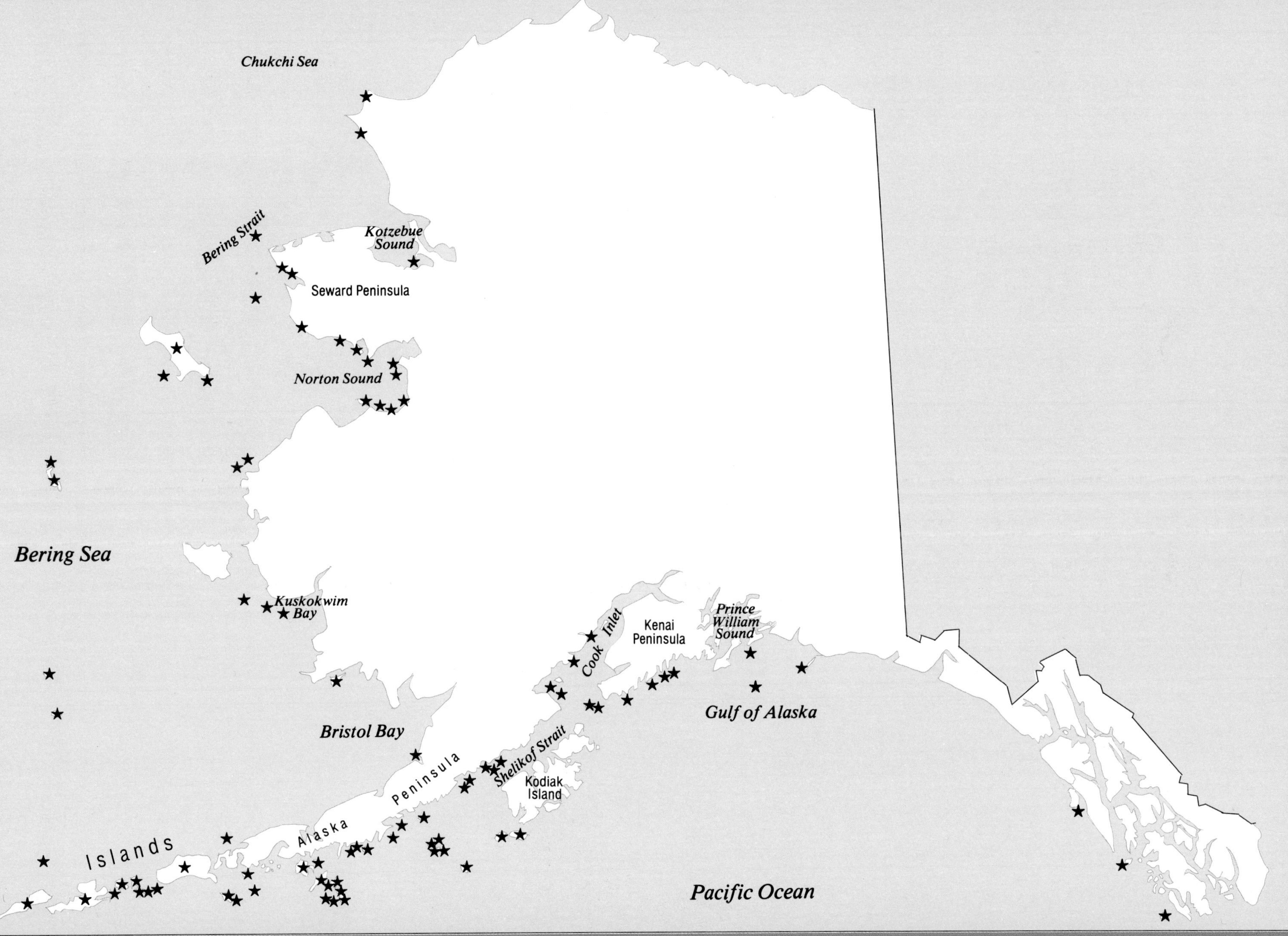

Arctic Ocean
Chukchi Sea
Bering Strait
Kotzebue Sound
Seward Peninsula
Norton Sound
Bering Sea
Kuskokwim Bay
Kenai Peninsula
Cook Inlet
Prince William Sound
Bristol Bay
Peninsula
Shelikof Strait
Kodiak Island
Gulf of Alaska
Alaska
Islands
Pacific Ocean

Alaska Peninsula National Wildlife Refuge

Arctic National Wildlife Refuge

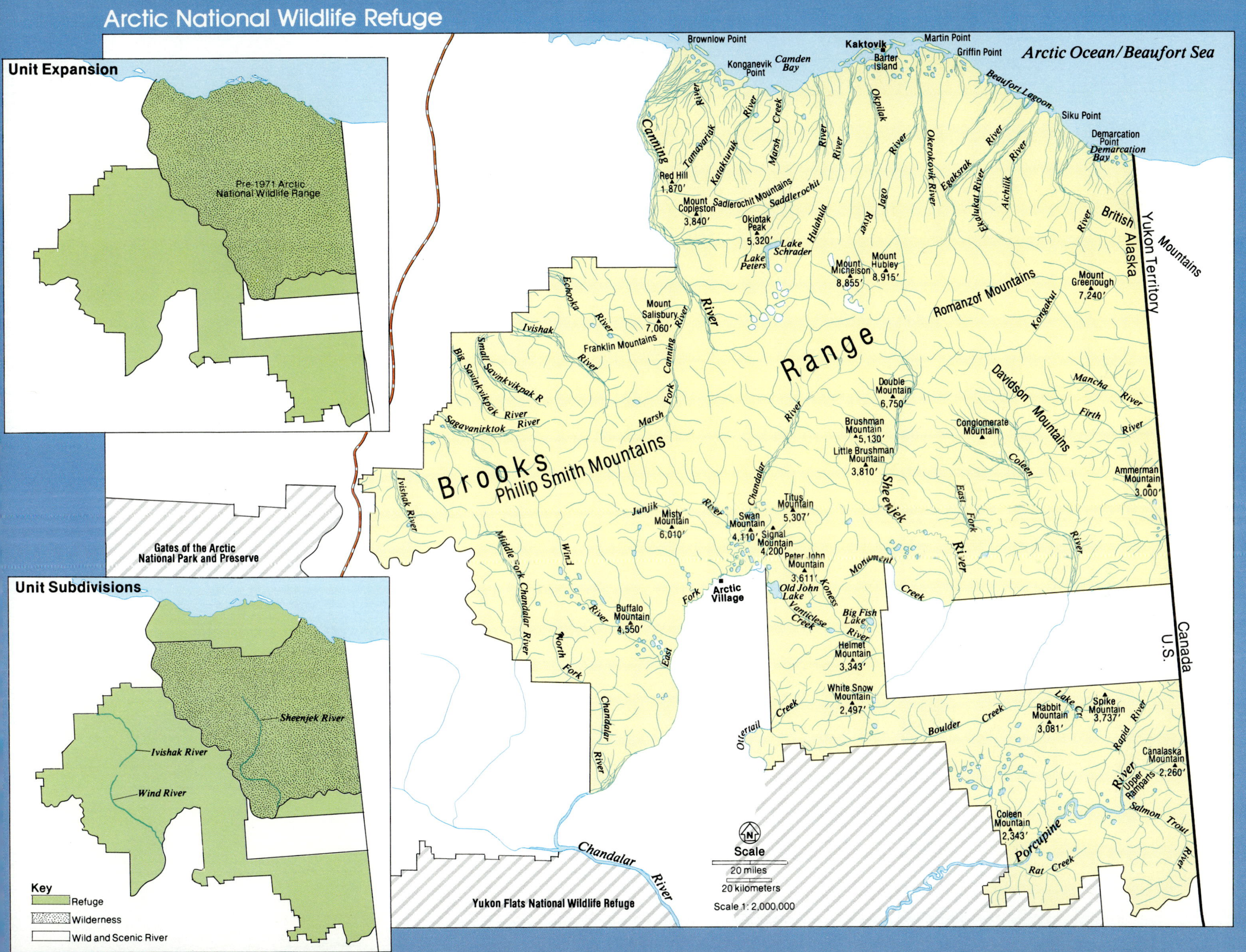

Becharof National Wildlife Refuge

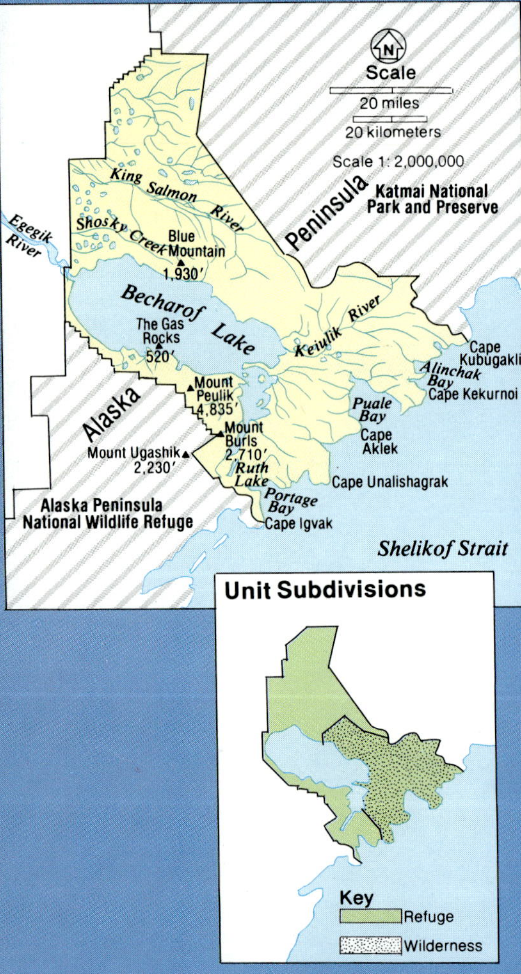

Innoko National Wildlife Refuge

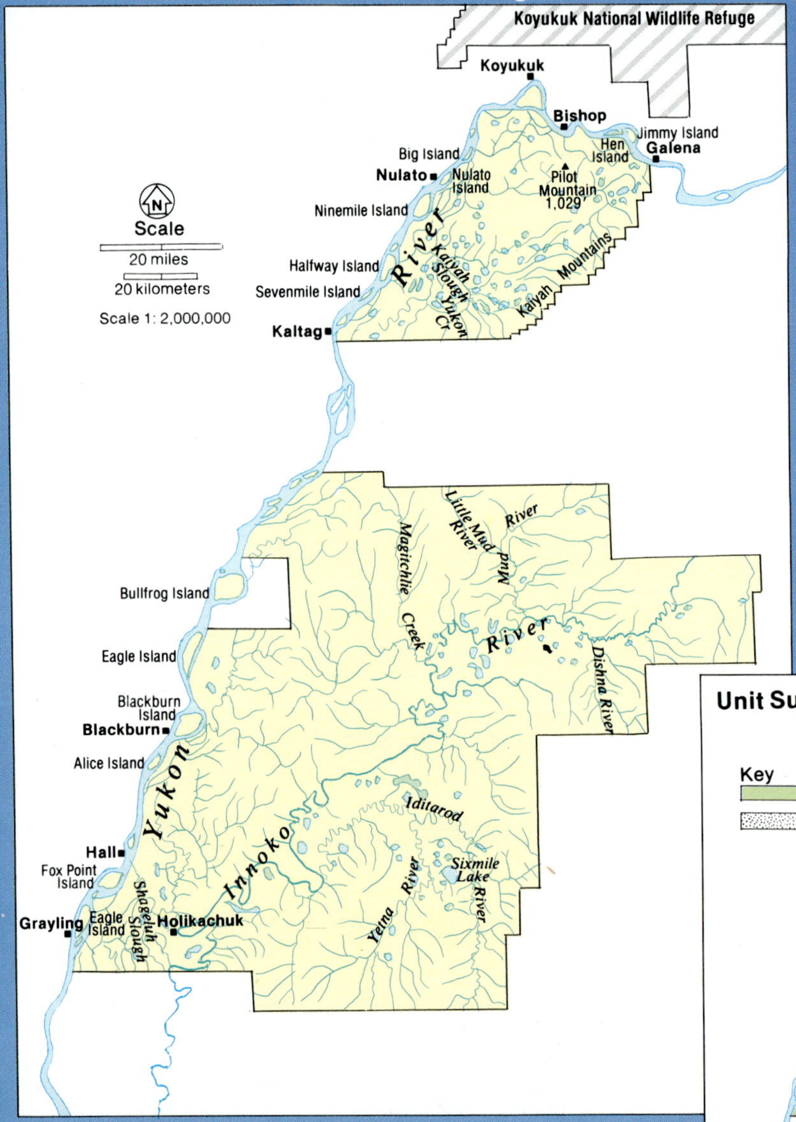

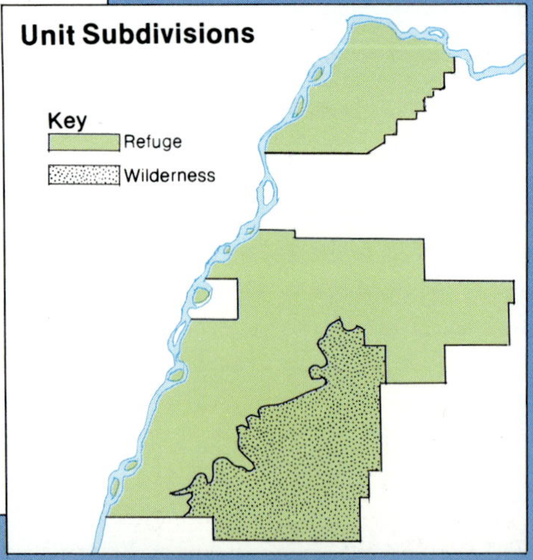

Izembek National Wildlife Refuge

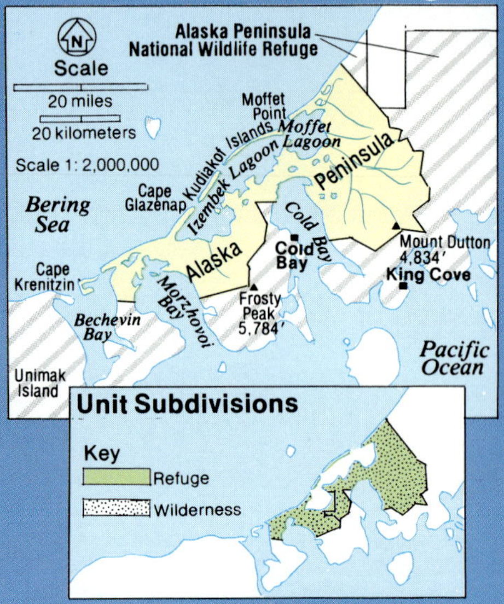

Kanuti
National Wildlife Refuge

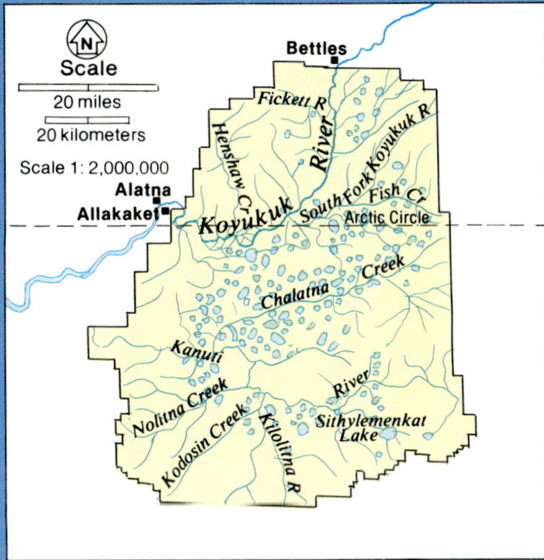

Kenai
National Wildlife Refuge

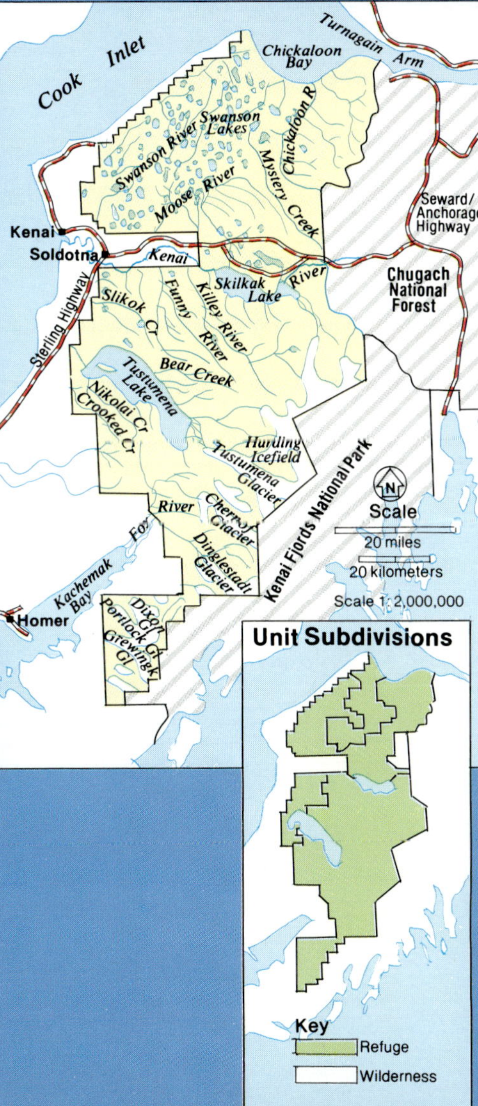

Unit Subdivisions

Kodiak National Wildlife Refuge

Koyukuk National Wildlife Refuge

Nowitna National Wildlife Refuge

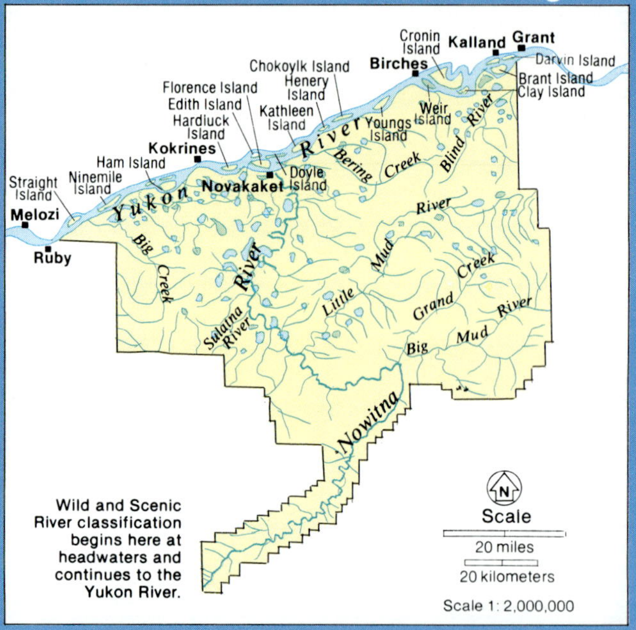

Unit Subdivisions

Selawik National Wildlife Refuge

Unit Subdivisions

Tetlin National Wildlife Refuge

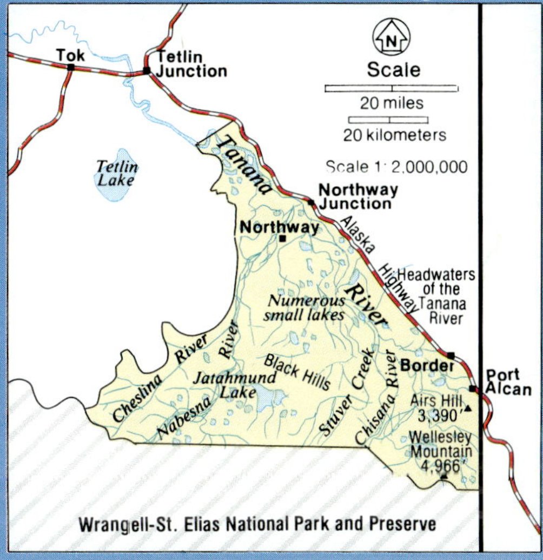

Togiak National Wildlife Refuge

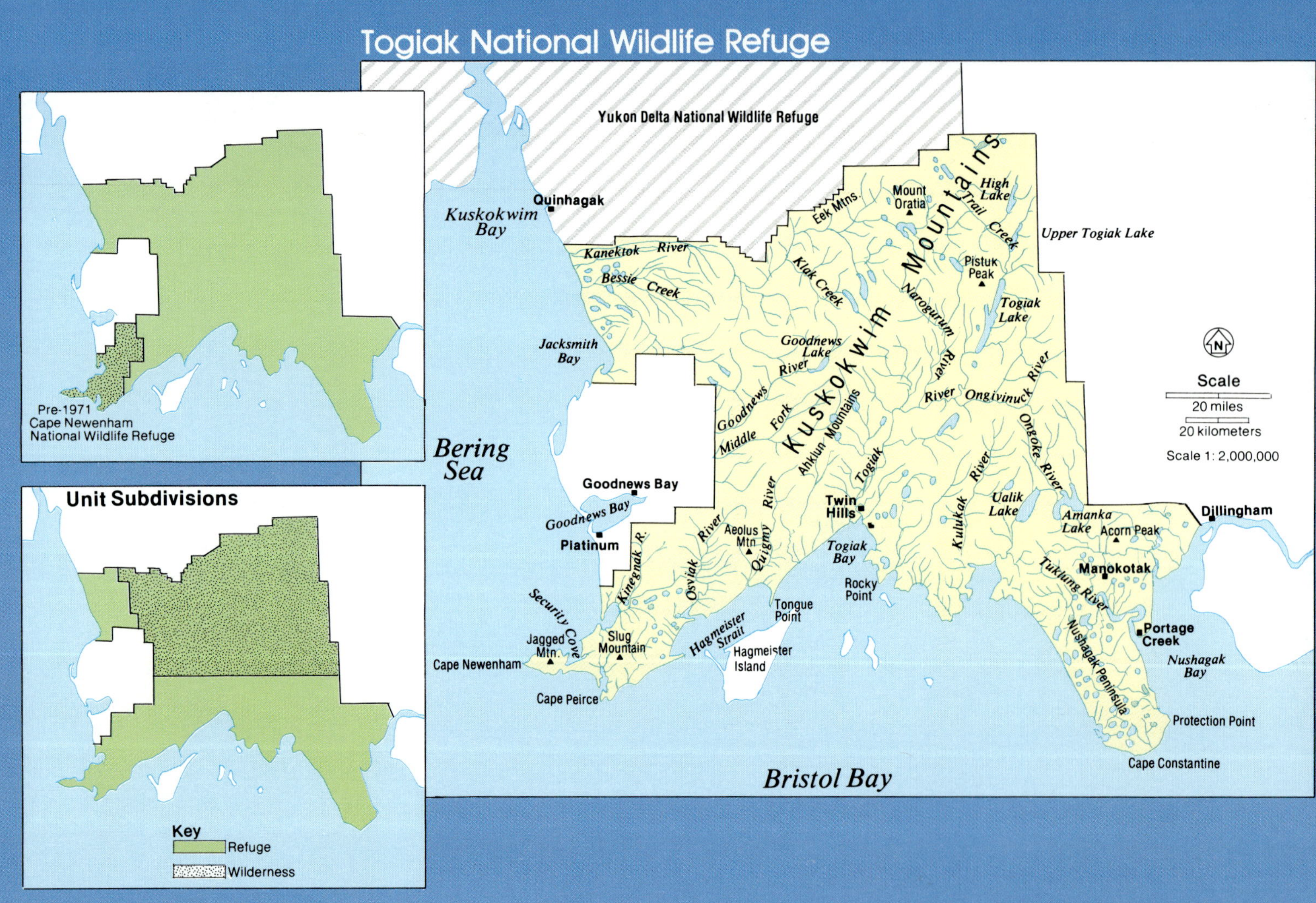

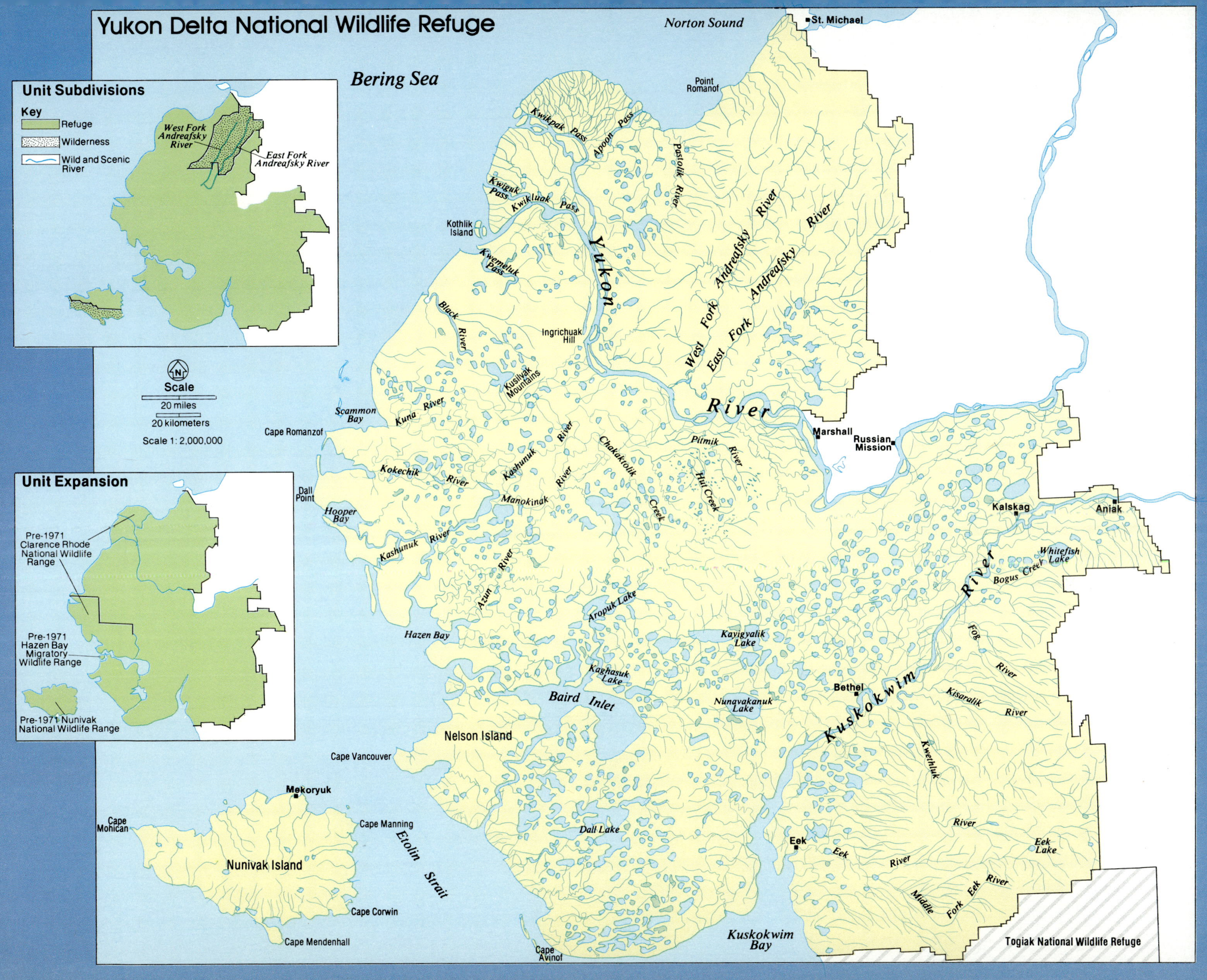
Yukon Delta National Wildlife Refuge
Norton Sound
St. Michael
Bering Sea
Unit Subdivisions
Key
Refuge
Wilderness
Wild and Scenic River
West Fork Andreafsky River
East Fork Andreafsky River
Point Romanof
Kwikpak Pass
Apoon Pass
Pastolik River
Kwiguk Pass
Kwikluak Pass
Kothlik Island
Kwemeluk Pass
Yukon
West Fork Andreafsky River
East Fork Andreafsky River
Black River
Ingrichuak Hill
Kusilvak Mountains
River
Scale
20 miles
20 kilometers
Scale 1: 2,000,000
Scammon Bay
Kuna River
Kashunuk River
River
Chakaktolik Creek
Pilmik River
Hul Creek
Marshall
Russian Mission
Cape Romanzof
Unit Expansion
Pre-1971 Clarence Rhode National Wildlife Range
Pre-1971 Hazen Bay Migratory Wildlife Range
Pre-1971 Nunivak National Wildlife Range
Dall Point
Kokechik
Manokinak River
Hooper Bay
Kashunuk River
Azun River
Kalskag
Aniak
Whitefish Lake
Bogus Creek
Hazen Bay
Aropuk Lake
Kayigyalik Lake
Fog River
Kaghasuk Lake
Baird Inlet
Nunavakanuk Lake
Bethel
Kisaralik River
Kuskokwim
Nelson Island
Cape Vancouver
Kwethluk
Mekoryuk
Cape Manning
Cape Mohican
Eziolin Strait
Nunivak Island
Dall Lake
Eek
Eek River
River
Eek Lake
Cape Corwin
Middle Fork Eek River
Cape Mendenhall
Cape Avinof
Kuskokwim Bay
Togiak National Wildlife Refuge

Yukon Flats National Wildlife Refuge

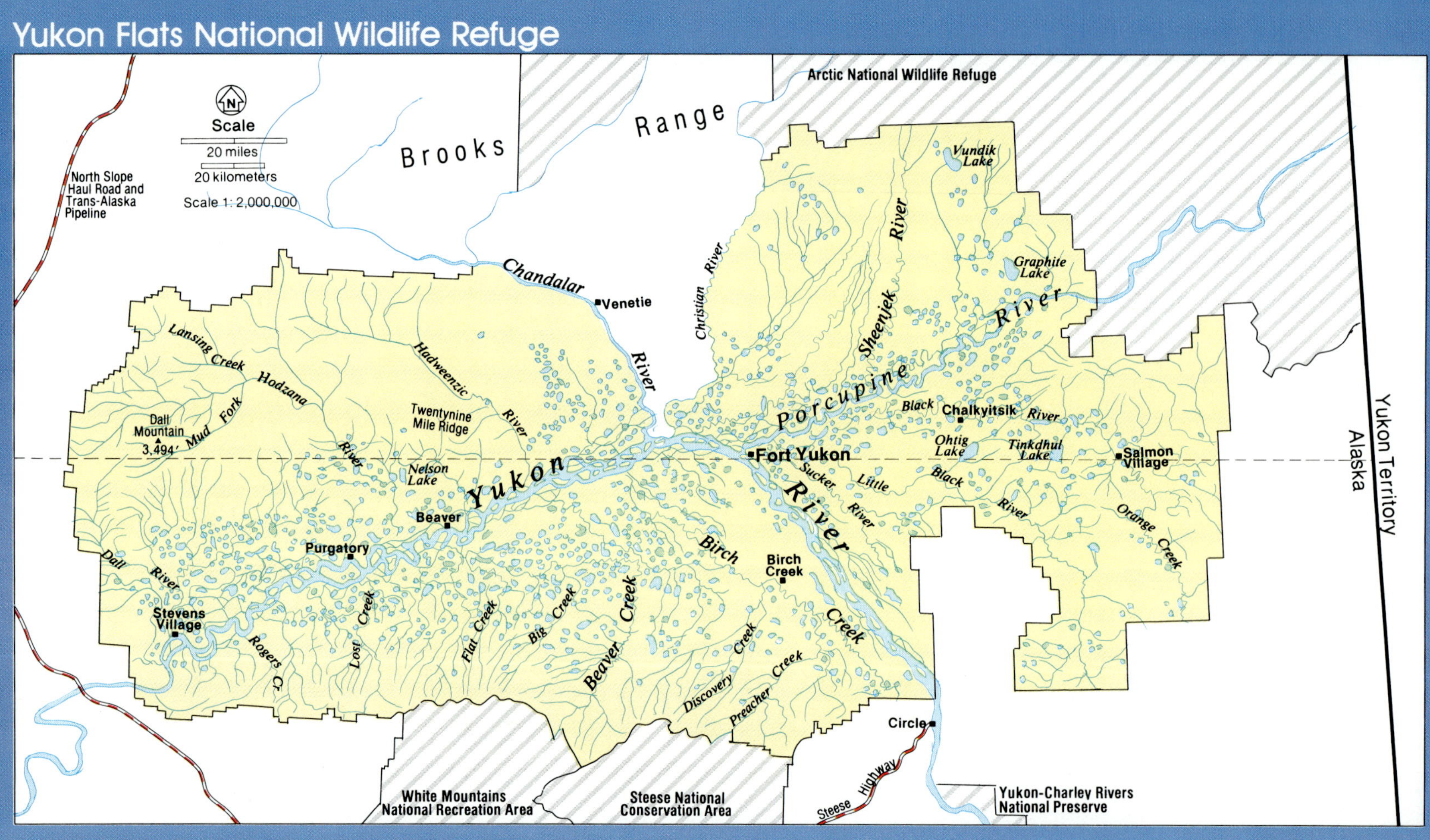

National Forest System

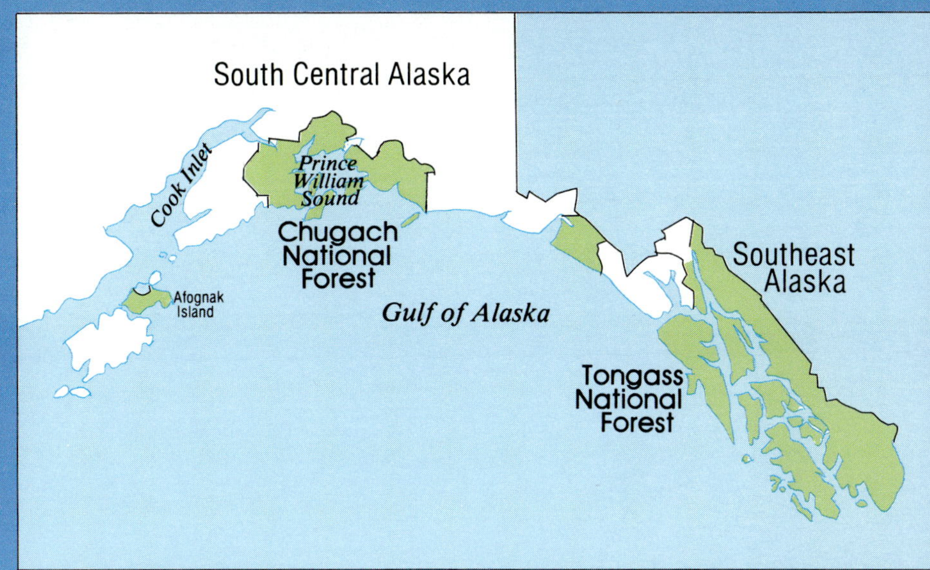

Chugach National Forest

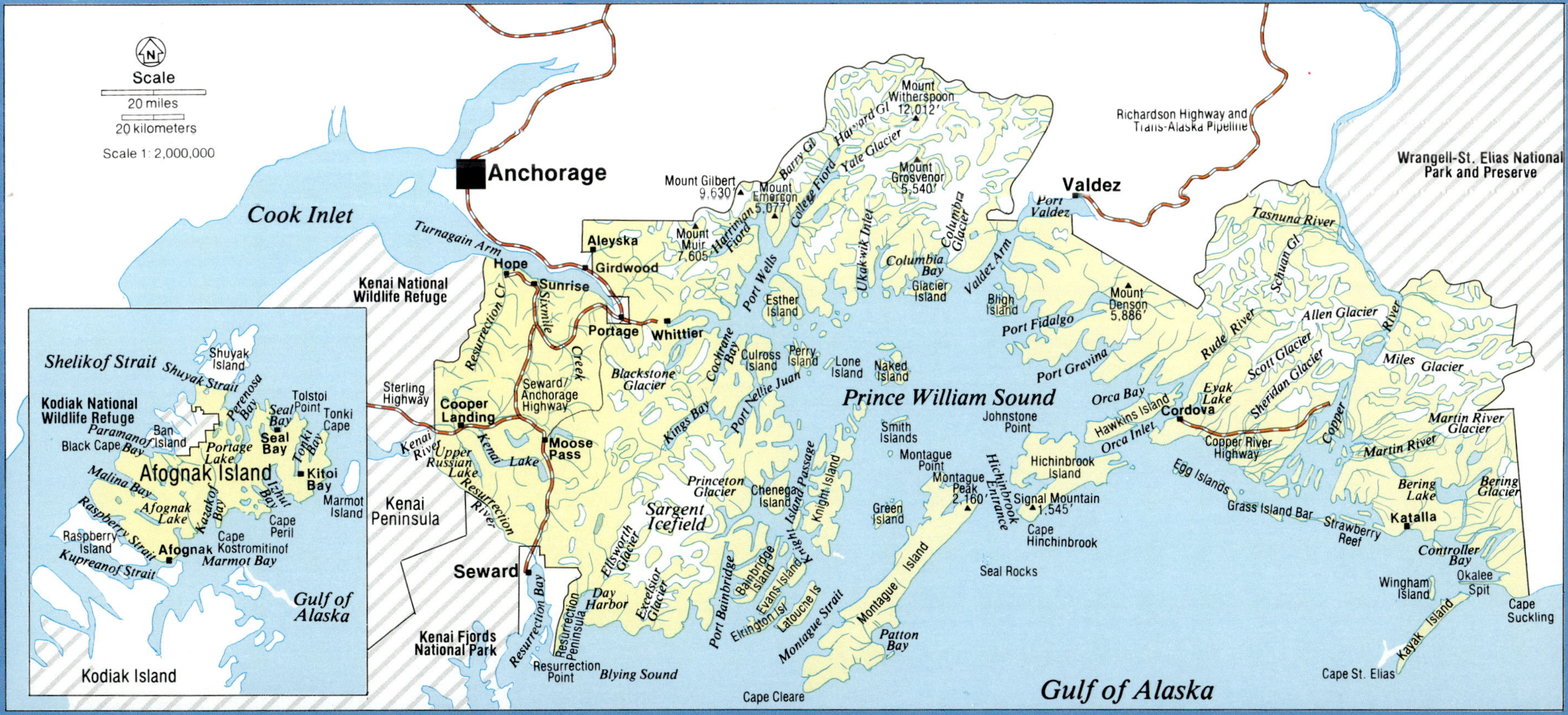

"""

Tongass National Forest

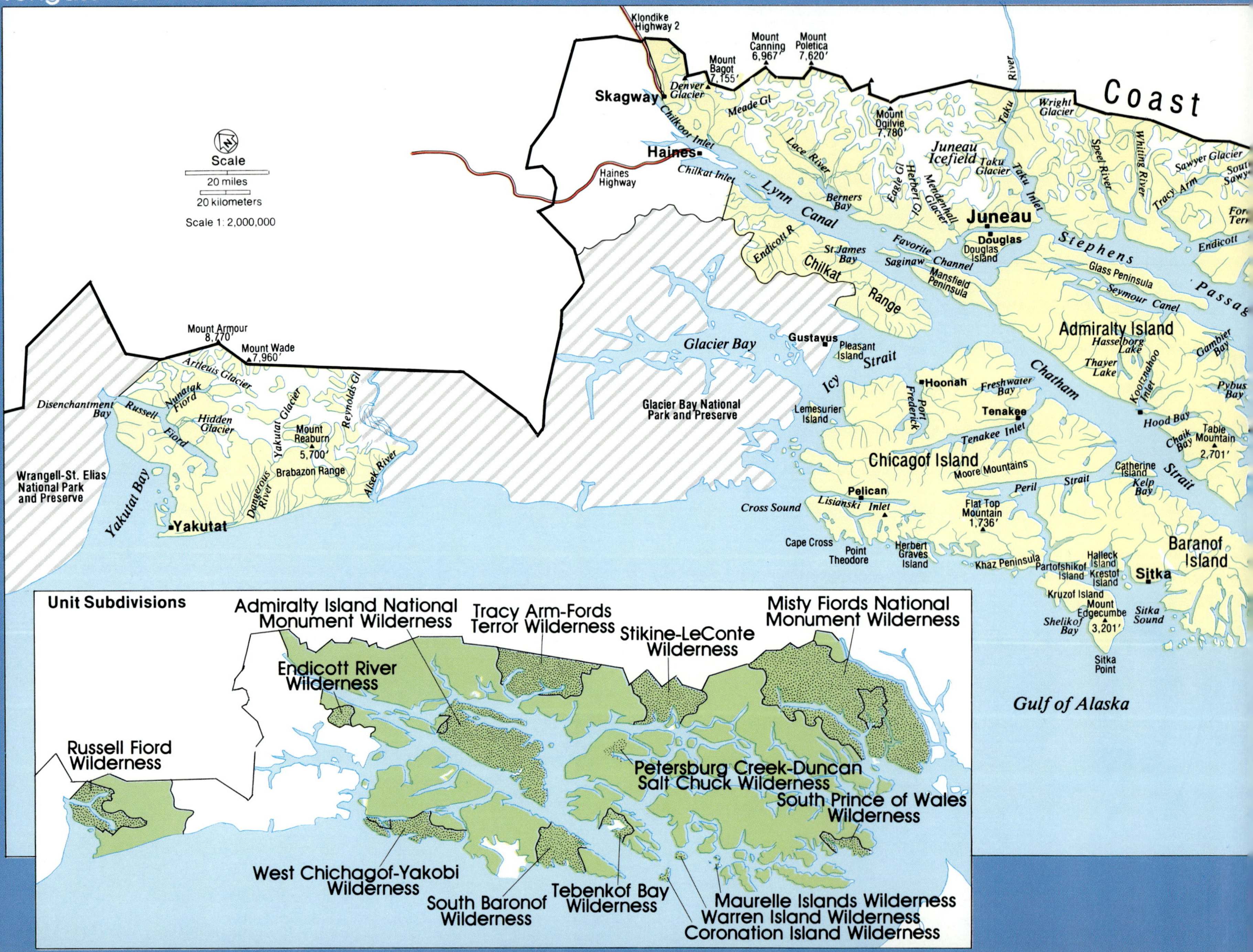

Klondike Highway 2

Mount Canning 6,967'
Mount Poletica 7,620'
Mount Bagot 7,155'
Denver Glacier
Skagway
Meade Gl
Mount Ogilvie 7,780'
Chilkoot Inlet
Haines
Haines Highway
Chilkat Inlet
Lace River
Berners Bay
Eagle Gl
Herbert Gl
Mendenhall Glacier
Taku Glacier
Taku Inlet
Wright Glacier
Whiting River
Sawyer Glacier
Tracy Arm
Sout Sawy
For Terr
Endicott

C o a s t

Juneau Icefield
Taku River
Speel River
Stephens
Passa

Endicott R
St James Bay
Favorite Channel
Saginaw Channel
Douglas Island
Mansfield Peninsula
Juneau
Douglas
Glass Peninsula
Seymour Canal

Lynn Canal
Chilkat Range

Mount Armour 8,770'
Mount Wade 7,960'
Artleuis Glacier
Nunatak Fiord
Hidden Glacier
Yakutat Glacier
Reynolds Gl
Mount Reaburn 5,700'
Alsek River
Brabazon Range
Dangerous River
Russell Fiord

Disenchantment Bay
Russell

Glacier Bay
Gustavus
Pleasant Island
Icy Strait
Lemesurier Island
Hoonah
Port Frederick
Freshwater Lake
Tenakee
Tenakee Inlet
Chatham
Hasselborg Lake
Thayer Lake
Kootznahoo Inlet
Gambier Bay
Pybus Bay

Glacier Bay National Park and Preserve

Admiralty Island

Hood Bay
Chalk Bay
Table Mountain 2,701'

Chicagof Island
Moore Mountains
Peril Strait
Pelican
Lisianski Inlet
Flat Top Mountain 1,736'
Cross Sound
Cape Cross
Point Theodore
Herbert Graves Island
Khaz Peninsula
Partofshikof Island
Krestof Island
Halleck Island
Catherine Island
Kelp Bay
Baranof Island
Sitka

Wrangell-St. Elias National Park and Preserve
Yakutat Bay
Yakutat

Kruzof Island
Mount Edgecumbe 3,201'
Shelikof Bay
Sitka Sound
Sitka Point

Gulf of Alaska

Unit Subdivisions

Admiralty Island National Monument Wilderness
Tracy Arm-Fords Terror Wilderness
Stikine-LeConte Wilderness
Misty Fiords National Monument Wilderness
Endicott River Wilderness
Russell Fiord Wilderness
Petersburg Creek-Duncan Salt Chuck Wilderness
South Prince of Wales Wilderness
West Chichagof-Yakobi Wilderness
South Baronof Wilderness
Tebenkof Bay Wilderness
Maurelle Islands Wilderness
Warren Island Wilderness
Coronation Island Wilderness

Scale
20 miles
20 kilometers
Scale 1: 2,000,000

Mountains
Dawes Glacier
North Baird Glacier
Baird Glacier
Mount T
8,001'
Devils
Thumb
9,077'
Kates
Needle
10,002'
Patterson Glacier
Castle
Mountain
7,329'
Stikine River
Wrangell
Peak
3,747'
Thomas
Bay
Fanshaw
Range
shaw
nd
hton
Petersburg
Wrangell
Wrangell Island
Mitkof Island
Wrangell
Narrows
Woronkofski
Island
Zimovia Strait
Bradfield Canal
Bell
Island
Burroughs
Bay
Behm
Canal
Leduc River
Walker
Cove
Behm
Ruggeds
Bay
Smeaton Bay
Portland
Canal
Hyder
Kupreanof
Island
Duncan
Canal
Woewodski
Island
Kake
ilton
Bay
Zarembo
Island
Etolin Island
Ernest Sound
Behm
Canal
Cleveland
Peninsula
Revillagigedo
Island
Carroll Inlet
Thorne
Arm
Boca de Quadra
Nakat Bay
Point
Nesbitt
Clarence
Ketchikan
Revillagigedo
Mary
Island
Channel
Cape Fox
Kuiu
Island
Conclusion
Island
Point
Barrie
Sumner
Island
Point
Baker
Capitan Passage
Shakan
Thorne
Bay
Kasaan
Kasaan Bay
Strait
Gravina
Island
Nichols Passage
Annette Island
Metlakatla
Duke
Island
Point
Ellis
Kosciusko
Island
Tuxekan
Island
Prince of Wales Island
Cholmondeley
Sound
Moira
Sound
Kendrick
Bay
Patterson
Point
Klawock
Hecate
Island
Craig
Hetta Inlet
Hydaburg
Goat
Island
Sukkwan
Island
Cordova
Bay
Cape Chacon
Warren
Island
San
Fernando
Island
Waterfall
Cape
Decision
Maurelle
Islands
Lulu
Island
Coronation
Island
Noyes
Islands
Sumez
Island
Long Island
Cape
Ommaney
Baker
Island
Bucareli Bay
Dall
Island
Cape Muzon
Cape
Addington
Pacific Ocean

Wild and Scenic Rivers System

For detail maps of the other 21 Wild and Scenic Rivers, refer to the map for the preservation unit through which the river flows (see chart, page 202).

Delta River and Gulkana River

Fortymile River

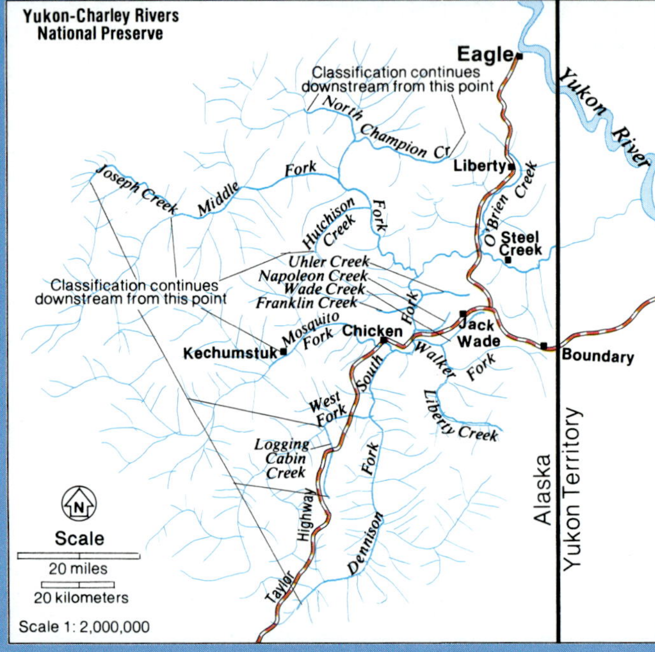

Unalakleet River

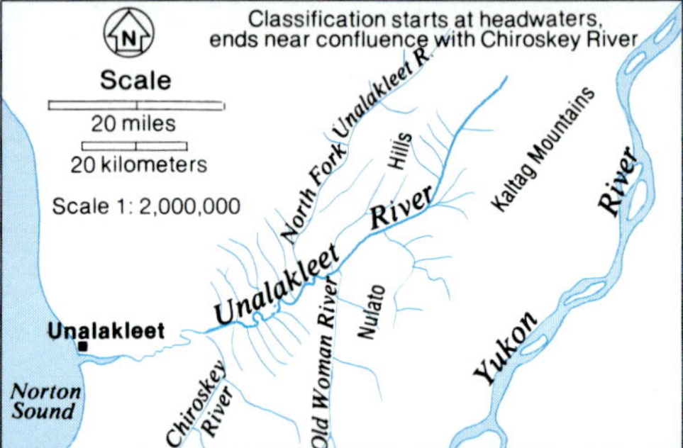

Bureau of Land Management System

Steese National Conservation Areas and White Mountains National Recreation Area

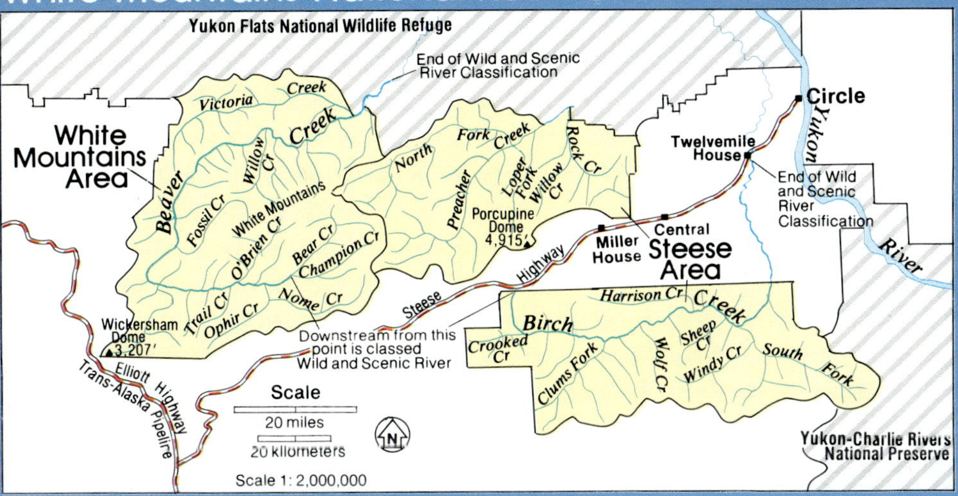

Alaska Geographic® Back Issues

The North Slope, Vol. 1, No. 1. Charter issue of *ALASKA GEOGRAPHIC®*. Out of print.

One Man's Wilderness, Vol. 1, No. 2. The story of a dream shared by many, fulfilled by few: a man goes into the bush, builds a cabin and shares his incredible wilderness experience. Color photos. 116 pages, $9.95

Admiralty . . . Island in Contention, Vol. 1, No. 3. An intimate and multifaceted view of Admiralty: its geological and historical past, its present-day geography, wildlife and sparse human population. Color photos. 78 pages, $5.00

Fisheries of the North Pacific: History, Species, Gear & Processes, Vol. 1, No. 4. Out of print.

The Alaska-Yukon Wild Flowers Guide, Vol. 2, No. 1. First Northland flower book with both large, color photos and detailed drawings of every species described. Features 160 species, common and scientific names and growing height. 112 pages, $10.95

Richard Harrington's Yukon, Vol. 2, No. 2. Out of print.

Prince William Sound, Vol. 2, No. 3. Out of print.

Yakutat: The Turbulent Crescent, Vol. 2, No. 4. Out of print.

Glacier Bay: Old Ice, New Land, Vol. 3, No. 1. The expansive wilderness of Southeastern Alaska's Glacier Bay National Monument unfolds in crisp text and color photographs. Records the flora and fauna of the area, its natural history, with hike and cruise information, plus a large-scale color map. 132 pages, $9.95

The Land: Eye of the Storm, Vol. 3, No. 2. Out of print.

Richard Harrington's Antarctic, Vol. 3, No. 3. The Canadian photojournalist guides readers through remote and little understood regions of the Antarctic and Subantarctic. More than 200 color photos and a large fold-out map. 104 pages, $8.95

The Silver Years of the Alaska Canned Salmon Industry: An Album of Historical Photos, Vol. 3, No. 4. Out of print.

Alaska's Volcanoes: Northern Link in the Ring of Fire, Vol. 4, No. 1. Scientific overview supplemented with eyewitness accounts of Alaska's historic volcano eruptions. Includes color and black-and-white photos and a schematic description of the effects of plate movement upon volcanic activity. 88 pages, $7.95

The Brooks Range: Environmental Watershed, Vol. 4, No. 2. Out of print.

Kodiak: Island of Change, Vol. 4, No. 3. Out of print.

Wilderness Proposals: Which Way for Alaska's Lands?, Vol. 4, No. 4. Out of print.

Cook Inlet Country, Vol. 5, No. 1. A visual tour of the region — its communities, big and small, and its countryside. Begins at the southern tip of the Kenai Peninsula, circles Turnagain Arm and Knik Arm for a close-up view of Anchorage, and visits the Matanuska and Susitna valleys and the wild, west side of the inlet. 230 color photos, separate map. 144 pages, $9.95

Southeast: Alaska's Panhandle, Vol. 5, No. 2. Explores Southeastern Alaska's maze of fjords and islands, mossy forests and glacier-draped mountains — from Dixon Entrance to Icy Bay, including all of the state's fabled Inside Passage. Along the way are profiles of every town, together with a look at the region's history, economy, people, attractions and future. Includes large fold-out map and seven area maps. 192 pages, $12.95.

Bristol Bay Basin, Vol. 5, No. 3. Explores the land and the people of the region known to many as the commercial salmon-fishing capital of Alaska. Illustrated with contemporary color and historic black-and-white photos. Includes a large fold-out map of the region. 96 pages, $9.95.

Alaska Whales and Whaling, Vol. 5, No. 4. The wonders of whales in Alaska — their life cycles, travels and travails — are examined, with an authoritative history of commercial and subsistence whaling in the North. Includes a fold-out poster of 14 major whale species in Alaska in perspective, color photos and illustrations, with historical photos and line drawings. 144 pages, $12.95.

Yukon-Kuskokwim Delta, Vol. 6, No. 1. Out of print.

Aurora Borealis: The Amazing Northern Lights, Vol. 6, No. 2. The northern lights — in ancient times seen as a dreadful forecast of doom, in modern days an inspiration to countless poets. Here one of the world's leading experts — Dr. S.-I. Akasofu of the University of Alaska — explains in an easily understood manner, aided by many diagrams and spectacular color and black-and-white photos, what causes the aurora, how it works, how and why scientists are studying it today and its implications for our future. 96 pages, $7.95.

Alaska's Native People, Vol. 6, No. 3. In the largest edition to date — result of several years of research — the editors examine the varied worlds of the Inupiat Eskimo, Yup'ik Eskimo, Athabascan, Aleut, Tlingit, Haida and Tsimshian. Most photos are by Lael Morgan, *ALASKA®* magazine's roving editor, who since 1974 has been gathering impressions and images from virtually every Native village in Alaska. Included are sensitive, informative articles by Native writers, plus a large, four-color map detailing the Native villages and defining the language areas. 304 pages, $19.95.

The Stikine, Vol. 6, No 4. River route to three Canadian gold strikes in the 1800s, the Stikine is the largest and most navigable of several rivers that flow from northwestern Canada through Southeastern Alaska on their way to the sea. This edition explores 400 miles of Stikine wilderness, recounts the river's paddlewheel past and looks into the future, wondering if the Stikine will survive as one of the North's great free-flowing rivers. Illustrated with contemporary color photos and historic black-and-white; includes a large fold-out map. 96 pages, $9.95.

Alaska's Great Interior, Vol. 7, No. 1. Alaska's rich Interior country, west from the Alaska-Yukon Territory border and including the huge drainage between the Alaska Range and the Brooks Range, is covered thoroughly. Included are the region's people, communities, history, economy, wilderness areas and wildlife. Illustrated with contemporary color and black-and-white photos. Includes a large fold-out map. 128 pages, $9.95.

A Photographic Geography of Alaska, Vol. 7, No. 2. An overview of the entire state — a visual tour through the six regions of Alaska: Southeast, Southcentral/Gulf Coast, Alaska Peninsula and Aleutians, Bering Sea Coast, Arctic and Interior. Plus a handy appendix of valuable information — "Facts About Alaska." Approximately 160 color and black-and-white photos and 35 maps. 192 pages, $14.95.

The Aleutians, Vol. 7, No. 3. The fog-shrouded Aleutians are many things — home of the Aleut, a tremendous wildlife spectacle, a major World War II battleground and now the heart of a thriving new commercial fishing industry. Roving editor Lael Morgan contributes most of the text; also included are contemporary color and black-and-white photographs, and a large fold-out map. 224 pages, $14.95.

Klondike Lost: A Decade of Photographs by Kinsey & Kinsey, Vol. 7, No. 4. An album of rare photographs and all-new text about the lost Klondike boom town of Grand Forks, second in size only to Dawson during the gold rush. Introduction by noted historian Pierre Berton: 138 pages, area maps and more than 100 historical photos, most never before published. $12.95.

Wrangell-Saint Elias, Vol. 8, No. 1. Mountains, including the continent's second- and fourth-highest peaks, dominate this international wilderness that sweeps from the Wrangell Mountains in Alaska to the southern Saint Elias range in Canada. The region draws backpackers, mountain climbers, and miners, and is home for a few hardy, year-round inhabitants. Illustrated with contemporary color and historical black-and-white photographs. Includes a large fold-out map. $9.95.

Alaska Mammals, Vol. 8, No. 2. From tiny ground squirrels to the powerful polar bear, and from the tundra hare to the magnificent whales inhabiting Alaska's waters, this volume includes 80 species of mammals found in Alaska. Included are beautiful color photographs and personal accounts of wildlife encounters. *The* book on Alaska's mammals — from Southeast to the Arctic, and beyond! $12.95.

The Kotzebue Basin, Vol. 8, No. 3. Examines northwestern Alaska's thriving trading area of Kotzebue Sound and the Kobuk and Noatak river basins, lifelines of the region's Inupiat Eskimos, early explorers, and present-day, hardy residents. Contemporary color and historical black-and-white photographs illustrate varied cultures and numerous physical attractions of the area. $12.95.

COMING ATTRACTION

Alaska's Glaciers, Vol. 9, No. 1. Examines in-depth the massive rivers of ice, their composition, exploration, present-day distribution and scientific significance. Illustrated with many contemporary color and historical black-and-white photos, the text includes separate discussions of more than a dozen glacial regions. To be distributed to members February 1982. Price to be announced.

Your $30.00 membership in The Alaska Geographic Society includes 4 subsequent issues of *ALASKA GEOGRAPHIC®*, the Society's official quarterly. Please add $4 for non-U.S. membership.

Additional membership information available upon request. Single copies of the *ALASKA GEOGRAPHIC®* back issues available, per listing here. When ordering please add $1 postage/handling per copy. To order back issues send your check or money order and volumes desired to:

The Alaska Geographic Society

Box 4-EEE, Anchorage, Alaska 99509